THE GREEN ROAD HOME

THE GREEN ROAD HOME

*A Caddie's Journal
of Life on the
Pro Golf Tour*

Michael Bamberger

CONTEMPORARY
BOOKS, INC.
CHICAGO • NEW YORK

Library of Congress Cataloging-in-Publication Data

Bamberger, Michael, 1960–
    The green road home.

    1. Bamberger, Michael, 1960–   2. Caddies—
United States—Biography.   3. Golf.   I. Title.
GV964.B36A34   1986   796.352′092′4 [B]   86-4377
ISBN 0-8092-5160-4
ISBN 0-8092-5159-0 (pbk.)

Lyrics from "Born in the U.S.A." on page 164 copyright © 1984
by Bruce Springsteen. Used by permission.

Published by Contemporary Books, Inc.
180 North Michigan Avenue, Chicago, Illinois 60601
Manufactured in the United States of America
Library of Congress Catalog Card Number: 86-4377
International Standard Book Number: 0-8092-5160-4 (cloth)
                                    0-8092-5159-0 (paper)

Published simultaneously in Canada by Beaverbooks, Ltd.
195 Allstate Parkway, Valleywood Business Park
Markham, Ontario L3R 4T8 Canada

For my mother, father, and brother—
Dorothy, Joseph, and David Bamberger

Home was never like this.
　　　　　　—Old American phrase

CONTENTS

TOURNAMENTS

The Honda Classic—Coral Springs, Florida

The U.S.F. & G. Classic—New Orleans, Louisiana

The Panasonic-Las Vegas Invitational—Las Vegas, Nevada

The Tournament Players Championship—Ponte Vedra, Florida

The Magnolia Classic—Hattiesburg, Mississippi

The Sea Pines Heritage Classic—Hilton Head Island, South Carolina

The Houston Open—The Woodlands, Texas

The Tallahassee Open—Tallahassee, Florida

The Byron Nelson Golf Classic—Irving, Texas

The Memorial Tournament—Dublin, Ohio

The Kemper Open—Bethesda, Maryland

The United States Open Regional Qualifying Rounds— Montclair, New Jersey

The Manufacturers Hanover Westchester Classic— Harrison, New York

The United States Open—Birmingham, Michigan

The Canadian Open—Oakville, Ontario, Canada

The British Open Qualifying Rounds—Deal, England

The British Open—Sandwich, England

The Dutch Open—Noordwijk, Holland

The Professional Golfers' Association Championship— Cherry Hills, Colorado

The Jerry Ford Invitational Golf Tournament—Vail, Colorado

The Metropolitan Open—West Caldwell, New Jersey

The B.C. Open—Endicott, New York

The Caddie Classic—Endicott, New York

1
A CADDIE IS BORN

I

IN MY YOUNGER and more cavity-prone years, my dentist's wife gave me her golf clubs and some advice to go with them.

"Here," she said one day as we stood in the waiting room, "try to use them more than I did." She had played twice in the past seven years.

The season was spring, the new grass smelled of hope, and I was a prize pupil in Mr. Greenlee's eighth-grade golf gym class. Everything about golf sounded good to me. I liked the friendly sounding names the first golfers gave their clubs: the spoon and the niblick, the mashie and the putter. I liked the sturdy sounding names of the companies that made them: Spalding and MacGregor, Wilson and Dunlop. And I liked the dashing sounding names of the early golfers: Tommy Armour and Joek Hutchison, Walter Hagen and Chick Evans.

Mrs. Libin's clubs didn't have a brand name, but they were not without style. Their grips were pink, the woods blue, and the yellow bag's ball pocket filled with Flying Ladies, or Lady Flites, or something unsuitable for a boy of fourteen. No matter; my excitement for the game was limitless. Whacking those plastic balls off Astroturf mats in gym class was thrilling. I couldn't wait to actually play.

That summer I joined the Bellport Golf Club, a village-owned course on the south shore of Long Island, where Dr. Libin played. Joining Bellport was not like becoming a member of Winged Foot, or Medinah, or the Royal and Ancient. It was more like joining a public library. Anyone under the age of twenty-one with fifty dollars could become a Class F member. We *Juniors*, as the Class Fs were also known, could play Monday through Thursday after 2:30 P.M., except for Wednesday, which was Doctors' Day, when the starting time for Juniors was 3:30 P.M. Sometimes, however, we could play earlier, at the Discretion of the Pro. (The Bellport Golf Club liked to use capital letters for emphasis, as in "Replace Your Divots.")

I seldom appealed to the Pro's Discretion. My parents were not members so I was completely without clout in the Discretion Department. Also, I was not from Bellport, but from Patchogue, one town west. Only Bellport residents, through the village trustees, hired and fired the Pro. Patchoguers had no say. Whether you lived in Antelope, Nebraska, or four miles down the road, if you weren't from Bellport you didn't matter.

They were a short four miles, I discovered in my first summer as a Class F. That summer I had a job as a stockboy at Patchogue Floral. My workday began at 7:00 A.M. and ended at 1:00 P.M. Each day after work I headed to the golf course by one of three methods: bus, bike, or thumb. The last of these was my favorite.

Hitchhiking with golf clubs is easier than you might think. There are fourteen million golfers in the United States and most of them own cars. Many car-owning golfers—no study has shown the exact percentage—are sympathetic to the plight of the carless golfer. You see few hitchhikers with golf clubs slung across their backs because such hitchhikers generally get rides quickly. On Wednesday afternoons I was often picked up by Dr. Libin himself.

By the end of that first summer of play I could break 100. By the end of the next summer I could break 90. And by the end of my third summer I could break 80 (once in a freakish while). There, like a summer romance at Labor Day, my game peaked. I made my high school team (anybody with a set of clubs could), and was even elected captain as a senior (more a tribute to my enthusiasm than my skill). But I wasn't especially good. I spent all winter reading golf instruction books and all summer playing, but I became no better.

One Doctors' Day, while waiting for a ruling from the Discretion of the Pro Department, a white convertible sports car galloped into the parking lot, while another car, dull by comparison, trotted in behind it. Two middle-aged men filed out of the dull car. Walter Rhodes, a man of wealth, flamboyance, and local fame, emerged from the sports car. I had glimpsed him before, usually marshalling a parade. But I had never seen him at the golf course. Curious, I strolled over to his car for a look.

He pulled a gleaming white bag out of the trunk.

"Are you looking for caddie work?" he asked.

"Yes," I said impetuously. I had never caddied before.

"Here you go," he said, hoisting the bag on my shoulder.

The two guys from the nondescript car shared an

electric cart. They spent most of their time traversing the fairways from the left rough to the right rough. Mr. Rhodes was a good player, a long and straight hitter. His playing partners were often out of earshot.

"Now this fellow," Mr. Rhodes said, pointing with a one iron to the large man slashing away in the right rough, "he's a commercial airline pilot. He flies the big ones, the 747s. You know what happens in your head when you fly one of those things, ordering everyone around? You figure you can do anything." He took a shot.

"And this fellow," now pointing with a putter to the wiry man involuntarily mowing the left rough, "he's a surgeon. Same psychology. When you're a surgeon at your operating table it's like, like owning a baseball team. You're in control.

"Now these two fellows are my closest friends—my ex-wife says they're my only friends—and when we go sailing in *my* boat I massage *their* egos. They don't know a thing about sailing. But I'll ask them questions. 'Say, Sky, think we need the spinnaker?' Or, 'Say, Slim, think we need to trim the jib?'

"They don't know that it's a setup. A psychological setup. And this is where I get my pay-off, right here on the golf course."

At first my job seemed easy. I handed him the clubs as he asked for them, cleaned the ball on the green, listened politely to his stories, and kept quiet. I liked my boss. His stories were funny and his candor unexpected. When he made a long putt on the third hole I let out a small cheer for him.

On the fourth tee Mr. Rhodes leaned toward me and said, "I've got an offer for you." This was when the book *The Godfather* was popular and people were always making offers.

"I'll pay you twenty dollars, straight out, or pay you ten dollars and ten percent of whatever I win."

A guaranteed twenty dollars seemed like a lot of

money for an afternoon's work; I was making $1.90 an hour at Patchogue Floral. I looked at Mr. Rhodes. His white teeth sparkled in the sun.

"I'll take the percent," I said.

"Nothing like a good caddie," Mr. Rhodes said to Sky and Slim. They looked at me doubtfully; I could hardly keep the big bag on my small shoulder.

The round progressed with the characteristic and pleasant languor of golf being played in the embracing heat of an August afternoon. The flags slept listlessly on the pins. The golfers' conversations were jovial, gentlemanly, and confidential. But their concentration was deep. Winning mattered.

Mr. Rhodes pushed his tee and ball through the hard ground on the eighteenth tee. He looked at his ball for a moment, and then the hole, sizing up the long par four with liberal doses of rough, a series of small, cleverly placed bushes and, running down the right side, a stream of tall oaks.

"Well, fellows," he said, "how do we stand?"

Sky, the pilot, who kept score like an accountant, gave a report: "We halved the front side, you're one down on the back, and one down on the match." Mr. Rhodes took it in.

"Then if I lose this hole," Mr. Rhodes said, "or tie it, I lose the back nine and I lose the match."

"Correct," said Sky.

Mr. Rhodes looked down on his ball and said: "If I make a double press and win the hole, then I win the back nine and the match, right?"

"Correct," said Sky, "But if you lose, or even tie, then you lose double."

Mr. Rhodes nodded. "But the only way I can actually win money is to press, correct?" asked Mr. Rhodes, smiling.

"Correct," said Sky, smiling back.

"Would you gentlemen be interested in accepting a double press here?" Mr. Rhodes asked.

"Naturally," said Sky.

"Of course," said Slim.

All three men hit good drives off the eighteenth tee. Mr. Rhodes hit it about twenty yards farther than the other two. Slim and Sky hit their second shots to the edge of the green leaving chips for birdies. It was likely that, between them, one would make a par. Mr. Rhodes would then need a birdie on this, the most difficult hole on the course, to win. I thought I saw beads of perspiration on Mr. Rhodes's nose as he stood over his ball in the eighteenth fairway. Mr. Rhodes did not appear to be a man accustomed to perspiring.

"What do I have?" he asked.

He caught me by surprise. He had barely said a word to me all day.

"How many yards do I have?" he asked.

I didn't know. From that spot the shot required a full three iron for me. That meant it was 180 yards, roughly, I guessed. The only thing I did know was that I couldn't let him sense my lack of confidence.

"One hundred and eighty-two yards, Mr. Rhodes," I said.

"What do you like?" he asked.

That was not a conversation-making question: He was between a four iron and a five iron.

"Smooth four, Mr. Rhodes," I said.

"That's what I like, too," he said, taking the club slowly and dramatically from my hand.

Mr. Rhodes eyed the shot, set up over the ball, waggled slowly, and hit the worst shot of his round, a sad topper that skidded down the fairway and stopped twenty yards short of the green.

He walked urgently to the ball and stood over it, arms folded across his chest. This time there was no question: There *were* beads of perspiration on his nose.

"And what do you like *here*?" Mr. Rhodes asked, as if it were my fault we were there in the first place.

"A little cut sand wedge," I said.

"I like the bump-and-run, myself," Mr. Rhodes said unconvincingly.

"You think you can get a bump-and-run to stop, hard as these greens are now?" It was late August and the whole golf course felt as if it had sat in a kiln for the month.

"Where would you put your little cut sand wedge?" Mr. Rhodes asked. He was getting slightly snooty now. This was not the same Mr. Rhodes who had bought me a Yoo Hoo at the Halfway House.

"In the middle of that big slope, five yards short and five yards to the left of the pin," I said.

Mr. Rhodes pulled the sand wedge out of the bag.

How sweet it would be if I could tell you that Mr. Rhodes hit the shot exactly where I told him to, that it took one soft bounce and rolled gently into the cup for a birdie. Mr. Rhodes did, however, the next best thing. He bladed the shot pathetically, catching the ball with the fat flange of the sand wedge so that it rolled off the club like a brutally thrown bowling ball. His ball sliced right past Slim's ball and Sky's ball and rolled directly at the hole smashing flush against the center of the pin. The ball popped two feet up and fell straight into the hole.

Mr. Rhodes had made his birdie.

"R.B.U., R.B.U.," Mr. Rhodes repeated as he staggered with jolly frivolity to the pin. He pulled his ball out of the hole. "R.B.U., R.B.U." He kissed his golf ball and continued his slinky walk.

I didn't learn what "R.B.U." meant until after Slim and Sky missed their chips for birdie and Mr. Rhodes had become the clear winner.

"R.B.U.," Mr. Rhodes said, slapping a crisp fifty dollar bill in my hand—as much as I'd make in three days at Patchogue Floral. "R.B.U."

It was Slim, the surgeon, who picked up on the quizzical expression latched on my face.

"R.B.U., boy, is Rotten But Useful," he said.

I couldn't tell if the appellation referred to the shot or to me. I didn't ask, so I still don't know.

II

Caddying at Bellport, sadly, proved to be an undependable career. A caddie there—and I was just about the only one—could go days without getting a bag, which did wonders for his putting, but little for his wallet. I needed a new way to make a living. Buoyed by a reasonable grade in College Freshman Composition, I wrote to *Golf Magazine*, *Golf Digest*, and *Golf Journal*, applying for summer jobs.

Writing to the editors of these magazines, I wondered about their jobs and the challenges they presented. These magazines—there are a dozen or so around the world—depend on a mix of feature and instructional articles for their success. But reader surveys show consistently that the instructional parts are best read.

Seemingly, there is a limit to what can be said about the golf swing. But month after month and year after year the golf magazines satisfy the desperate craving of the golfing public for any and all golf tips. The editors, ever creative, are forever cooking up new recipes for the old golf swing. Just when you think every idea has been explored and exhausted, and nothing will help your game, a new issue arrives with a brand new batch of hints. Putt with your eyes closed. Play in your bare feet. Swing with your shoulders, not with your head. Swing with your head, not with your heart. Hitting a sand wedge is like throwing a Frisbee. Putting is like throwing horseshoes, or darts, or boccie balls. The golf swing is like a pendulum. The golf swing is like a penny falling off the Empire State Building. The golf swing is like a rock attached to a string.

Nobody ever writes asking just exactly *how* the golf

swing is like a rock attached to a string. Nor, for that matter, does anyone ask how you attach a rock *to* a string. You don't want to stir up trouble. The circulation department may cut off your subscription.

The rejection letters came quickly; I didn't want to spend a summer in an office anyhow, I rationalized in a freshman way. What I really wanted to do—this was a period when people talked about what they *really* wanted to do—was to caddie on the professional golf tour. I wrote to two golfers, Randy Erskine and John Fought, picking their names at random from the near bottom of a P.G.A. Tour money order list.

Fought, whose last name rhymes with *coat*, was the 1977 U.S. Amateur champion, and had just joined the Tour. He was considered an outstanding prospect, although no one could figure out why he listed accounting, his major at Brigham Young, as a special interest in the Tour's media guide.

Erskine, whose last name rhymes with *good gin*, was considered one of the Tour's most likable players, but one of its lesser putters. His best finish was a second in the 1976 Buick Open, which was played in his home state of Michigan. His days as an outstanding prospect ended shortly after his graduation from the University of Michigan.

Professional golfers, unlike magazine editors, do not receive scores of letters from college students looking for summer jobs and, therefore, do not efficiently send out stock "thanks, but" letters.

Weeks passed. I received no replies. I called Erskine at his home in Michigan. (His number was listed; Fought's was not.)

"Hello, is Randy there?"

"No, he's out on the Tour. This is Mrs. Erskine, his wife. May I help?" she asked. I explained my purpose.

"Oh, yes," Mrs. Erskine said, "Randy received your letter. He thought it was very . . . amusing."

"Amusing?"

"Well," said Mrs. Erskine, "let's just say that it's been, oh, quite a while since somebody has written to him out of the blue and asked him for a caddie job."

"How long?" I asked.

"Oh, well, hmmmm," said Mrs. Erskine, "come to think of it, I can't remember it ever happening before."

That brought conversation to a stop. Then Mrs. Erskine said, "Why don't I give you his number? He's playing in Florida now." She sounded like a nice woman.

I reached Randy at a Holiday Inn.

"You're the guy who wrote me the letter," he said, memory coming back. He was flipping the television channel switch. "When did you want to start?" he asked.

"How about the Kemper Open in Charlotte in May?"

"Kemper, let's see, let's see. Yes, I'm already qualified for Kemper. Kemper. Fine. Why don't we meet at the first tee at seven on the Tuesday before the tournament?" Randy asked.

"Great, I'll see you there," I said.

"Okay," he said.

"I really appreciate it. Thanks a lot. I can't wait," I said.

"Okay," he said. Cool guy, I thought to myself.

Several days later I received a letter written with neat penmanship on good stationery in all capital letters. It looked like a telegram. It read:

I AM VERY SORRY FOR NOT HAVING AN-SWERED YOUR LETTER BEFORE NOW. IT TOOK A WHILE TO REACH ME WHILE I WAS ON TOUR.

IN RESPONSE TO YOUR WANTING TO CADDIE FOR ME, I CANNOT COMMIT TO GUARANTEE YOU A JOB FOR ANY LENGTH OF TIME. I AM

SOMEWHAT PARTICULAR. IF A GUY DOES
HAVE THE POTENTIAL TO BE MY KIND OF
CADDIE, I WILL TRAIN HIM AND GIVE HIM
THE JOB. HOWEVER, SOME GUYS DON'T HAVE
THE RIGHT ATTITUDE TO START WITH. I HOPE
YOU CAN UNDERSTAND WHAT I AM SAYING. I
AM MORE THAN WILLING TO GIVE YOU A
CHANCE TO WORK. AND YOU MAY BE EX-
ACTLY WHAT I AM LOOKING FOR. BUT I CAN-
NOT GUARANTEE YOU THAT I WILL KEEP YOU
AS LONG AS YOU WANT.

WHAT I SUGGEST IS THAT YOU LET ME
KNOW WHAT TOURNAMENT YOU WOULD LIKE
TO WORK AND I WILL MAKE ARRANGEMENTS
FOR YOU TO WORK FOR ME. WE WILL GIVE
YOU A GOOD TEST. IF YOU WORK OUT THEN
THE JOB WILL BE YOURS UNTIL WE DECIDE
OTHERWISE. IF THINGS DON'T WORK OUT
THEN I WOULD BE FREE TO MAKE A CHANGE.
YOU MUST KNOW THIS IN ADVANCE.

IF YOU ARE STILL INTERESTED, LET ME
KNOW.

> SINCERELY,
> John Fought

Fought went on to win two tournaments that year.
He won $108,000. He was the rookie of the year. And
he did it without me on his bag, a fact which tempted
me to kick myself every day for a year.

Erskine was at a different point in his career. His
Tour days were winding down. Caddying for Randy
Erskine in the 1979 Kemper Open is a romantic
memory, of sorts, to me now. I remember how close
we were to making the thirty-six-hole cut, how exciting it was, and how disappointing it was, in the end,
when we didn't. I also remember how determined
that missed cut made Randy.

"The last thing I wanna do while I'm still out here

is qualify for the U.S. Open," he said after the
Kemper. "I've never been in one. There's nothing I'd
like more."

On the Monday after the Kemper Open, at the
Charlotte Country Club, there was a one-day, thirty-
six-hole U.S. Open regional qualifying round, the
entrance examination of the U.S. Open. The only
preparation course was practice. We played seventy-
two practice holes during the Kemper Open
weekend.

"If I get into this thing, I'm gonna give you a
hundred bucks for the day," Erskine said early on
that Monday morning. We played immediately behind Arnold Palmer, who attracted a large gallery
even for this, a prequalifying round. The crowd
excited Erskine, but not his golf game. The putts
missed all day.

"Here," he said, handing me $100 anyway. "It's not
your fault I can't putt."

Despite Randy's poor showing, I found the week
intoxicating. My past semester's boondoggle with
calculus seemed as if it had happened in a different
lifetime. At Randy's invitation, I came to dinner with
him and a bunch of his golfing buddies. Their conversation was framed in hope for the next tournament
down the road and good stories from tournaments
past.

"If my putter gets hot and I win a tournament in
the next month, I could be out here another ten
years," said Randy over a Burger King burger.

I called home and shared with my parents my
great Tour life lesson: I had learned, I claimed with
presophomore wisdom, more in a week than I could
in a *summer* working in some office. I outlined my
plans, to see how far my Patchogue Floral savings
could take me on the Tour. And if Randy's putter got
hot, I'd be looking at some big checks down the road.

That's wonderful, my parents said. They were
delighted for me.

Did I know about a letter from the dean? I made an "A" in English, and an "F" in calculus. Did I know I was on academic probation? I'd better come home and take a summer course to make up the credit, and show the seriousness of my intent.

III

By senior year of college, the caddie dream was near-dead.

Other dreams replaced it. Chiefly, being a newspaperman, making a living from a typewriter. Equipped with decent grades in English, and a short history in math, I managed to get a job on the *Vineyard Gazette*, the newspaper of Martha's Vineyard, an island six miles off the southeast coast of Massachusetts.

Martha's Vineyard is a resort, but not in the tradition of Pinehurst, North Carolina, or La Quinta, California, or Grossinger, New York. The summer people, many of them city dwellers, sail, fly, and drive great distances to the island so that they may work on their houses, yards, and gardens. Gardening is big.

Of course, not everybody who comes to Martha's Vineyard owns a house, yard, and garden. For these people there are hotels and two lovely public golf courses with lovely sounding names: Mink Meadows and Farm Neck. And, although few will admit it, there are summer colonists with houses, yards, and gardens who actually prefer playing golf to posting "No Trespassing" signs. For these people there are two private courses: the nine-hole Edgartown Golf Club and a six-hole unnamed track governed by the Inland Ballwatchers' Society.

A dirt path called East Elbow Road passes through the Ballwatchers' rugged six. The road, which gets sporadic traffic from fishermen in jeeps and home owners in station wagons, is a dangerous route. Golf balls squatting in the middle of East Elbow Road are treated like a cattle crossing in the Midwest. One sits in one's vehicle—no one would drive a mere car down East Elbow Road—until the golfer plays his shot.

One of the Ballwatchers is a famous writer, a nocturnal worker seen on the links every day, spending a disproportionate amount of that time playing shots off East Elbow Road. Sometimes he'll wave vehicles through, rather than have a gallery for his road shots. More often, though, he is oblivious to observers. He is immersed in his game.

The nine-hole Edgartown Golf Club feels like a miniature U.S. Open course. Although the holes are short, they are of classical design, hilly doglegs bending left and right with elevated, curving greens and deep pot bunkers. It is an elegant layout that borders the Vineyard Sound and is laid out on softly rolling hills. The membership of the club comprises some of the richest and oldest of the Vineyard's summer people. Their golf course is kept in pristine condition. I know this because in the fall and spring I used to sneak onto the golf course regularly; I lived just off its eighth hole.

The Vineyard's weather authorities are fond of saying that the island has no spring, but that, I think, is a slight overstatement. The Vineyard spring, it seems to me, comprises about four days dispersed unevenly and unpredictably between New Year's Day and Independence Day. These are cool days— you can feel the air against your cheeks—but they are blue and dry days, too, accompanied by pleasant northerly breezes.

Early on the morning of one such day, I met my *Gazette* colleague and golf partner, Andy Shanley, at the golf course.

Andy, playing with borrowed clubs and walking hand in hand with his three-year-old son Colin between shots, played his own brand of flawless golf. (That's not the same as flawless golf, which doesn't exist. The remarkable quality of Shanley's game is that the flaws don't bother him.) The birds sang, the grass seemed to turn greener before our eyes, and the golf balls made delightful soft *thud* sounds when they landed, gently, on the spongy greens. The last remains of snow, hiding in the always-shaded corners of bunkers, melted away. We didn't talk much—a "Good shot" here, a "Well played" there—and recorded no scores. Our footprints down the wet fairways provided us with all we needed to know. The round had been a long time coming, for the winter had been difficult and harsh; it was an exodus from a dormant winter to the promise of spring.

That afternoon I returned to a book, *Golf in the Kingdom*, and to a chapter called "Singing the Praises of Golf." The author, Michael Murphy, quotes a Scot called Shivas Irons who sings these praises:

" 'My friends,' he said, 'devoted discipline and grace will bring ye knowin's and powers everywhere, in all your life, in all your works if they're good works, in all your loves if they're good loves. Ye'll come away from the links with a new hold on life, that is certain if ye play the game with all your heart.' "

I felt a new hold on life!

He also says:

" 'Fascination frees our journey through the worlds and opens the doors to where we want to go.' "

I felt a need to journey!

From Shivas Irons my mind wandered to a descriptive passage in Bobby Jones's biography, telling how Jones wrote letters home during a transatlantic sailing between the U.S. Open and the British Open. It suggests a wonderful image: Bobby Jones, the greatest golfer of his day (and an amateur!), sitting in a cabin of a gently rocking ship, writing home, assessing his achievements and his aspirations. His journey was truly through the worlds. How inspiring!

I felt a dormant desire reawakening in me.

2
BASIC TRAINING

I

I WAS SURPRISED how willing Brad Faxon was to grant me a tryout. I wrote to him, and then called him after two rounds of the 1985 Bing Crosby National Pro-Am. Brad was a stroke off the lead.

"I'm not sure how long this could work out, but I'll give you a chance," Brad said. "Caddying is not the most lucrative profession in the world, you know."

"I know," I said.

"Seems like certain caddies are always borrowing money," Brad said.

There was a pause. I think Brad wanted this to set in.

"And the work itself—it's not as easy as it looks. Carrying the bag, that's the least of it."

"I know," I said.

"And, although the golf tour goes to a lot of beautiful places, the caddies usually wind up staying in cheap dives off the highway," Brad said.

"I love a good cheap dive," I said.

"And, although there are a lot of parties and dinners for the players, the officials, and the press, there isn't anything like that for the caddies, you know," Brad said.

"I know."

"Okay," said Brad, whose deep voice and mature manner belied his youth. He was twenty-three years old. "I just want you to know what you're getting into."

"What I'm worried about," I said, "is doing a good job, so I can keep my job. What do you think makes for a good caddie?"

"Well," said Brad, "you've got to have all the basics."

"Basics," I wrote on a piece of scrap paper.

"You know: Keep the ball clean, the clubs clean, give accurate yardages, keep things dry in the rain, keep things organized," Brad said.

"Ball clean, club clean, yards good, dry rain, organ," I wrote down.

"That's the easy stuff," Brad said.

"EZ," I wrote down.

"It's the intangibles, the stuff you can't articulate, those are the things that separate the good caddie from the poor one," Brad said.

"Intangibles toughest," I wrote down.

"Does that help?" Brad asked, obviously anxious to get back to something, probably the practice tee, or the putting green, or to one of those player parties.

"Oh, *yes*," I said, "yes, yes, yes."

Brad Faxon graduated from school—the Tour Qualifying School—in the fall of 1983, along with fifty-seven other golfers. He had a solid amateur record: He twice won the Rhode Island Amateur and twice won the New England Amateur; he played on the 1983 Walker Cup team and was named an All-American in 1982 and 1983. In 1983, while a senior at

Furman University, Faxon won three national awards as college player of the year. This record did not earn Brad the annual sportswriters' title of "possibly the next Nicklaus," although he was nominated. Three other players from his class were more highly touted: Willie Wood, one of Brad's closest friends and a winner of five national junior titles; Corey Pavin, who won three tournaments overseas in 1983; and Joey Sindelar, who broke most of Jack Nicklaus's college golf records at Ohio State.

Still, Brad's credentials were impressive, and no close observer of golf was too surprised when he finished the 1984 golf season in a respectable eighty-second place on the money-earning list, making $71,688. He was fourth among his classmates, finishing behind Pavin, who was number eighteen on the money list, Sindelar, who was number fifty-nine, and Wood, who was number sixty-one. Most important, for Brad, was that he finished in the top 125, the prerequisite for guaranteed exemption for the following year's Tour. Of the top 125, no one was younger than Brad.

Brad and I made arrangements to meet at the Honda Classic when the Tour moved east, to Florida, in February 1985. When our time came I packed, flew to Miami, rented a car, and drove north to Coral Springs.

It doesn't take long to realize that the Honda Classic, played at a golf course–real estate fortress called Eagle Trace, is a significant event in Coral Springs, the sort of event that inspires newspapers to special sections. The paper there, the *News/Sun-Sentinel*, published a sixteen-page special section on the Sunday before the tournament, complete with color photographs, maps, golf course diagrams, and a dozen articles, one of which detailed the most strategic places to watch. The advertisements in this section were mostly for real estate.

"This is the life," read one advertisement, for a real estate-resort complex called St. Andrews, Boca Raton. "The privileged life."

"Eagle Trace," another advertisement stated. "It says you've arrived."

"Discover a course so private," said an advertisement for a real estate development called Boca Grove Plantation, "Gary Player wanted it for his own backyard."

In many of these recently sprung Florida towns, the newspapers depend upon real estate advertisements for their survival, and real estate companies depend upon the lure of golf for theirs.

Besides golf and real estate, there's not much actually happening *in* Coral Springs—if you want to go to the dog track, or to jai alai, or the beach, you have to drive; driving may be Florida's second favorite pastime.

Coral Springs is a place where people come to live, not to visit and, consequently, it has few hotels. There was, of course, a Holiday Inn. The golf Tour doesn't go anywhere that doesn't have a Holiday Inn. This was the closest hotel to Eagle Trace, and many of the players stay there. Along a commercial highway there were cheaper motels nestled conveniently between gas stations and fast-food restaurants.

"And, although the golf tour goes to a lot of beautiful places, the caddies usually wind up staying in cheap dives off the highway," Brad had said.

"I love a good, cheap dive," I had answered.

Hmmmm. A good cheap dive is one thing, but an overpriced cheap dive quite another. I decided to drive the commercial strip. I made myself a deal: If I came across one motel where all the lights were working, I'd stay there.

I began the drive. There was an "—otel," and there was a "mo—el". There was a "—ruckers Welcome" and there was a "—lean Rooms." I didn't want to press my luck. At the first chance I made a U-turn and headed for the Holiday Inn.

The week before the Honda Classic, the Tour convened in Miami for the Doral-Eastern Open. On the concluding Sunday of that tournament, some of the players were checking in at the next stop. Bill Kratzert carried his big, orange Power-Bilt golf bag into the Holiday Inn lobby. Outside the hotel George Archer and Hubert Green swatted flies and swapped stories.

"You wearin' a girdle, George?" Green asked, looking up. Archer is six feet, five inches tall.

"Nah," said Archer. "This thing is enough of a pain." He pointed to a white bandage wrapped around his forearm.

"Ya look so skinny, George," Green said, poking Archer in his slight stomach, "that I figured you must be wearin' a girdle." The grown men laughed easily on the warm, soft Florida evening.

I checked into my room and thought about my seemingly modest goal: to caddie on the tour for six months or until my money ran out, whichever came first; to see as much of the country as possible; to learn as much as possible about the game of golf; to learn as much as possible about the people who play the game professionally; to become, in some small way, part of the Tour.

My first goal was to win the job from Brad, who had never had a steady caddie on the Tour.

Through the West Coast leg of the Tour, Brad had made $12,415, making him number sixty-four on the money list, $182,210 behind the money leader Mark O'Meara, and $9,970 ahead of number 125, David Thore, who had earned $2,435. Since a caddie's salary is dependent, in part, on the performance of his player, as Brad's caddie during that part of the Tour, I would have earned more than David Thore; Mark O'Meara's caddie earned more than Brad.

A professional Tour caddie is paid a weekly salary, which is between $200 and $300 a week, depending upon the financial status and generosity of the player and the experience of the caddie. Of greater importance is the caddie's percentage: he, or she—there is an occasional female caddie on the Tour—generally receives five percent of his player's winnings. If a player makes the cut, finishes in the middle of the field, and earns $2,000, the caddie receives five percent of that ($100), plus his salary (say $250), and makes $350 for the week.

A $2,000 week is average for Brad, mediocre for O'Meara, and good for Thore. In any given week, about half the field does not survive the thirty-six-hole cut. The cut players leave for the next stop without a paycheck. David Thore misses many more cuts than he makes. Brad missed the cut fourteen times in the thirty-three tournaments he entered in 1984. Even O'Meara, who finished second on the 1984 money list, missed eight cuts in the thirty-two tournaments he entered. In a missed cut the caddie gets his weekly salary and the weekend off. This does not please him. One needs to play on the weekends, and play well, to make a decent check.

Financially, and spiritually, the Tour caddie lives on chance: One good tournament can save a year. First-place finishes are usually worth at least $72,000; some are worth twice that. In the spirit of victory, and sometimes by prior agreement, a winning player will write a caddie a check for ten percent of his keep. In Mark O'Meara's West Coast tear, he earned most of his $194,000 in two tournaments—$90,000 for the Hawaiian Open title in early February and $90,000 for winning the Crosby the week before that.

Tom Janus, O'Meara's affable and confident caddie, made $18,000 for the two weeks. Some caddies could live for two years on that, and tell stories for a lifetime.

II

"Can I borrow your pen?" a caddie, wearing a blue Andy Williams–San Diego cap, asked me. He looked vaguely familiar. Hadn't he been Woody Blackburn's caddie when Blackburn won at San Diego a few weeks earlier?

He took the pen and made a mark in his caddie yardage book. I was at Eagle Trace the day before Brad was due to arrive, trying to become familiar with Tour life in a nervous hurry.

"Where could I get one of those yardage books?" I asked the caddie who had my pen. I sensed they were hard to get.

"See that guy with the red hat and the white shirt?" He pointed toward a cement patio outside the bag room, which served as the caddie yard.

"Thanks," I said, stuffing the pen back into my pocket. I went over to the man with the red hat and the white shirt and, I could see now, tattoos on his forearms. He was talking with another caddie.

"Excuse me," I said, "but do you have any yardage books?"

"Any what?" he asked.

"Yardage books?"

"Why would I have any yardage books?" the man with the tattoos wanted to know.

"One of the caddies thought you might have. . . ."

"One of the caddies was wrong," the man said, returning to his conversation with the other caddie.

Feeling slightly humiliated, and more than slightly awkward, I climbed back up the hill to the practice putting green and sat down: Breaking into the world of the caddies was going to be hard.

A distinctive looking man with silver-gray hair stood in front of me. He was Angelo Argea, who had caddied for Nicklaus for over a decade.

"Angie!" a young caddie called to Angelo. They shook hands. "S'up?" the caddie asked.

"Nothing, man," Angelo said back, smiling and continuing to shake his hand. "Nothing at all," he said, as if nothing could be further from the truth. Everything was up.

"You still doin' your book?" the caddie asked.

"For you, man, sure," Angelo said, "only for you." Out of his back pocket came half a dozen yardage books, held together by a rubber band. With motions graceful and deliberate, he popped the rubber band off the books and onto his free left hand. With his right thumb he slid the top book off the pile. He looked at the other caddie, then popped the rubber band back in place and returned the resulting neat pile of yardage books to his back pocket. He folded his arms over his chest and stood with his feet three feet apart. He was a measured, steady, graceful man.

"How much, ten?" the caddie asked.

"Oh, no," said Angelo. "I know where you guys are coming from. Just six." Angelo's hands didn't move as the caddie dug into his front pockets and started pulling out crumpled single dollar bills, one by one. He got six of them neatly ordered and only then handed them to Angelo.

"Thanks," said the caddie as he inserted the money between a sliver Angelo created between his index and middle fingers.

"Thank *you*," said Angelo. He broke up his position to shake the caddie's hand. "Play good this week," he said.

When the other caddie walked off, Angelo pocketed the money.

The transaction didn't look so difficult.

"Do you have any more of those for sale?" I asked.

" 'Course I do, my friend," Angelo said, repeating his graceful procedure as he pulled the books out of his back pocket and removed the rubber band.

"Six?" I asked.

"Well," said Angelo, "normally they're eight. But I'll let it go for six."

I handed him the money.

"Who you working for?" Angelo asked.

"Brad Faxon."

Angelo nodded slowly, impressed.

"How long you been with him?"

"This is my first week."

"Friend of his from home, I suppose? You know Brad from Massachusetts?"

"Well, sort of. I guess you could say that."

"You from Massachusetts yourself?"

"I've lived there."

"But you're not from there."

"Well, no, not from there." I said.

"Where you from?" Angelo asked.

"New York," I said.

"New York City?"

"Well, no, New York State."

"Where?"

"Patchogue," I said. "On the south shore of Long Island."

"Oh, Patchogue, Patchogue. I know Patchogue," Angelo said.

"You do?"

"Oh, sure. Lot of us guys know Patchogue."

"How's that?"

"Well, you got to drive through Patchogue to get out to Shinnecock Hills," he said. "Patchogue, sure, Patchogue. Why didn't you just say that?"

"It didn't occur to me that you would have heard of it," I said.

"Oh, sure, we've heard of it. We've heard everything out here," Angelo said. "Patchogue. Just say that. Out here we like to know where people are from."

He returned his sunglasses from the top of his head to the bridge of his nose and smiled. We shook hands. It seemed that Angelo did a lot of smiling and shaking hands. That was all. Angelo, retired celebrity caddie, had to attend to other business: A small crowd had developed around the putting green, and Angelo wanted to know why.

Charley Pride, the singer, was trying to make a downhill, curling, twelve-foot putt on the practice green as he waited to tee off in the pro-am being played that day. A crowd had gathered, including a photographer intent on getting a shot of Pride, the crowd, and the putt going in the hole.

Pride stroked the twelve-footer. The ball sat on the left lip but refused to fall in.

"One more, one more," the photographer said.

"Okay, okay, one more," Pride said for the fifth time.

He missed again. The crowd hissed.

"One more, one more," the photographer said.

"Okay, okay, one more," said Pride.

A miss. Another miss. Another miss. More hissing.

Pride set down the ball, looked over the line, peered into the cup, and, finally, rolled the ball into it. The crowd whooped with pleasure; the photographer literally twirled with delight.

"I got it, I got it," he said, cheering for himself.

"Yep," said Pride, "you got it."

Pride worked his way over to the practice tee. The crowd followed him. I suppose they wanted to see what his *next* trick was going to be.

At the entrance to the practice tee an attractive woman sat in a lawn chair with a shoe box underneath it. Every so often a player or a caddie would come up to her and hand her ten dollars. She would then dip into the shoe box in which she carried several dozen yardage books.

"Excuse me," I said after she had made a sale and before she returned to her novel. "Who is allowed to buy those books?"

"Anybody who wants to," she said. "Players, caddies, spectators. Anybody with ten dollars." She smiled.

"What's the difference between this book," I asked,

pulling the Angelo book out of my pocket, "and your book?"

"This book is better," she said, pointing to her book. Her direct manner was convincing. I shelled out ten bucks.

I had just bought the Book, as it is called on the Tour, which, after the towel, is the caddie's most important aid. The Book diagrams each hole of a golf course, showing bunkers, water, out-of-bounds markers, trees, and, most important, sprinkler heads. Sprinkler heads, and certain other significant landmarks, are marked in the Book with numbers. These numbers tell the distance from the landmark to the front of the green. They are an invaluable aid in club selection.

The Book is prepared by George L. Lucas II, a retired Tour caddie, who travels the country a few weeks ahead of the Tour schedule gathering data for his books. He continually revises them, showing a new tee, a new green, a new bunker. Yet, for all the Book's detail, Lucas needs but one day and one junior assistant to do his research. His method is simple, proven, and unpatented, but wholly his own. He stands on the front edge of a green with a fishing rod and reel, wound with 300 yards of line. The reel is rigged to measure yards as the line goes out. Lucas directs his assistant, usually a local boy, to various landmarks, reels the line in until it is taut, and notes the yardage in a notebook.

The players consider the yardages extremely accurate. Only a few don't use them. Jack Nicklaus, who was one of the first players to employ a yardage book, uses his own yardage books, many of which he made in the 1960s. His caddie, though, double-checks the figures with the Book, and occasionally finds contradictions. Bernhard Langer, the West German player, makes his own books, measuring the course with a surveyor's wheel. Seldom seen in the United States, the surveyor's wheel is widely used among caddies and players in Europe. They believe it is the most accurate method of determining yardage. The Americans, basically, trust George.

But not completely. There is an endless, feverish quest among caddies and players to find mistakes. When somebody discovers a difference of two or three yards, general pandemonium erupts, complete with philosophical debate that throws into question not only that particular book, but the entire institution of yardages by George.

Not everyone is caught up in the yardage game. Most of the Australian caddies on the U.S. Tour don't care about the surveyor's wheel or the Book. "Show me the player who can differentiate between 203 yards and 207 yards," an Australian caddie told me once. "I want to be on his bag."

The Lucas book is filled with cryptic notes and his own brand of humor. For instance, of hole seven at Eagle Trace, a 193-yard par three, Lucas warns:

"If pin is cut near back left area, more accurate yardage will be obtained if you subtract approximate pin from back left measurement because green depth varies from thirty-six to forty-two depending upon which tee you use. P.S. Read that again—I didn't get it the first time either."

Sometimes Lucas gives his opinion of the par on the hole. On a par four of 470 yards, Lucas might write on the top of the diagram: "No. 10, 470 yards, par $4\frac{7}{16}$."

Some of the yardages in the Book are marked with the initials J.I.C., which stands for Just In Case. There are yardages from a course's more awkward locations, where a player is not supposed to put his ball but inevitably does. In extreme cases Lucas marks the yardages J.I.C.Y.F.U. and J.I.C.Y.R.F.U. These dour witticisms are supposed to perk up the troubled golfer.

Angelo Argea's yardage book is a less detailed version of the Book. Argea's book does not show the

contours of the green with the precision that Lucas's
book does, nor does it get the shape of the bunkers as
accurately. About the only thing it has that the Book
doesn't is a letter from the author inside. Angelo's
growing ego was one of the problems Nicklaus cited,
privately, when the famous team went their separate
ways.

I brought the Book to bed with me that night,
trying to become familiar with it, nervous for the
next morning when I would finally meet Brad. My
mind wandered.

"Morning, Brad. Oh, you've never played Eagle
Trace before? Well, the first hole is a short par four,
just 396 yards, but it's tight. You can hit driver, but
you've got to hit it big, through the bottleneck in the
fairway 240 yards out. And you've got to watch out
for the grass bunkers on the right. I think we might
want to play short of the trouble off the tee with, say,
a two iron. Won't leave us with more than an eight or
a nine iron to the green. It's the sort of green where
you *want* to be hitting a full shot into it, if you know
what I mean.

"Now, on number two, you want to hit a driver. . . ."
I was asleep before we had played the front nine.

III

I met Brad's golf bag before I met Brad, a large
black Titleist bag with Brad's name painted on it in
white block letters. A fresh white towel was wrapped
around the necks of the golf clubs, in the same spirit
in which a boxer puts a fresh towel around his neck
before a bout. The dew sparkled in the early morning
sun. It was 7:00 A.M. and the day promised to be hot
and still. I looked around for Brad, not precisely sure
what to look for. I had seen him only on television.

"You lookin' for Brad?" a caddie sitting on a bag
nearby asked.

"Yes," I said.

"Just sit tight; he'll be back in a couple of minutes," he said.

Did my uneasiness show through that obviously?

I looked at the other caddies: They looked comfortable waiting. Some sat on the ends of bags. Some stood in small groups eating doughnuts out of paper bags. One was sprawled on a picnic table in the caddie yard. Is it possible to learn that sort of casualness?

Brad suddenly appeared. We shook hands enthusiastically. "Warm up these eggs, would ya?" Brad asked, handing me a sleeve of new balls. Golfers like to play with warm golf balls. The warmer they are, the farther they'll fly. Warming up the eggs meant stuffing the balls in my pockets.

Brad resembles a giraffe, and I mean that nicely. The giraffe, after all, is a graceful, gentle animal. Brad is tall and thin and his hair color is between orange and blond. He has a long neck and, halfway down it, a prominent Adam's apple, which explains his especially deep, mature-sounding voice. Later, I was often slightly surprised to hear Brad describing a Bruce Springsteen concert, or driving a Porsche at high speeds, or making fun of a tacky hat. His voice and choice of subject matter seemed incongruous.

We walked toward the first tee. "You're a southpaw, eh, Mike?" Brad asked, noting that I was carrying the bag on my left shoulder.

"Just in caddying and hockey. Everything else I do righty," I said.

"What happened to your Rangers last night?" Brad asked.

"They got whopped, huh?"

"Twelve to four."

"St. John's–Georgetown on ESPN tomorrow night," Brad said.

"That should be a good one," I said.

"You see *Killing Fields* yet?" Brad asked.

"Great movie," I said.

"Heard it was awesome."

"Grammys tonight," Brad said.

"Who do you like?"

"Springsteen," said Brad. "I think Springsteen's gonna sweep the whole thing."

Just when I was beginning to think that Brad had an inexhaustible supply of interests and conversation topics, we reached the first tee. Our conversation came to an abrupt end. And for the next five hours Brad concentrated solely on golf.

I cleaned the clubs and the balls and replaced the divots and, for a short while, the whole environment felt as familiar as the Bellport Golf Club. Then Hale Irwin caught up to us in the fifth fairway.

"Hey, Brad," said Irwin.

"Hi, Hale," said Brad. "Did you want to play through?"

"Thanks," said Irwin. He blasted a three-wood shot home on the par five.

"Can you make it to my tournament?" Irwin asked, walking toward his shot before it settled. Irwin, like many of the players, has his own small charity-raising tournament.

"Yes, thank you," said Brad. "Wouldn't miss it."

Hale Irwin may not capture the imagination of the golfing public the way other golfers of similar, or even lesser, accomplishment might. Images of Craig Stadler are probably more formed in the minds of golf fans. But, among the pros, Hale Irwin is revered for being one of the game's most consistent scorers, one of the game's best shot-makers, and, most important, a winner of the U.S. Open not once, but twice. He doesn't have the presence of Nicklaus. He doesn't have the glib charisma of Trevino. He doesn't have the guts of Watson. Television announcers pick up on that kind of stuff. Irwin's colleagues do not. Going into 1985, he was the fourth-leading money winner in the history of the game. Brad watched intently as Irwin made that three-wood shot.

The practice rounds did not help my skills in using the yardage book. By the time I figured out which sprinkler head in the book corresponded with which sprinkler head in the fairway, Brad would already be standing over his ball. Brad carried a yardage book, too, and was quick at figuring out the yardages. (Or I was slow.)

His concentration was enormous, and the shots fantastic, long, high, and gently curving depending on the requirements of the shot. He never left his long putts short of the hole and he nailed his short putts squarely into the back center of the cup, in the same manner of a good foul shot in basketball hitting the back of the rim. His shots landed softly with lots of spin and his chip shots ran to the hole with authority. It was an impressive display. Later, I learned that all of the good players can play that way in practice rounds, as long as their games are working. The winners are those who can play like that all week long.

When we finished our practice round it was noon and the course had become crowded with spectators. Brad, after signing autographs, told me to watch the bag and wait for him on the putting green while he went into the clubhouse for lunch. He said I should grab lunch, too, and that after lunch *we* would putt.

"Good luck finding lunch here," Brad said.

I said the grilled hamburgers smelled good.

"Junk food," Brad said. He was smiling, but serious.

I asked him what he would have for lunch.

"Probably three turkey sandwiches on whole wheat, some fruit, trail mix, and juice," he said.

"Three sandwiches?" I asked.

"I'm trying to put on weight," said Brad, who weighs 170 pounds when he's home and 160 pounds when he's on the Tour.

When Brad returned from lunch he did not look

remotely bloated, or in need of a siesta. The temperature was ninety, life was moving, generally, leisurely, and Brad had more energy than he did at 7:00 A.M., which was considerable.

"Let's make some putts," Brad said. And that is how he spent his afternoon. Making putts. Hundreds of them.

Brad explained that his psychologist, Dr. Bob Rotella, who advises many professional athletes, had Brad on a strict putting program: fifty straight three-footers one day, forty straight four-footers the second day, and thirty straight five-footers on the third day. Under the program, whenever Brad feels uncomfortable with his putting stroke, he goes back to the three-footers and builds himself up again to the five-footers.

With great care Brad searched the green for a perfectly level three-foot putt. He put down three balls and began putting. My job was to count putts and throw the balls back to him. Our talk was spare.

"How many that time?" he asked once.

"Twenty-seven," I said.

He putted in silence until he missed.

"How many that time?"

"Thirty-four."

"Stroke's good; concentration isn't."

Every putt received a full effort: practice stroke, address, look at the hole, look at the ball, stroke.

The putts rolled in, again and again and again, almost all of them in the center of the hole and firm. If a putt went in off-center, Brad's face would crinkle into a disturbed expression.

"What am I up to?" Brad asked. He had lost count due to several interruptions: a caddie asked for a job for Las Vegas; a Hogan company representative said his new driver would arrive soon; Willie Wood wanted to make arrangements to watch the St. John's–Georgetown game.

"Forty-seven," I said.

He made number forty-eight. He made number forty-nine.

"This is for the U.S. Open," he said, looking at number fifty. He popped it in and said immediately, "Let's take some long putts, then we'll hit some balls."

I looked at my watch. It was 3:30 P.M. Brad had been putting for over two hours. Brad may love the game, I thought to myself, and it may be a game, but what he's doing now is work.

Most of golf's most familiar figures were on the putting green and at the practice tee: Nicklaus, Irwin, Seve Ballesteros, Peter Jacobsen, Curtis Strange, Johnny Miller, Hubert Green, John Mahaffey, Andy Bean, Payne Stewart, Gary Koch, J. C. Snead, Calvin Peete, Greg Norman, Raymond Floyd, Craig Stadler, Hal Sutton, Mark O'Meara, Fred Couples, Tom Kite, Ben Crenshaw, Bruce Lietzke, George Burns, George Archer, Denis Watson, Bob Eastwood, Nick Faldo, Bernhard Langer. The Honda Classic drew an impressive field. The good tournaments always do.

The most important tournaments, to professionals, are the four majors: the U.S. Open, the Masters, the British Open, and the Professional Golfers' Association Championship. After these, the most coveted title is the Tournament Players Championship, and then the Memorial Tournament. The T.P.C. is played at the Tournament Players Club in Ponte Vedra, Florida, at the headquarters of the P.G.A. Tour. Officials and players consider the T.P.C. their showpiece. The Memorial is Nicklaus's own tournament. Players come at his invitation and play a course he designed.

Some argue that the Tournament of Champions and the World Series of Golf, both tournaments with large purses whose fields are limited to those who have won tournaments in the preceding year, are of equal importance. Others argue that these tournaments are merely television-inspired commercial golfing shows. Regardless, they are prized tournaments.

After these, the most sought titles are the old Tour stops played, for the most part, on rugged, stern golf courses: the Western Open, which began in 1899 and is played at the Butler National Golf Club, outside Chicago; the Los Angeles Open, which began in 1926 and is played at the Riviera Country Club; the Bing Crosby National Pro-Am, which began in 1937 and is played on three courses on the Monterey Peninsula, including the Pebble Beach Golf Club; the Colonial National Invitation, which began in 1947 and is played on the Colonial Country Club, outside Dallas; and the Bay Hill Classic, which began only in 1966, but requires an invitation from Arnold Palmer. It is played at the Bay Hill Club, outside Orlando.

Most of the game's leading players make certain to play in these thirteen tournaments. For Nicklaus, Watson, Trevino, and Irwin, these thirteen tournaments will account for at least half their playing schedule. In these tournaments, Watson has tallied fourteen of his thirty-one victories, and Nicklaus has won thirty-one of his seventy titles.

But the golf year is not limited to those thirteen events; the 1985 P.G.A. Tour schedule comprised forty-seven tournaments. At least eight other tournaments annually get top players; all offer something to distinguish themselves. At the Bob Hope Classic the golfers are treated luxuriously. The Hawaiian Open is a relaxed, fun tournament; some players bring their families and consider the week a working vacation. The Panasonic–Las Vegas Invitational is played on three mediocre courses, but the $950,000 purse is the biggest of the year; just about everybody who is eligible to play will do so. The players admire the Sea Pines Heritage Classic, played on Hilton Head Island, South Carolina; it is a well-run tournament played on one of the country's best courses. The

Byron Nelson Classic, because it is an old tournament, because it honors one of the game's great
players, and because it has a healthy purse, gets a
good field.

Three other tournaments attract the top players,
not only because they have large purses but because
they are played on courses owned by the P.G.A. Tour.
These are the Houston Open, played at the Tournament Players Club at the Woodlands; the Sammy
Davis, Jr.-Greater Hartford Open, which is played at
the Tournament Players Club of Connecticut; and the
Honda Classic. To pass on these tournaments would
be something akin to missing your own birthday
party.

We walked out to the Honda Classic practice tee.
Brad wedged his way between John Mahaffey and
Willie Wood and started beating balls. Seve Ballesteros was practicing at one end and Johnny Miller at
the other. Just about everybody was there and working hard. This was serious golf.

IV

By three in the morning, back at the Holiday Inn, I
realized something dramatic had happened during
the course of the day. My neck had grown several
puffy inches in diameter. Any motion that caused the
skin to fold at all, even little, everyday things like
moving my head, bending an arm, or blinking, pro-
voked pain. I was quite sunburned. At 3:30 A.M. I was
in the car in search of aid. The only place open in
Coral Springs, the front desk said, was a 7-Eleven.

"Oh, you've got it bad," the woman behind the
counter said when I asked her to point me to the skin
care department.

She did not say this menacingly; actually, she said
it kindly. With arms bright pink, I must have presented an odd sight. But she was an odd sight, too: Do
you recall ever seeing a grandmother working the

cash register at a 7-Eleven at four in the morning?

"My grandson, he's seventeen, and he was visiting us and he got it real bad, too," she said. "We went to the beach, him with his skinny white legs. When we came back they were elephant legs. Pink elephant legs. We told him, vinegar and water, half and half, that's the thing to do. He said he wanted to go to the hospital. He thought he was dying. So we took him to the hospital. Know what they said? Vinegar and water, half and half. My grandson, he didn't want to do it, thought it was grandmother advice. Know something? It worked. Took the hurt right out of his legs."

I bought a fifty-nine-cent bottle of vinegar. I also bought an eight-ounce jar of Golden Harvest Sun Burn Relief Lotion and three ounces of Solarcaine Lotion and Golden Harvest Sun Block Number 15.

Nothing stopped the burn. Not even the vinegar and water. I waited for sunrise and headed to Eagle Trace, this time in a long-sleeved shirt, sunglasses, a hat and dripping in sun block. Brad laughed when he saw me.

"When you get through the Tour school, they bring in a dermatologist at the end. He talks about skin care," said Brad. "Clinique, number nineteen—the strongest stuff they got—that's the ticket," said Brad.

I hoisted the bag on my shoulder and tried to keep my yelp to myself. My lesson was a day late. The only thing I could prove now was my toughness. I turned up my collar and marched into the sun.

V

Our tee time was for 7:38 A.M. on Thursday morning for the first round of the Honda Classic. We were the dew sweepers.

On tournament days, Brad arrives at the golf course one hour before his tee time, time enough to putt, chip, and hit a bucket of balls at a leisurely pace. You wouldn't want to arrive much more than an hour before your tee time, he said: Butterflies might set in. But you wouldn't want to arrive too much later, either, he said: Hastiness might set in. The preround warm-up is not the time to think about swing mechanics, he said. It's not a time to think at all. It's a time to feel the swing, to get loose, to get comfortable.

When I arrived at the course it was not yet dawn and there was an eerie, beautiful serenity over the golf course. Fog banks had rolled in; they were especially dense over the ponds and in the valleys. The ground and the bushes were dripping with dew. If you scraped your leg against one your pants would be soaking wet, and your leg cold. Before the sun rises, a February day in Florida has all the wet-cool of Martha's Vineyard in early spring. My sneakers were wet and squeaky and blades of recently cut grass clung to their sides and to the tops of the toes.

The caddies arrived first on this day. Some of the more nocturnal ones came straight from the conclusion of a night out. For others, the early start was a way of life. A few caddies carried the morning's paper, but the fog was too thick to read.

Some of the caddies walked to the golf course. Who knows from where they came, or for how long they walked. Some hitched rides in with marshalls, scorekeepers, and volunteers. A few of the battered caddie cars that limp across the United States from Tour stop to Tour stop brought a few more. For me, the whole scene and setting were exciting; for the (caddie) pros, it was another day.

The good caddie arrives before his player. The statement is small but important: I'm here to take care of you, the caddie is saying. The caddies wait for their players to arrive near the entrance to the clubhouse, which they cannot enter.

I was not surprised to see Brad pull his clubs out of

his car trunk, even though most of the players leave their bags in the bag room. Bringing his clubs home each night is another part of his deliberate, careful approach to the game, an approach that includes seeing a nutritionist and sports psychologist and arriving precisely an hour before his tee time. He warmed up in the lifting fog and emerging light. We worked our way over to the first tee. There, Brad chatted with his playing partners, David Ogrin and Mike Donald.

"I heard you won a Cadillac," Brad said to Donald.

Donald, courtesy of a hole-in-one a few weeks earlier, had won the car.

"I'm trying to get a Porsche out of the deal," said Donald.

"How's that?" asked Brad.

"The guy who owns the Cadillac dealership has a brother who owns a Porsche dealership. They're trying to work out a trade so I can get the Porsche for a couple of grand," said Donald.

"That's not a bad deal," said Brad.

"God knows I'm too cheap to get a Porsche any other way," said Donald.

Although Brad made all pars on the front nine, the round did not begin well. He did not hit the ball with nearly the authority he had in the practice rounds. He sprayed the ball to unexplored places, some of them right off the Book. But he got some breaks, too. A ball that could have rolled into the water was held up by a clump of grass. Several putts rimmed the lip and fell in when they could have stayed out.

To be more than generous to myself, I was less than stellar as a caddie. My intentions were good; my performance was not. I had many indications that things were not going well. For instance, after tee shots Brad walked down the fairway with Mike Donald's caddie, Greg Rita, who is called Boats. (His feet are the size of a small yacht.) Boats caddies for

Gil Morgan when Morgan plays, which is in about twenty-three tournaments a year. That leaves Boats with about twenty other tournaments a year to fill. Boats went to the same high school as Bruce Edwards, who caddies for Tom Watson. Boats and Bruce are good friends. This association, and his ability, make Boats one of the more sought-after caddies. In their fairway walks, Brad and he discussed the outcome of the St. John's–Georgetown game, the Grammy Awards, and which weeks Boats could work for Brad in the future. This last topic, naturally, was worrisome to me.

As the round progressed, I tried harder and harder to do a good job. But, as you know from taking a driver's license test, or from playing golf, the harder you try the worse you usually do. The work, and this refers to what Brad calls the "basics," not the intangibles, *is* harder than it looks. First, you must know where each player is all the time. Walking ahead of another player, and into the line of his shot, is an offense on par with a member of the chorus walking upstage from a play's star. Green etiquette is especially tricky. It is unlikely that a caddie, wearing tennis or basketball sneakers, could do physical damage by walking in the line of a putt, but that is not the issue. The issue is that a golfer cannot make a putt if a caddie steps in his line. The player will be too startled by the grand faux pas.

The caddie must also know which player will make the final putt on each hole; the caddie whose player makes the final putt is responsible for putting the pin back. Should a caddie, in a fit of absentmindedness, forget this responsibility, he will, undoubtedly, be reminded by the caddie stuck with the task, and, at the next tee, said caddie's tone will not be pleasant: "I'm not here to do your work," he might say.

The caddie must anticipate. On some greens he must have the player's driver, or three wood, or one iron, ready to hand him. Many players change balls every third hole; they get bent out of shape even on good shots. The caddie must have the new eggs ready and warm. On the ninth hole the player needs his scorecard, which the caddie usually holds for him, to give to the scorekeepers. The caddie must have it ready. The ninth hole, halfway through a round, is also a natural time for a player to dip into his bag for a banana or an apple or a Snickers bar. The good caddie knows his player's stomach as well as he knows his game and dips into the bag for him. At any given moment, and sometimes several times in the course of a single hole, a player may take on or off a sweater or rain gear or a jacket. The caddie folds the article and puts it back in the bag. And this must be done with a minimum of fuss, for no player wants a reputation for being overly concerned with the care of his clothing.

Just like responsibilities in the office, the caddie must sometimes face all his tasks at once. If he is experienced and competent, a caddie handles these all-at-once situations instinctively. If he is a neophyte, these situations are recipes for disaster.

On the ninth hole Brad pushed his drive badly into the rough. His second shot was treacherous: His ball had burrowed its way to the bottom of an entangled congregation of grass, and he was still 220 yards away from the hole on a ferocious par four. The shot was a blind one; Brad could not see the top of the pin from where he stood, nor any part of the green; a sizable hill was in his way. We climbed to the top of the hill to get a view of the shot. Brad positioned me in a line between his ball and the pin so he would know where to play the shot. He returned to the ball, taking a five iron with him, the least-lofted club he could hit out of that lie, and addressed the ball, using me for his line. He set up and waved me to the side. He had his line. With a great flurry of swing and flying grass, Brad played his shot. The ball squirted out of the high grass softly, moving like a knuckle ball, flew over the top of the hill by ten yards, flew one hundred yards, and rolled twenty more.

Brad was not pleased with the shot and, gripping the club with one hand, smashed it into the ground. The display of temper was atypical for him; he was clearly upset. I waited for him at the top of the hill to take his club. (Golfers like to get rid of their clubs as quickly as possible after mediocre shots.)

"Don't ever stand in my view while I'm making a shot again," Brad said. He was curt, but not hostile.

"I'm sorry," I said. I felt sheepish. "I thought when you waved me right you wanted me to stay on top of the hill to watch the shot."

"A caddie should never be in a player's line of vision when he is making a shot," Brad said. "You should have come back down to the ball."

Although he is a thorough New Englander, Brad is seldom terse. I had obviously blundered. Considerably.

We walked in silence. I felt stupid. The ball was in J.I.C.Y.F.U. territory, and so was I.

By the time I located the sprinkler head nearest to the ball, Brad had already figured out the yardage.

"I've got ninety-five yards," Brad said. Yardages between seventy and one hundred twenty are the most important to determine precisely. In that range the player must make refined decisions between sand wedges and pitching wedges, and how hard to hit them.

A good, experienced caddie might have said, "Ninety-five yards; that's what I've got, too. Let's put in on the pin and save par."

Brad knocked a sand wedge to ten feet by himself.

Brad's ten-footer was the last putt; both Ogrin and Donald had tapped in after taking longer putts. I had the pin. Brad would need a new ball after putting

out. I had failed a caddie basic: I would not have his
new ball ready and warm. As he stood over his putt,
I realized he would need his driver and scorecard
here, too. It was too late to pull out the driver; doing
so would risk distracting him. I felt my pockets for
the scorecard. I couldn't find it. The situation was
serious. The group behind us stood in the fairway,
waiting to play their shots. Our group was in jeopardy of being assessed a two-stroke penalty for slow
play.

Brad made his putt to save par. I put the pin back
in the hole and ran back to the bag, where Brad
stood. I pulled out the driver, stumbling with the
head cover and handed him the club.

"New ball?" asked Brad.

"I'll have to get one out of the bag," I said.

"Scorecard?" he asked.

I stared at him blankly, not knowing what to say.
Cold sweat. Everywhere. He yanked it out of my shirt
pocket.

No question about it, I was screwing up.

"Come on, they're waiting. Go to the tee," Brad
said, and we walked to the tenth tee. Brad reached
into the bag and grabbed a new package of balls,
which he handed to me. He took off his sweater and
handed me that, too. He took out a banana and
started to peel it. Ogrin and Donald played their tee
shots. After they played their shots, Brad handed me
his banana.

Brad hit his tee shot; this one again pushed to the
right. Brad wanted to get rid of the driver as soon as
he was off the tee. He handed me that, too. He looked
at me, juggling the sweater, the package of balls, the
half-eaten banana, and the driver.

"Your hands are too full," he said, taking back his
banana.

Brad walked toward his ball as I folded and put
away the sweater. I took the golf balls out of their

package, stuffed them in my pockets, threw out the package, put the headcover back on the driver, and put the driver back in the bag. The towel needed water on this hot day quickly growing hotter. I gave it some from the water cooler on the now deserted tenth tee.

I ran down the fairway. A good caddie always beats his man to the ball. That's one of the basics. Forget about the intangibles.

VI

Brad arrived at Eagle Trace early on Friday, even though we had a late tee time. He wanted to work on his putting. I sat at the hole and threw balls back to Brad as he putted. I was nervous on two counts: My poor performance had rattled me, and I knew that if we failed to make the thirty-six-hole cut, my career as Brad's caddie was sunk. We needed to play well.

"Caddying's not so easy, huh," Brad said as I threw back three shiny Titleist 90s.

"No, it's not."

"It's hard work," Brad said.

Brad is not a prima donna; he simply has high expectations, for himself and for those who work for him. He expects things to go smoothly. No player can afford to worry about his caddie: Playing the game for five concentrated hours is difficult enough. The good caddie helps funnel all the player's concentration to his shot-making; he is a valued companion in moments of pressure; he is a scapegoat in times of poor play; he is a cheerleading coach in times of waning interest. These seemingly contradictory rules *do* make the caddie's job "hard work."

On the second day my caddying improved. On the ninth green, for instance, I had Brad's ball, scorecard, and driver ready. Brad's play improved, too. Through twenty-seven holes, he was still even par, just as he had been the day before, but the pars came more easily. They were two-putt pars, not scramblers. It seemed just a question of time before the birdies would start falling.

But they didn't, and by the fifteenth hole we were on the edge of making or missing the cut.

Brad hit a good, strategic tee shot there, in the middle of a fairway, practically on top of a sprinkler head marked by a number, 155.

"One fifty-five to the front, the pin's twenty yards back, 175 all the way," Brad said. He took out a six iron, and started to consider the shot.

"Brad," I said, taking a chance, plunging into his concentration with the rattle of potato chips being eaten in a library. "I think that's sprinkler head *number* 155. According to the Book, the yardage to the front is 135." Brad pulled out his book. If I was wrong I was cooked. If I was right it was a big save.

"Yep," said Brad. He handed me the six iron. "One thirty-five to the front, plus twenty, 155 to the hole," he said. He took out an eight iron and knocked it stiff. He made the putt for birdie.

The six iron would have been far too much. He would have "airmailed" the green, as the golfers say, and we would have been fortunate to make a bogey.

"I was just testing you," Brad said with a smile after the putt. He was under par for the first time in the tournament. All we had to do was par in to make the cut.

We made the cut by a shot. My contribution was small, but not insignificant. Had Brad hit that six iron, we probably would have missed the cut. Our moods lifted.

My caddying improved on the weekend. Although I wasn't coaxing Brad out of hard nine irons in favor of smooth eights, or urging him to play downhill twelve foot putts with double breaks on the left lip, I was, at least, getting the basics down. Brad didn't have to worry about me constantly; I wasn't in the way. I thought things had gone pretty well. Then it came time for Brad to pay me.

"Well, I *am* going to pay you," Brad said.

He wrote me a check for $305, $250 for the weekly salary and $55, which constituted five percent of his winnings.

I asked him if I could work for him in the future; the question came out in garbled words and a shaky voice.

"I'm going to have to think about that," Brad said. "You improved as the week progressed, that's for sure. Had you asked me after Thursday, it would have been a definite 'No.' "

I felt slightly hopeful.

"I'd say why don't we try it again for next week, at Bay Hill, but I've already made another arrangement with somebody for that week," Brad said.

"Maybe I could get a bag there, work on my caddie technique, and we could hook up the following week in New Orleans?" I asked. Caddies and players *hook up* unless they *go their separate ways.*

"Maybe New Orleans," Brad said. "I wouldn't suggest you go up to Bay Hill. It's an invitational, and the field is limited to about a hundred. As it is, a lot of the regular caddies aren't going to get bags. I think you'd have a hard time landing something up there. I'll give you a call when I make a decision about New Orleans," Brad said.

I hope I'm not fired, I thought as I flew back to New York, calculating my losses for the week, which were $350; I just hope I'm not fired.

3
CAJUN CADDIE

I

MY WORST FEAR came true. Brad fired me.

I got the word in New Orleans. I had flown there on the Saturday of the Bay Hill Classic, on the only cheap flight I could get.

I called Brad Sunday afternoon at the conclusion of Bay Hill.

"I don't think it's going to work out for New Orleans," was all he said.

My heart sunk. I didn't ask if that meant just for New Orleans, or for New Orleans and after. I didn't want to know the answer.

New Orleans, which is what the players call the U.S.F.&G. Classic, played at the Lakewood Country Club, does not attract many of the Tour's leading players, leaving spots available for some of the Tour's lower-ranked players. These players do not have the luxury of knowing in what tournaments they will play. Therefore, they do not have the luxury of

47

arranging for a caddie before a tournament. So I still had a chance for a bag. But I needed to move quickly.

I headed out to the golf course with Wally Brewer, the young manager of the Grenoble House, where I was staying. Wally wanted to offer a discounted rate for golfers through the tournament's hospitality desk. He was trying to drum up business for the historic hotel his family had recently purchased.

The Lakewood Country Club is built directly on a commercial highway, ten miles from New Orleans's French Quarter, home of the Grenoble House. Dusk was approaching; the course and the clubhouse were quiet. A lone player worked on the putting green. I knew the golfer: He was Bill Britton, one of New York's top amateur golfers when I was in high school. When he made the three straight putts, I walked over and introduced myself.

"What'd you do, move down to New Orleans to take a job?" Bill asked. He had a slight accent that revealed his Staten Island upbringing. I found the familiarity of it comforting.

"Actually, I'm here for the tournament. I'm trying to get started as a Tour caddie," I said.

I mentioned, briefly, my tryout with Brad. Did he need a caddie for the week?

"Actually, I do," Bill said. "Why don't we give it a try tomorrow? We'll see how it works out."

And in a single conversation all my despair over Brad Faxon dissipated. I had a bag! The warm, sweet, early evening air blended with the smell of freshly cut grass and suddenly the Lakewood Country Club filled me with all the hope I once felt at the Edgartown Golf Club, at Bellport, and in Mr. Greenlee's eighth-grade golf gym class.

Bill and I met at the golf course at eight the next morning. We played a practice round and, between shots, got acquainted. At one point our conversation turned to newspapers.

"There's a guy on the *Staten Island Advance* who writes about golf. I think he's a good writer, a nice guy. They've given me a lot of ink over the years," Bill said. "Every time I come back to the island after having been out on the Tour for a while we'll talk and he'll write something up. I know what the first paragraph's going to say before I even see the paper: 'Life on the Tour sure is tough if you're not a super-star. Staten Island golfer Bill Britton knows.' And they'll have a nice story about how I'm working really hard on my game but I'm not making any big checks and how there's a lot of travel and a lot of hotels and a lot of expense. By the end, he's usually cheerleading for me to play better.

"There's really only one reason I'd like to be written up in the paper," Bill said, "and that's for playing good golf."

Bill Britton, a trim five-foot, seven-inch, twenty-nine-year-old, was going through a difficult time when we met in New Orleans. He was playing poorly, and had been for two years, since the end of 1982. In 1982, his second year on the tour, Bill played well, earning $75,328 and finishing fifty-seventh on the money list. At the end of the season, he placed second in the Walt Disney Classic when he lost a play-off to Hal Sutton. It was Sutton's first win as a professional. It was the last time Bill played outstanding golf.

Bill plays with Hogan clubs and takes that master golfer's approach to the game: endless practice, fierce determination, constant attention to swing mechanics. He has certain Hogan mannerisms: the deliberate gait, the erect posture, the tight, controlled gestures. Bill speaks the same way: measured, precise, always with care. His model is a great one; many professional golfers considered Hogan at his prime to be golf's best shot maker ever. By choosing Hogan as an ideal, Bill revealed something about himself and his deepest attitude about the game. Bill's ideal was not the player who had won the most money or the most tournaments, and not the longest hitter in the game or the most glamorous. He chose Hogan, the great shot maker. Everything else flows from shot making. To some, everything else would mean fame, wealth, position, prosperity. To Hogan, and to Britton, it meant, and means, good golf scores.

By the time Bill was in high school, Hogan had long retired from tournament golf, returning to Texas, where he could hit balls and design clubs out of the public eye. His clubs, classic and simple, appealed to Bill. No nonsense.

Bill learned to play golf from Jim Albus when Albus was a driving-range teaching pro on Staten Island. He gave Bill a grip, some golf balls, and a start. Bill's age was then in single digits, and his scores in triple digits. By the time Bill was in high school, Jim Albus had graduated to a top club-pro job at the Piping Rock Golf Club, on Long Island. Bill bought a set of Hogan Apex irons in the Piping Rock pro shop that he used all through high school and college. Bill became a good golfer with those irons. He took them with him when he made it to the Tour. The Hogan company responded: They gave Bill a big red, white, and blue Hogan bag and complete Hogan wardrobe: trousers and shirts and sweaters. Everything had Hogan's signature on it. Bill Britton was shrouded in his golf hero. For two years—his first two years on the tour—Bill played a Ben Hogan-style game. He was straight. He hit a lot of greens in regulation. He scored consistently around par. Sometimes he scored a great deal lower. It was on a Sunday in the October of his second year that Bill shot a 64 to catch Hal Sutton in the Walt Disney Classic.

A few months later, at the end of the season, Bill

retired those Hogan clubs. They were worn-out. You seldom see worn-out clubs in amateur circles. On the Tour it happens every week.

When a professional's clubs wear out, the sweet spot on the face becomes dull in color. The scoring lines on the face, which impart spin on the ball, lose all sense of definition, as if you have drawn a line in the soft sand on the edge of the ocean. In extreme cases the sweet spot can actually become concave and render the clubs in violation of United States Golf Association rules.

Bill intended to retire only the clubs; unintentionally, part of his game was retired with them. When I met Bill in New Orleans, he was searching for the missing parts of his game. The search was two years old, and going strong.

Bill hit balls on the driving range for a couple of hours and then putted for a couple of hours: just a regular ten-hour practice day.

Whether it was because we were both from New York, or because it had been a while since Bill had a caddie who cared about his golf game, I don't know, but Bill and I struck up an immediate rapport as golfer and caddie. My caddie skills were improving and Bill seemed to reward effort, and value it.

"I'm glad I found you," Bill said at the end of the day. "You've got the job. I pay $200 for the week and five percent; is that OK?" Bill asked.

"That's fine," I said, ecstatic.

The golf Tour, I thought to myself, does not begin and end with Brad Faxon.

II

Back at the Grenoble House, Wally Brewer and his all-purpose assistant, John Rowland, drank beer and cooked steaks on a grill beside the pool, which was next to the Jacuzzi. They were discussing strategy. John had a date and would not be able to tend to one of his usual duties: the after-dinner distribution of chocolate mint candies on the bed of each guest. Wally was to pinch hit.

"It's best to put the candies right on the pillows," John said. "If you put them on the bedspread, the colors blend and the guests don't see them."

I asked Wally if he had any luck drawing guests through the tournament office.

"Not only didn't I get any golfers, I didn't get Jerry Ford, Jimmy Carter, or Eddie Murphy either," Wally said in mock disgust.

John explained: Murphy was coming to New Orleans to do a show. Ford and Carter were here for a debate. "That's my date," John said, looking embarrassed. "She's into that stuff; so is my father. If I don't go, he'd really start wondering." He was talking about the debate.

John's father, the Reverend Richard Rowland, was Dean of the New Orleans Christ Church Cathedral. But John was more interested in money than God, and on this he and his father differed. The Grenoble House job was only part of the budding John Rowland empire. He also owned Southern Hospitality Systems, a party catering business. He made no pretense about why he was going to the debate: to please his date; to please his father; and to please himself. The debate was an important opportunity to make contacts. Or, as he put it: "Anybody who's anybody will be at the thing. Wanna come?"

"Absolutely," I said.

Wally couldn't make it. He had just begun at the hotel as its interim manager. Normally, he was the advertising and promotion department of Precision Tune, a chain of car tune-up shops that his family also owned. When Wally wasn't promoting Precision

Tune, or writing advertising copy for it, he was adjusting carburetors and changing oil. That was much of the time. Sitting at the Grenoble House pool, sipping beer, cooking up ways to coax Eddie Murphy to the hotel, he clearly enjoyed his new position and the opportunity it afforded him to practice his relaxed management style.

Before we left for the debate I called the *Boston Globe*, where I had a contact dating back to my Vineyard days, and made arrangements to cover the debate for the paper.

A press conference preceded the debate, for which every reporter in New Orleans evidently took a crash course in U.S.-U.S.S.R. relations. Chernenko had just died, and President Reagan had announced that Vice President Bush would represent the United States at the funeral. That was the day's big news story.

The first group of questions put to Carter and Ford asked if they thought Reagan should go to the funeral himself. The second set of questions involved the state of relations between the Soviet Union and the United States. Then came questions about the Star Wars defense package, the size of the military budget, the escalating arms race, and the use of economic sanctions against the Soviet Union. Carter and Ford dutifully answered these questions, as they no doubt had hundreds of times before. When the press conference came to an end, all the reporters crammed around Carter and Ford to ask the questions for which there was no chance earlier.

"Mr. Ford," I asked, "how's your golf game been this year?"

He had played better at the Bob Hope than he had at the Bing Crosby, but both are great tournaments. He rattled off his schedule, which was extensive, and concluded by saying that he hadn't hit anybody with a golf ball in a long time.

I asked him who his favorite professional golfer was.

"Oh," said Ford, "they're all such great guys." And then he took a question about funeral diplomacy.

I had my lead:

New Orleans—In this city, where residents discuss the Louisiana Purchase as if it were a current event, it seemed like the good old days for a few hours Wednesday night.

Jimmy Carter told a few Amy stories. Jerry Ford reeled off his golf schedule, committed to memory. . . .

III

Much is made, usually by country-club teaching pros with middle-aged female pupils, of the claim that length is an unimportant quality for golf success. This is a myth, and is proven to be one each week on the Tour. Survival there is dependent, in part, on hitting the ball long distances.

Bill is a short hitter, by the inhuman standards of the Tour, and and that puts him at a decided disadvantage. In New Orleans we played with Robert Wrenn and Bill Sander, both of whom are long hitters. Sander, the 1977 U.S. Amateur champion, is especially long. He is about thirty yards longer than Bill off the tee, and a club longer with the irons, meaning he can hit a six iron as far as Bill can hit a five iron. In play these differences translate dramatically.

The fifth hole at Lakewood Country Club is a 410-yard par four. Halfway down the fairway, about 230 yards off the tee, the fairway thins considerably, making for a tight landing area for tee shots, with a series of trees on the right and a twenty-five-yard-deep bunker on the left. Two hundred fifty-five yards off the tee the fairway begins to broaden again. There are fewer trees on the right; there is no bunker on the left.

In a typical Bill Britton 240-yard tee shot, all the hole's challenges come into play. Bill Sander's typical 270-yard drive sails right over the more difficult spots. Britton's 240-yard tee shot leaves him with 170 yards to the hole, a five-iron shot. Sander's 270-yard drive leaves him with 140 yards to the hole, a nine-iron shot. Bill Britton is now asked to be as accurate with a five iron as Bill Sander is with a nine iron. And that assumes Britton is not playing out of a bunker or trees.

Out of necessity, Bill Britton has developed a style of golf game that is distincly different from that of many of his longer-hitting colleagues. His game, when it is on, is to keep the ball in play, hit a lot of fairways, hit a lot of greens. He is a better than average putter, straighter with a five iron than many others are with a seven, a good bunker player, and, most importantly, a sound strategist. Golfers, especially non-long ball hitters, are forever reminding themselves to play their own game. Bill does this steadfastly. Still, it must be psychologically difficult to see other players blowing the ball thirty yards beyond his own.

After his unhappy first-round score of 75, Bill went straight to the practice tee. He didn't say anything. He just started beating balls.

IV

Back at the Grenoble House, John was grilling steaks again. I joined him.

"You doing anything tonight?" he asked.

"No plans," I said.

"You want to join Wally and me and three gorgeous girls to drive around New Orleans in a limo and then party with Eddie Murphy?" John asked. He tucked his back shirttail in his trousers; it was often falling out.

"I don't have anything better planned," I said.

John left me with the steaks and went off to distribute mint chocolates. Wally arrived.

"I don't know who the girls are, where the limo's from, or how we're getting into a party with Eddie Murphy," said Wally. "This is a John-inspired evening, and I'm dubious about the whole thing."

We went to a bar in the French Quarter where the limo was supposed to come by. There were five people in the bar: the three of us, the golfer Rex Caldwell, and his caddie. Ten minutes later we were the only three. A half hour later Wally made a move to leave the bartender by himself.

"We've been stood up," Wally said.

"No, they're going to come, I'm sure of it," John, an enthusiast and an optimist, said.

"How are you so sure?" Wally said.

"They work for me," John said. The three women were part of John's Southern Hospitality Systems.

"The three girls?" Wally asked.

"The limo driver, too," John said. "Some of the parties like to have a limo and driver handy, just in case," he said.

We waited another ten minutes. John's employees were now forty-five minutes late.

John's beeper beeped, and he left to make a telephone call. Just then the limousine driver came through the door. John returned with a triumphant smile and we piled into the car, where there *were* three women drinking champagne. One of them, who *was* strikingly attractive, had evidently been drinking champagne for some time. She was nearly incomprehensible, although that didn't seem to bother John in the slightest. John introduced her as Trish, and she extended a limp hand to Wally and me. She was

John's date, she explained lavishly. John beamed. The other two women discussed wines.

As promised, we drove around New Orleans in a limousine and drank champagne.

Trish was a self-styled Southern aristocrat. When she said to John, "Oh, I am so terribly hungry; this champagne has gone right to my head," it was with the dramatic flair that blended the best of Scarlett O'Hara and Daisy Buchanan. John instructed the driver to New Orleans's most expensive hotel. We were going to dinner.

While John talked with the maître d', I helped Trish stand up. She was at the toppling stage and I thought it might be difficult to pick her up off the floor in her tight, sequined evening dress.

We sat down for dinner and Trish clasped her hands around John's shoulder and said, "Oh, what *shall* I have?"

Wally and I looked at each other: Had she really said that?

"Anything you want, babe," John replied.

Wally and I looked at each other: Had he really said that?

Trish took John at his word. She ordered a manhattan. She ordered a dozen oysters and a bowl of french onion soup. She ordered a filet mignon and a caesar salad. She looked for a partner to share a liver pâté. She ordered a bottle of wine, and told the waiter to chill an after-dinner champagne and to begin a chocolate soufflé for dessert. She ordered $100 worth of food. At least.

John sank in his chair. His order was brief. "Bring me a beer," he said.

While we waited for our food, Trish began to explain her theory of marriage: A marriage works only if both parties are rich. Her oysters came and she plowed through them.

"The richer, the better," she said.

She sucked on her manhattan. While poking at the french onion soup, she returned to her marriage theory, which staggered to a slurred end. Her face fell into her propped-up cleavage; she was out.

The waiter came by to pick up the appetizer plates. "Was the lady done with her oysters?" he asked John.

"Yes," said John, "Very done." His beeper went off and he abruptly marched off to the nearest telephone.

Conversation had dried up without Trish. Wally made sure Trish's head did not crash into the table.

I walked over to John at the telephone. He was talking to one of his fraternity brothers, who had beeped him for a report. There were bets, no doubt, at the house.

"You know how much this bitch is gonna cost me?" John yelled into the telephone. "More than I've made in the past month, that's for sure."

It was hard to feel sorry for John; he had created the mess. But it was harder not to feel sorry for him.

"John," I asked, "think we better call it a night?"

"Have they brought out the dinners yet?" John asked.

"No," I said.

John hung up the phone, stormed over to the bar and grabbed the limo driver by his coat.

"The party's over, buddy," said John in a sudden burst of boldness. "Take the girls home."

An awkward minute later, Wally, John, and I sat at the table, separated by three empty chairs.

Wally was the first to laugh out loud. I quickly followed suit.

"Very funny," said John, loosening his tie. "You know what this is gonna cost me?"

"Expensive lesson, huh, John?" Wally asked.

"Yeah," said John. He looked dour and defeated. All was quiet.

Suddenly, John perked up.

"Hey, let's see if we can get into that Eddie Murphy party!" he said.

"I got a better idea," Wally said. "Let's go to some cheap bar for a beer." He slapped John on the shoulder. "My treat."

V

By my preround calculation, Bill needed to shoot 68 in the second round to make the cut. With every bogey he made in the Friday round, his chances became dimmer and dimmer. So did the skies. A storm was coming. By the time we finished the front nine, Bill had virtually no chance of making the cut. He needed to birdie about every hole on the back side to make it. That has never been done on the Tour, and this seemed an unlikely time for it to happen.

The humidity continued to increase, the skies continued to darken, and Bill's total over par continued to rise. The rain began as the eight of us—three players, three caddies, a scorekeeper, and a standard bearer carrying the scores—stood on the tee. The light rain became hard as Bill Sander played his shot. A moment later, in the distance, there was a rumble of thunder. Bill Britton waited a few seconds to see if the officials would sound the siren marking the official postponement of play. Thunder and lightning, by the rules, require an official suspension. The rain was pouring now. Bill debated not playing his shot. A golfer, by the rules, may call his own suspension of play if he feels endangered. He put the ball on the tee. The grip of his club was drenched and water beads the size of small grapes dripped off the brim of his hat. Bill took his time setting up the shot. The siren did not sound. Bill was out of the tournament but still wanted every shot to count.

He pushed his shot badly. His ball rolled into a pond. Just as he came off the tee the siren blew. Play was postponed, but his shot counted. Bill smashed his driver into the ground and clipped the grass with a swift kick. I offered him the umbrella, but he didn't want it. He walked down the fairway by himself, frustrated. I fetched the ball out of the pond and he marked the point of entry with a tee.

"I shouldn't have played that shot," he said, more to himself than to me. "I shouldn't have played that shot."

We walked back to the clubhouse in silence. (I could enter only because I was returning clubs to the locker room.) The mood inside was festive, the way a ski lodge is during a blizzard. The pelting rain broke the seal of internal pressure that makes the tension of tournament golf so private. Golfers, club members, and tournament officials, rubbing towels through their hair and drinking merrily, recounted how far away *they* were from the clubhouse when the skies blackened. Bill was not part of the festivity. He made a single shot the subject of his frustration. But the real frustration, I'm sure, was deeper.

We met at 6:30 the next morning to finish the two and a half holes. When we came in, he took the bag from me. Our too short weekend was over.

"You did a good job," Bill said. "You can work for me any time you want to."

"How about next week?" I asked, referring to the Las Vegas Invitational.

"No, I didn't get in," he said. By not finishing among the top 125 money winners in 1984, Bill was not an automatically exempt player for 1985. Whether he got into tournaments depended, in part, on how many of the exempt players choose to play a particular tournament. Las Vegas had the biggest purse of the year, and almost anybody who could tee it up would.

"Are you going to Las Vegas?" Bill asked.

"I don't know. It's a long way to go without having a bag lined up," I said. As Bill asked the question, a familiar caddie passed us.

"Killer, my man," Bill said. I recognized Killer immediately; he had caddied for Irwin in Irwin's prime.

"Mike here's wondering about Las Vegas," Bill said to Killer. "Think he can get something out there?" Only one caddie had been on the Tour longer than Killer; Killer had wisdom.

"You can't get no *player* now," Killer said, "but you can get an amateur."

"How would that pay?" Bill asked. I was flattered by the interest he took in my welfare. It was a mark of his decency.

"You can do all right," Killer said. Then he turned to me.

"You wanna travel the Tour?" he asked.

"Yes," I said.

"Get yourself someone to travel with; got to have someone to travel with," Killer said.

"I've got a friend I can stay with in Las Vegas," I said.

"That don't matter," said Killer. "Rent's cheap in Las Vegas. Food's cheap in Las Vegas. Cheap town. For ninety-nine cents you can eat all the breakfast you want. But you got to get somebody to travel with." Killer was sharing wisdom.

"Thanks a lot, Killer," I said.

"Okay, babe," Killer said.

"Thanks, Killer," Bill said.

"Okay, babe," Killer said.

I left Bill with his golf bag and a weekend off that he didn't want. I was sad for him. But his desire was inspiring. And he actually wanted me to work for him. I was sad, too, to be leaving New Orleans; I enjoyed Wally and John and the Grenoble House. In my second week on the Tour I was feeling its transiency. In a vague way, I felt myself becoming a part—an insignificant part, yes, but a part nonetheless—of tournament golf. Have you ever noticed how good that can feel, becoming part of something bigger and more important than yourself?

4
THE TWO-FISTED GOLFER

I

WHEN I ARRIVED at the Las Vegas Country Club at
7:00 A.M. on the Monday before the tournament,
Killer was already there. Killer believes in getting to
a golf course early. Or maybe he just does it.

"Hey, babe," Killer said, "you got a bag yet?"

"No," I said, "I hope to line something up today."

Killer nodded. In twenty-five years of caddying on
the Tour, he's seen caddies sweating over bags, or the
lack of them, before.

Although it is unnerving for a caddie to arrive at a
tournament without a bag, the Panasonic–Las Vegas
Invitational offered, seemingly, ample opportunity to
work. As Killer explained, most of the professionals
were already spoken for, but there were also 576
amateurs competing. The Panasonic is a five-day
tournament played over three golf courses. For the
first three days, four amateurs play with each professional. After the third round, on Friday, the profes-

sional field is cut to the top seventy, plus ties. The top thirty amateurs also make the cut, and they play on Saturday to determine the winning pro-am team.

There is no prize money for the amateurs, of course; they pay $2,000 to play in the tournament, and their most valued prize is the chance to play on national television. The $2,000 also gets them invitations to parties where, they hope, some of the other, better-known amateurs will be: Dean Martin, or Glen Campbell, or Charley Pride. The amateurs are, generally, businessmen in search of a tax write-off, a reason to go to Las Vegas, and an excuse to vacate the office for a week without having to take a vacation. There are many more applicants than there are spots.

By mid-morning dozens of caddies had arrived at the course. Some were Tour caddies, but most were students at the University of Nevada, Las Vegas, responding to signs posted there, or the marginally employed looking for a week's work. A few were regular full-time Las Vegas caddies. The caddie master, Mike Weiner, a silver-haired man wearing yellow pants and white clogs, was in charge of organizing the caddies. I asked him what the procedure was for getting an amateur bag.

"No procedure," Weiner said. "Last year we assigned the amateurs to the caddies. But this year we decided to do it different, to let the amateurs choose their own caddies and let them make arrangements with the caddies themselves, just like the players do. We think that will make it more of an experience for them."

What it really did was test the ingenuity of the caddies.

Early on Monday the caddies waited in a roped-off area, outside the bag room. After they registered in the clubhouse, the amateurs were told that if they wanted to hire a caddie they could look over the available lot in the caddie yard. They didn't have to take a caddie; electric carts were available, too.

At every pro-am, regardless of its size, there are a number of amateurs who insist on taking a caddie. These are serious players. They are not always good, but they are serious. They are defenders of tradition. In Scotland, the number of these Americans defending tradition increases dramatically, for, once at the Birthplace, any American with a putter and driver in his bag becomes a serious player. It is widely held that the caddies in Scotland are capable of shaping brilliant rounds from the hands of the most miserable twenty-nine handicapper. Back at their home clubs, these same players are back in the cart. There are exceptions: At Winged Foot, in New York, for instance, you wouldn't make a move without a caddie. To do so would be an unacceptable break in tradition. You'd be lucky to be invited back to the grill room, let alone the first tee. But the Las Vegas Country Club is not Winged Foot, and few amateurs came by the caddie yard. The caddies were stewing. And scheming.

Six caddies crept up to the rear clubhouse door, from which the amateurs exited after registering and before going to the first tee. Some caddies sat on a railing, hoping to be noticed. (The caddie seeking employment has a certain hungry look about him.) Others, not believing in the psychology of body language, were bolder: "Need a caddie?" they would ask, or, "Excuse me, sir, are you set for a caddie for the week?" Neither line was effective. Later in the day, the same technique was employed at the front door of the clubhouse. There, though, it was difficult to establish a strategic position and keep it. Periodically, the doorman shooed all the caddies away, as if they were irritating gnats.

The caddie yard did not see an amateur for hours. I grew nervous about my prospects for a bag. I checked the progress at the clubhouse door.

The situation there had evolved. The valet parking attendant was out, and arriving cars were now finding their own parking spots. The more inventive and bold caddies were running to the cars as they pulled into spots. These caddies met the drivers and passengers and pulled their golf bags out of back trunks for them. They carried the golf bags to the clubhouse, often two at a time, and while walking made their caddie pitch.

About half of these caddies landed jobs, probably because the amateur was overwhelmed by the pitch, or had sufficient time to size up the caddie, or saw how pleasant it is to see somebody else carrying his own bag. Failing to win a job, these caddies received tips for carrying the bags.

I got bold.

A yellow Cadillac with a black roof pulled in. A short man with a fat cigar climbed out of the car, opened the trunk, and yanked out a golf bag.

"Can I give you a hand with your bag to the clubhouse?" I asked.

He pulled the fat cigar out of his mouth and said, "What, you don't think I can handle it myself?" He pounded shut the trunk, turned on his heels, and left me in a cloud of cigar smoke.

A mint-condition Volkswagen Bug pulled in a few spaces away. A tall, lithe man emerged, grabbing a small canvas golf bag off the back seat. I didn't bother to ask him.

A brown Chevrolet station wagon pulled in, but another caddie beat me to the car. He carried off two bags.

A silver Jaguar pulled in. The driver pulled an expensive leather bag out of the trunk. I walked over to him.

"Can I give you a hand with your bag?" I asked.

"You U.N.-L.V. guys," he said, "always trying to hustle a buck. Reminds me of when I was an undergraduate there." He left me admiring the car.

I needed a lesson, so I watched as a pea-green Mercedes pulled in. The driver grabbed the bag off the back seat. "Here, I'll take that for you," the caddie said, pulling the bag from the driver. Assertiveness, I reasoned, was the key.

A white Porsche pulled in. I was at the car before it came to a full stop. A minute passed until the driver emerged; he was fidgeting with an alarm system. Finally, he pulled out his golf bag. I started to take it from him. "Here, I'll take it from you," I said in imitation.

"No, you won't," the driver said. He grabbed the bag back. I felt ridiculous.

Frustrated and humiliated, I retreated from the parking lot. I walked back to the caddie yard. There the same caddies sat. I sat with them as mid-afternoon turned into late afternoon. Finally, I decided to leave the Las Vegas Country Club. I had had enough of it for one day.

Walking through the parking lot on the way out, I saw Al Geiberger, who in his prime was one of the game's best players. At that moment, though, he was wandering around the parking lot with his bag on his back.

"Are you looking for a caddie, Mr. Geiberger?" I asked. I recognized him from his old Skippy peanut butter advertisements.

"Actually, I am," Geiberger said. His eyes roamed the parking lot.

"Do you need somebody for the week?" I asked.

"I might," he said. "I was supposed to meet a friend's son here, but I haven't seen him all day. Are you looking for a bag?"

"Yes," I said.

"Well, I'm not sure if he's going to make it," Geiberger said. "Why don't you give me a call tomorrow morning? I'll know for sure what the story is by then. I'm staying at the Golden Nugget."

"What time should I call?" I asked.

"Is 9:00 A.M. too early?" Geiberger asked. He was forty-seven years old and had left 8:00 A.M. practice rounds behind with the Skippy advertisements.

I returned to my hotel room feeling hopeful. Geiberger, or "Mr. 59," as it said underneath his name on his red Spalding golf bag, is a small part of golf legend, the only player to shoot below 60 in a P.G.A. tournament. He once shot 59 at the Colonial Country Club, in the 1977 Memphis Classic. That round, played on one of the country's most demanding golf courses, a 7,200-yard par 72, is considered a nearly perfect round: He shot 59 with six pars, eleven birdies, and an eagle. To work for Geiberger would be an honor.

My hope ended with the 9:00 A.M. call. "I'm sorry," Geiberger said. "My friend's son did show up." He seemed to feel genuinely bad for me. "Are you caddying on the Tour?" he asked. "I'm not playing again until Greensboro, and I've got somebody there, but maybe we could meet somewhere down the line. Call me the week before Houston, maybe we can work something out for that week."

I dreaded another day of tracking down amateurs, but there was nothing else to do: I had to get a bag.

II

As I arrived at the front door of the golf course clubhouse the next morning, a battered taxicab pulled up. Two men got out of the back and the cab driver grabbed two bags out of the trunk.

"Do either of you need a caddie for the week?" I asked. My enthusiasm for another day of rejection was not high.

The shorter of the two, with the more expensive bag, said, "Thanks, but I'm going to take a cart."

"You're gonna ride?" said the other in a voice that revealed his home state. This was a Texan. "Well, then I'm gonna *have* to walk." He looked at the other man, who was his brother-in-law.

"What a *sally*," the tall Texan said.

The tall man's name was Lee Roy Pearson III. He was from Ranger, Texas, "from *real* Texas," as he put it. He was a head over six feet and had a huge, square chin about the size of a floor tile and a voice that probably could carry several fairways. I learned about the remarkable carrying quality of Lee Roy's voice while we played a practice round with Jimmy Adams, his brother-in-law, and two Alabamans.

"What you got over there in Ranger, Texas?" one of the Alabamans asked Lee Roy as they warmed up on the practice putting green. They were separated by fifty yards and a strong wind.

"Nothin'," Lee Roy answered, speaking normally and putting a pinch between his cheek and gum, " 'cept oil."

I imagined Ranger, Texas, as a place where nobody needs telephones.

"I'm gonna show you," Lee Roy said as he put his peg in the ground on the first tee, "the shot that made me famous." In college Lee Roy once nearly beat Tom Kite.

The hole was a par four, a gently curving dogleg to the right with acres of room on the left and a row of houses on the right, separated from the golf course by a chain-link fence.

"I'm gonna put the power fade on this baby," he said.

Nicklaus is the master of the power fade: a long, high tee shot, which sails softly with a slight left-to-right movement, lands gently, and rolls only a short distance. The power fade is a controlled shot, elegant and powerful.

Lee Roy took a mighty whack at the ball and sent it flying. It was a monstrous hit by any standards. The ball started straight down the center of the fairway but, after nearly three full seconds in the air, it began to slice wickedly. It rested, finally, in a swimming pool on the other side of the out-of-bounds fence.

"Doggone it, doggone it, doggone it," Lee Roy muttered. He strolled down the center of the fairway and pretended to be upset. Regardless of its wildness, it was an impressive shot. The Alabamans were in awe.

Jimmy Adams, the brother-in-law, came up behind me in his cart. "Don't worry about that shot," he said. "Lee Roy's a helluva player once he finds his game."

I saw Lee Roy's ball on the other side of the fence, at the bottom of a swimming pool. A middle-aged man and woman were sunbathing on either side of the pool. They must have been startled by the sudden arrival to their peaceful setting.

"Sorry about that intrusion," I said. The man dismissed me with the wave of his hand and without removing the opaque glasses that covered his eyes. Next to the fence was an oversized sand bucket, filled with shiny golf balls.

Lee Roy made a modest confession as we walked down the first fairway. "See here," he said, "I'm what you call a two-fisted golfer." He lifted his hands. He held two cans of Coors. "I'll start playin' now."

Properly fueled, Lee Roy did begin to play well. Carrying an honest six handicap, Lee Roy had a fine, powerful, upright swing. From tee to green he was nearly professional in quality. On the putting greens, however, he was a different animal; he might as well have been putting with a broomstick. Still, from holes numbers two through seventeen, he played well and, excluding number one, where he took an "X," he was only a couple of shots over par.

The eighteenth hole at the Las Vegas Country Club

is a short par five that bends slightly to the right. It
has a man-made pond in front of a green-painted
green. The eighteenth is similar to the first in that
the right side of the fairway is defined by an out-of-
bounds fence. The one on eighteen separates the golf
course from the parking lot. The prevailing breeze is
down hole. After about 260 yards, the fairway slopes
down and is as hard as the plains of Texas. A player
wants to smash a drive here and catch the downsloping hard fairway. The good tee shot will set up
only a medium-length second shot into the par five
with a wonderful opportunity for a birdie and a
chance for an eagle.

Lee Roy, who plays golf in the manner that some
people hunt, wanted an eagle. He sized up the hole,
handed me his beer, and said, "You know what I'm
gonna play here, don't you?"

"The power fade?" I asked. He had announced
power fades on every hole except the par threes.

"You betcha," he said.

He let one go, this one even longer and wilder than
the one on the first tee. The ball took one huge bounce
in the club's parking lot, jumped fifty yards up and
fifty yards right, bounced, jumped high and right
again, and rolled over a two-lane road. It settled in
the Hilton parking lot, a par four away from the
eighteenth tee.

"Doggone it, doggone it, doggone it," Lee Roy
muttered with a certain joy, pointing up the distinct
advantage to being a two-fisted golfer, particularly
on a hot day when you've had nothing to eat. Jimmy
Adams tallied up his brother-in-law's card for him:
two over par, with two "X"s.

III

When Tour caddies want to make conversation,
which seldom happens since conversation among

them is usually spontaneous and vigorous, they might
ask, "Where are you staying this week?" Finding a
place to stay, week after week, tournament after
tournament, is a common bond among caddies, and,
for that matter, among caddies and players, although
a player will seldom ask a caddie where he is staying.
Usually, he'd rather not know.

I was embarrassed to answer that I was staying at
the Hilton, the same Hilton into which Lee Roy
Pearson III nearly sliced his ball off the eighteenth
tee. Caddies don't stay at Hiltons, but in this case I
was vindicated by the facts.

A friend, Andrew Clurman, the midwestern manager for *Skiing* magazine, was staying at the hotel,
one of about 3,000 representatives of the skiing industry assembled for the Ski Industries of America
Annual Trade Show. He kindly took me on as a
roommate, gave me an identity (Alan Greenberg,
editor, *Skiing*), and invited me to an endless stream
of ski gatherings. We ate smoked salmon and drank
Aquavit with the Norwegian Trade Council. We
gambled. We tried on handmade earmuffs courtesy
of Marceau Sports, Minnetonka, Minnesota. We
gambled. We saw ski movies. We gambled. The food
and drinks and movies were free. The gambling was
not.

This engaging activity cast a new light on our
friendship, for we had become friends in the puritan-
ical light of a Martha's Vineyard winter, far away
from the neon of Las Vegas. Raw immigrants to this
world, we watched studiously as Adam West gave
television gambling lessons on the Hilton's educa-
tional cable station. The films were old: The dry look
had been in vogue when they were made, and West,
apparently, had had an uncomfortable time adjusting to it. There were other signs of age. Nehru suits,
for instance.

In one film, West showed how to play "blackjack, or

twenty-one, as it is sometimes called," speaking as if reading from an encyclopedia, although he was clearly reading from cue cards. He dealt a fictitious round to show how the game worked. When the deal was done he flipped the cards to see how the players fared.

"Let's see here. John took a hit on seventeen and drew five, so he's over. Jane split on sevens and drew an eight and nine for a fifteen and a sixteen—not good enough to beat the dealer's eighteen. Ted, let's see what you did. You drew a picture card on sixteen for twenty-six—you're way over. And Sally? Sally took a hit on fourteen and drew eight for twenty-two, too bad." He turned to Sally. "Sorry, Sally," Batman said in his reassuring baritone, "but you're a loser, too."

Andrew and I approached the blackjack tables with that inspired phrase intoned in our heads: "Sorry, but you're a loser, too." We lost until we became weary, which was fairly early, thanks to the Norwegian Trade Council and their Aquavit.

IV

Lee Roy Pearson III—could you imagine a better name for a Texas oil man?—is a male chauvinist, he'll acknowledge. Men are no better or worse than women, but the sexes play different roles. According to Lee Roy, women should garden and men should mow the lawn. Women should cook and men should clean. The garage, that is. But there is one thing women should not do. They should not play in pro-ams. So when I met Lee Roy at the practice range of the Desert Inn golf course, one of the three courses on which the tournament was played, it was with a certain tongue-in-cheek disgust that he leaned down and whispered, "Do you see what we have on our team? A *woman!*"

By the third hole it became evident that Mary Finsterwald, a sixty-nine-year-old Californian who played off the white tees and paid her $2,000 to play just like everybody else, was holding the team together. Lee Roy, being competitive and having a large bet with his brother-in-law over whose amateur team would come on top, quickly became Mary's biggest cheerleader.

Her shots, although short, were straight, and her handicap entitled her to two strokes on nine of the holes. Every time she made a natural bogey on one of those holes, she contributed a birdie to the team. Contributing birdies is the best way to make friends in a high-stakes pro-am.

Although Lee Roy was consistently outdriving Mike Bright, the professional in our group, he did nothing to contribute to the team score, which is tallied by counting the best score in the group on each hole. Inspired, though, by his two-fisted state and Mary's golf, Lee Roy was in good spirits. He had lost "a large sum of money" on the blackjack tables the night before—by his standards that meant a good-sized five digit number. Mary was his ticket to getting some of that back.

"Let it rip, Mary," he said on several tees, trying to encourage her. She swung her driver as if it had the weight of an axe—you could get into a discussion of the SALT treaty in the time it took Mary to swing. Her tee shots—calling them "drives" would be an overstatement—putted along for 125 yards. They were always straight and they were always 125 yards.

"All right!" Lee Roy applauded after another patented Mary Finsterwald drive. He fell to his knees to be at her height and raised his hand to his shoulder for a high five. Mary beamed at Lee Roy's half-drunk Texan charm. Lee Roy beamed back. He was making money, and Mary was making it for him.

V

In almost every pro-am group, one player comes to play or, rather, to win. Although he may be a good golfer, chances are better that he is, at best, mediocre. He is also humorless and compensates for his colorless personality with golf attire that would compete favorably with an exotic African bird. *Competition* is a key word in this man's life vocabulary. Green, naturally, is one of his favorite color themes, although he also favors lavender and many pastels.

We had such a man in our group the second day (the amateur groups change for each round). A man named Dick Melville. Our professional for this round was an Englishman named Ken Brown, one of the finest players in Europe and a good part-time player on the American tour.

In attire Brown and Melville were totally dissimilar. That is because Brown, who lives in rumpled sweaters with elbow patches and baggy pants, is an anomaly among professionals. Melville, on the other hand, who carried an unreliable sixteen handicap and fifty extra pounds, dressed out of the P.G.A. catalogue. White alligator-skin shoes. Dark lavender polyester pants. (Tour players don't like to call that material *polyester*; they prefer *double-knit*, or, their favorite euphemism, *Tour wear*.) He wore a white Wilson visor and his caddie, a bona fide Tour caddie with a yardage book, carried a professional-size Wilson bag, the red and white model, just like the ones the pros use. Melville's name was painted on it in black script lettering. It was an expensive outfitting, but coming to Las Vegas from Los Angeles to play a week of tournament golf is not exactly cheap either.

Ken Brown, who is considered one of the best putters in golf, is also one of the slowest. He sometimes spends as much as a full minute to line up a three-footer and is occasionally penalized for his slow play. Most of the golfing public understands that the professional has his livelihood at stake when he spends sixty seconds lining up a three-foot putt. Most fans accept this technique without emulating it. Moreover, the good putter sees subtleties in a three-foot putt—a spike mark, a ball mark, a gentle break—to which most of us are oblivious. As slow as Ken Brown was on the greens, Dick Melville was even slower, in part thanks to Melville's caddie, who took Melville almost as seriously as Melville took himself. Together they spent upwards of two minutes lining up ten-footers, looking at the putt from as many as six different angles. In reading putts, Melville's caddie, whom Lee Roy named Skeets, liked to stand over the hole and peer into it with enormous effort and concentration, as if the secrets of the break were being discussed by putting elves meeting in secret darkness at the bottom of the hole. Invariably, Melville's putts missed, and when they did, caddie Skeets would smash the pin back into the hole, crushing the elves. Melville, in perfect imitation of a touring professional, would throw his putter against the bag in disgust and grimace. I think he was practicing the grimace for Saturday's round on television. Grimacing on television is something Tour players do all the time.

I read putts for Lee Roy, although not with Skeets's fanfare. Lee Roy actually holed a few for a change, which made the round especially enjoyable. Every time he made one, Lee Roy gave me a ten-dollar bill, and I fetched two beers for him. When I returned I'd hand the beers over to Lee Roy, and try to hand back the change. "Nah," he'd say. "Keep that, for the good read."

On the back nine Lee Roy Pearson, Jr., Lee Roy's father, joined us. On the eleventh hole I gave Lee Roy a good read for a natural birdie from eleven feet. He made the putt, forked over ten dollars, and told me to get some beers. I returned with two for Lee Roy III and one for Lee Roy, Jr. When I handed Mr. Pearson his beer he said, "Why, thank you, son," as if it was among the kindest gestures anyone had ever extended him. Lee Roy Pearson, Jr., was a happy man with a cold beer.

The three of us walked buoyantly down the eleventh fairway. Spirits were high: the day was beautiful; Lee Roy was playing well; the Coors were cold. With Mary's fine showing in the first round and Lee Roy's own good performance in the second, he was faring well, both in the tournament and, more importantly, in his side bets with his brother-in-law.

On the sixteenth green of the Tropicana Hotel golf course, Ken Brown holed a long putt to save par. Lee Roy had a chance for another natural birdie from fifteen feet. Melville had a chance for a handicap birdie from ten feet (he received a stroke on the hole).

Melville, ever the strategist, said to Lee Roy, "Maybe I should putt here first. If I miss, then you'll have the chance to charge for the birdie. But if you putt first and miss, well, that leaves me with a lot of pressure to make my putt. See what I'm getting at here?"

"Well, hell, Dick," Lee Roy said in return, "I'm gonna *charge* my birdie putt if I putt first or second. I was taught by my dad that who's ever away putts first. I've been playing that way all of my life. Don't see any reason to change now."

Lee Roy and I lined up his putt, which took about three seconds. Lee Roy rolled it. His putting method is to hit the ball so hard that all the break is taken out of the putt. The ball crashed into the center of the hole for a birdie. The team didn't need Melville's birdie try anymore. Melville picked up, smoldering, and said unconvincingly, "What a lovely putt."

Skeets smashed the pin in the hole and charged up to me. Melville had given him a cigar and a Wilson cap and, with his beard and mirrored sunglasses, he had a menacing appearance. He stood so close that the lighted end of his cigar was nearly in my mouth. "I can't be doing your work for you," he growled. The reference was to his putting back the pin after Lee Roy made his putt. It was my pin to put back.

My mood was dampened, but only for a minute. Lee Roy came up to me and said, "Caddie Skeets over there in the shades, he gives me the *creeps*."

He forked over ten dollars; his hands were empty.

VI

The third round began with a certain amount of tension. Lee Roy was in contention to be one of the amateurs to make the Friday cut and play before a national television audience on Saturday.

"Wouldn't the boys back in Ranger love that!" Lee Roy said. " 'Looky here,' they'd say, 'if that isn't ole Lee Roy Pearson on the TV,' " Lee Roy said, painting the scene back home.

He needed to play well, and there was every promise that he would: He had shown up three minutes before his tee time, which he swore was the secret to his success in the second round. Conversely, he argued, arriving thirty minutes before his tee time and hitting a practice bucket had been the root of all his problems in the first.

Lee Roy stood on that first tee of the Las Vegas Country Club, a hole that we had played once before, memorably.

He put the ball on the tee and said, "I got to do it, I just got to prove to myself that I can do it."

Oh, no, I thought to myself, the power fade.

I looked at Lee Roy.

He nodded back. "That's right," he said, "the power fade."

He reared back and fired. This one, unlike his opening shot in the practice round, did not start in

the center of the fairway and *then* slice uncontrollably. It began slicing the moment it left the tee. This
one had no chance of landing in a pool just over the
out-of-bounds fence. It cleared the house behind the
pool. This was a spectacular slice.

"Doggone it," said Lee Roy. "Doggone it, doggone
it, doggone it." This time he meant it.

"Jack Brown," he said to a buddy of his in the
gallery, "get me a couple of beers."

The shot was, sad to report, not atypical for the
day. Sadder to report, Lee Roy was having one of the
better rounds in his group. Whatever hope we had of
making the cut was completely diminished by the
time we reached the ninth hole.

Nick Price, a good-natured South African professional who plays the American Tour full time, and
well, waited until the eighteenth tee before giving
Lee Roy a tip.

"Lee Roy," Price said, "where I come from we have
a little saying."

Price paused as he bent over Lee Roy's tee and ball
and raised it about an inch.

"Tee it high," Price said, "and let it fly."

He smiled at Lee Roy, but Lee Roy was unim-
pressed. The hole, the very hole where Lee Roy had
committed his Hilton parking lot atrocity, called for
Lee Roy's old power fade.

"Tee it high and let it fly?" Lee Roy said.

"Yes, that's right," said Price, "tee it high and let it
fly."

"Jack Brown," Lee Roy called to his friend in the
gallery, who had taken my job as beer supplier, "I'm
gonna tee it high, and let it fly."

The resulting shot was extraordinary. The ball
sailed off the tee ferociously and, unlike any shot Lee
Roy had hit all week, hooked wildly. The shot went as
far left as it did forward, and settled not one, but two
fairways away from the eighteenth fairway.

Walking to the ball, Lee Roy hung his head low,

like a child does after a scolding. He suddenly became remorseful, a mood I had not seen in him in four days.

"You know," he said, "nothin' bothered me until this. This is goin' too far. A duck hook. I haven't hit a duck hook since high school. I'm supposed to be the 'A' player in the group, the guy the team can count on. And what have I done? Absolutely nothing. Are all these people gonna go home and say, 'That boy from Ranger, Texas, Lee Roy Pearson, he sure can play?' Hell, no. They're gonna say, 'Lee Roy Pearson—what a bum.'" He handed over the driver gently, a defeated man.

When the round was finished, Lee Roy suggested I drive with him to his hotel to see if Jimmy Adams had made the cut.

"Tell you what," Lee Roy said. "If he did make the cut, there's no way he's gonna ride in that cart in front of national TV. No brother-in-law of mine is gonna ride a cart. He needs a caddie."

We rode over (in a limousine posing as a shuttle van) from the Las Vegas Country Club to the Frontier Hotel, where Lee Roy and a score of Texans in town for the tournament were staying. At the Frontier, Lee Roy handed me $250 from a billfold that held several thousand dollars and said, "I'm gonna pay you as if I was playing tomorrow 'cause Lord knows I should be. Hell, you did everything you could to help out these worthless old bones." Lee Roy was in his mid-thirties and fit, but he consistently made a good case for sympathy. I was delighted to have the extra fifty dollars—we had agreed on fifty dollars a day (with me taking care of his clubs at night; "I don't want to look at the things," he had said after his first inauspicious round). With $250 I would almost break even for the week.

"Let's go see if Jimmy Adams made the cut," Lee Roy said, making a maze around blackjack tables

and roulette wheels and poker tables, up one flight of
steps, down one corridor, around a corner, and, finally, to a set of double doors. Lee Roy swung them
open as if he were in a Western. (Lee Roy was born to
be in Westerns.)

There were tables of food with meats and cheeses
and fish and fruit. There were several bars. There
was a dessert table. It was an impressive spread.
Serving it all were women in red satin cocktail-
waitress dresses. Long-legged, slender women. There
were more women in the place than men.

"Jimmy Adams, did you make the cut?" Lee Roy
asked his brother-in-law.

Jimmy shook his head. "But I gave it a good go," he
said.

Lee Roy growled and headed for the bar.

VII

The Panasonic–Las Vegas Invitational makes no
pretense to be anything other than a commercial
event. It bills itself as "golf's richest tournament,"
and the free-enterprise system was evident everywhere. Between the putting green and the driving
range there was a row of tents. One sold metal-
headed woods. Another sold wood-shafted irons. Still
another sold glass-headed putters (although not too
many of them).

The least commercial (and most expensive) of these
tents sold classic clubs, mint condition woods, irons,
putters, and wedges from the golden age of club
making, and the bronze age of persimmon curing.
Many believe that the best persimmon was cured in
the late 1940s and early 1950s, and that the woods
made with that stock have never been equaled.

Bob Goalby, the 1968 Masters champion and now
an NBC golf commentator, came into the tent. He
started picking up the old clubs with his muscular

hands, handling the clubs with gentleness and reverence, feeling the weight of the head and the soundness of the construction with easy, full waggles. He gripped the clubs lightly; his hands so encased the grips that you could sense not only his power, but his accuracy, too. You could see that his were hands that could manipulate a golf ball.

He picked up an old Wilson driver, a Denny Shute model.

"What do you think, Mr. Goalby?" one of the salesmen asked respectfully.

"What do I think?" Goalby asked back. He wagged the club, brushed his thumb against the face, and said, "I think I could put it in my bag and play it, that's what I think."

Goalby reached into his pocket for a billfold. The salesman grinned from ear to ear, and not because he had made a sale.

"I'll tell you," Goalby said to the salesman, "the last thing I expected to do was to come in here and buy a club. You know how many clubs I have? Hundreds and hundreds. You think I need more clubs? You think I need another driver? But I've got a contract with Wilson, and I should be playing a Wilson driver, and this feels good. You see this name here?" He raised the sole plate up to the salesman's eye level. " 'Denny Shute.' I played with Denny Shute. He was a gentleman, and he could play the game."

Densmore Shute won the 1933 British Open, the P.G.A. Championship in 1936 and 1937, and was twice the runner-up in the U.S. Open.

The half-dozen of us in the tent began peppering Goalby, a man who bridges golf eras, with questions—about Denny Shute, about winning the Masters. I asked him about the changing role of the caddie.

"You know, when I first started caddying, the club pro as we know him today didn't exist," he said. "He was more like a caddie master, but he did a lot more. He cleaned the clubs and gave lessons. He wasn't allowed in the clubhouse, unless he ran the bar, too, which he often did. Keeping him out of the clubhouse didn't bother him because he didn't really want to be in there anyhow. He wouldn't feel comfortable in there.

"When I first came on the Tour you couldn't use the same caddie more than two weeks in a row. They [the tournament officials] didn't want the caddies and the players to become too familiar. They were probably afraid there was going to be cheating. There probably was, to a limited extent, although I never saw any.

"Now everything's changed. This group of caddies we have today is by far the best ever. They're more than caddies now. They're valets. They're more than that. They serve as a buffer between the golfer and the world at large. They control the crowds. If a guy needs a new shaft put in, he might have the caddie run the club over to the repair shop. If a guy needs a plane reservation, the caddie might make the calls.

"Fifteen years ago you had a very different breed of caddie. You had some winos. You had some drug problems. Some of the guys were running away from alimony payments. Some were running from the law. Today you've got a group of bright, energetic caddies who know what they're doing. They have to. It's become a business, like everything's become a business. The yardage book is definitely part of it, part of making caddying a business.

"Almost everybody thinks that Jack [Nicklaus] invented the yardage book, and he certainly was one of the first to use them. But the person who invented the idea was Miller Barber.

"Years ago all that was done differently. Hogan, for instance, would stand in the middle of a fairway, even with a big elm with a dead limb, and he'd

remember that three years ago he'd hit a five iron
from there, in a soft rain with the wind slightly in his
face, and that it was perfect. This time there's no
wind. He'd stare down the shot, smoking hard on that
cigarette of his, and he'd say to the caddie, 'Six iron.'
That's all there was to it. I never heard him have a
conversation with a caddie that was longer than two
words. What does it tell you about Hogan, about the
game he played? He played with *feel*."

Goalby looked at his watch. He was due at the
broadcast booth. Too bad; he probably would have
gone on for hours, and the six of us in the classic clubs
tent would not have moved an inch.

VIII

On Sunday evening after the tournament—Curtis
Strange won the title and $171,000—I had a long
wait for a flight to Florida, where the next tournament was being played. I took thirty dollars from my
limited resources and dedicated them to blackjack.
My plan was to get back the hundred dollars I was
down for the week and quit. I had five hours to do it.
My flight, the caddie flight, the cheapest there was,
left at 2:30 A.M.

I was doing something right, although I'm not
certain what it was. Maybe it was the advice. A
matronly woman from Brooklyn sitting next to me
said at one point: "Never, never ever split tens.
Haven't you ever played before?" Adam West never
said not to split tens, so I didn't know.

Soon I was up $100, and even for the week. My plan
said quit. But I felt lucky, as they say in Las Vegas,
and I went double or nothing on my winnings. I won.
I was now up $200, and $100 for the week. Gambling
intoxication took over. I decided to play one more
hand and this, I said, would really be it. I placed
another $100 bet. I won. I was up $300 for the night

and $200 for the week. In an evening's worth of blackjack I had nearly doubled what I earned in four days of caddying.

It was midnight; I still had a two-and-a-half-hour wait for my flight. Feeling gleeful, I went to the bar.

A short while later an attractive woman in a red evening dress came up to me and began a conversation.

"Want to go to a party?" she asked.

"Sure," I said, "but I've got to catch a plane in a couple of hours."

"That's okay. This party won't take that long," she said. Won't take that long? I must have looked at her oddly.

"You do want to go to a party, don't you?" she asked.

"I think so," I said.

"For $200 I'll take you to the best party you've ever been to."

I finally understood my good fortune. It wasn't so good. And it wasn't me.

"I think you've got the wrong guy."

"Too bad for you," she said. She walked away.

As I got up from the bar, a couple sat down. He was wearing a rhinestone-studded denim coat and she a wedding dress.

This must be Las Vegas, I thought to myself. It was time to leave. I headed to the airport, two hours before my flight.

5
FROM THE BOOTH
AT FOURTEEN

I

EVERY CADDIE ON THE TOUR knows Chuckles, I was
told by a caddie while we were en route to Florida. A
score of caddies took this middle-of-the-night flight.
It featured a two-hour layover in Houston, which
provided a good opportunity to learn something without appearing *too* inquisitive. Professional caddies
are wary of people who are too inquisitive.

"Chuckles?" I asked.

"You know, Chuck Will, from CBS. Everybody's
gotta call Chuckles sooner or later. You get sacked.
Your man doesn't show. You don't have a bag. You call
Chuckles." Chuck Will, CBS associate director for
golf, gave bagless caddies temporary jobs.

We were headed for Ponte Vedra, Florida, for the
Tournament Players Championship, the fifth most
important tournament of the year. I didn't have a bag
lined up and my chances of getting one were slim.
The T.P.C., played on a grueling track against the

87

strongest field of the year and for a large sum of money, is an event for which players commit themselves—to the tournament and to caddies—weeks in advance.

I arrived at the golf club late Monday afternoon and spoke with Brad Faxon for the first time since Eagle Trace. He was sitting in his car (in Florida, where Brad lives, he drives from tournament to tournament), eating a granola bar and adjusting the car radio to Jacksonville's music stations.

"Well, I saw you in New Orleans, I saw you in Las Vegas, and now you're here in Florida," said Brad, "so I guess you must be serious about becoming a caddie."

"It's a tough business, but I'm learning," I said.

"Who'd you have in New Orleans?" Brad asked.

"Bill Britton."

"Play any good?"

"Missed the cut."

"Even close?"

"No."

"Wonder what happened to him," Brad said. "You know he nearly won a tournament in 1982, lost in a play-off to Sutton, and then he hasn't been heard from since. You wonder how that can happen."

Brad's eyes drifted off into the setting Florida sun. Any time a player misses a cut, as Brad had in Las Vegas, he can't help but think about his future in the game. It may be only a passing thought, but it is a thought.

"You got a bag for this week?" Brad asked.

"No," I said.

"It's a tough week to get a bag," said Brad. "Looks like CBS for you." He handed me a quart of fresh-squeezed orange juice and a box of granola. "I've got more of this stuff than even I can handle," he said, and sped off, late for a dinner date.

I found a telephone and called CBS.

"Is Chuck Will there?" I asked.

"This is Chuck Will," the other voice said.

"I'm a caddie who . . ."

"Yeah, yeah, yeah, blah, blah, blah; you're a caddie without a bag and you want a job for the week and this is your life story," Will said. "Right? Come by and see me."

"Where are you?" I asked.

"In the trailer, behind the garbage compactor," he said.

I found my way to the CBS trailer (behind the garbage compactor) and entered it, a long, thin rectangle crowded with desks, papers, televisions, and Styrofoam cups. Many Styrofoam cups. They were all over the place, including on Chuck Will's desk, which was marked by a large sign: "CHUCK WILL'S DESK." Standing at the desk, with a small piece of paper in his left hand, was a fit man with a weathered face locked in a grimace. He had the stubborn look of a high school math teacher–football coach, who knows his kids can do better if only they'd push themselves, practice a little discipline.

Chuckles looked at the piece of paper in his hand, and then looked at me.

"Michael Barnblatt?" he asked, reading off the paper.

"Michael Bamberger," I said.

Will dropped his glasses to the tip of his nose and looked at me. "If I wanted you, Bamberger, I would have asked for you, you asshole," he said.

At random, he picked up one of the Styrofoam cups on his desk and said, "Let's see if you can do something right. There's coffee in the next tent. Get me a cup. Black." He handed me a Styrofoam cup that appeared to be several coffees old.

When I returned, a caddie called Beaufort stood at Chuck Will's desk. Beaufort, who is about the size of a golf bag, was looking smaller by the moment.

"You come in here and you tell me you want a job," Will said to Beaufort in a tone of controlled rage. He dug into the deepest depths of a file next to his desk and took out an index card with two dozen names on it. Next to each name was an amount of money. Thin black lines were drawn through most of the names.

"You see this?" Will asked Beaufort. "Can you see this? This card dates back to 1980. 1980. One-nine-eight-oh. That's five years ago." Beaufort nodded his head as if he were getting an after-school detention lecture. Will held out his right hand to demonstrate the number five with his fingers. "It says here that I lent you forty dollars in 1980, and your name is not crossed off, which means you did not pay me back. You come in here looking for a job, but you don't pay me the forty dollars you owe me, and you don't even have the decency to mention it."

"I can't pay you back right now. I don't have the money," Beaufort said. "If I had a job, I could pay you back."

"I don't give a shit about the money," Will said. "You think I could care less about the money? My accountant wrote it off as a loss years ago. It's not the money. 'I could pay you back. I could pay you back.' Go on, get out of here. I don't have any work for you."

Beaufort turned on his worn sneakers and began to walk out of the trailer. It had been many years since he had had a good regular bag, and that showed.

"Understand," Will said in a softer voice as Beaufort exited, "that it's not the money. It's the principle of the thing, right? You understand that. See you sometime down the line."

Beaufort nodded and walked out of the trailer. Will returned to his seat at the desk, and exhaled deeply, but not with the theatrical quality with which he went through his tirade. I moved the coffee to his desk. He grabbed it the moment I set it down.

"Bamberger," Will said, "are you Jewish?"

"Yes," I said.

"You better be with a name like that. OK, you're hired. I'll fill you in on the job tomorrow," Will said. I started moving toward the door.

"And, Bamberger," Will said, "you know you're not going to get rich from this. But we'll give you enough money to help you get down the road." I put a hand on the trailer door.

"Bamberger," Will called out, "who do you work for?"

"Bill Britton," I said. (This was not the time, obviously, to get into a long explanation of my shaky start as a Tour caddie.)

"Billy Britton," said Will. "He's a good friend of mine. He once worked for me here, when he was a senior at Florida. He can play the game. He's determined. Maybe a little too much so. Maybe if he took it a little easier he'd play better. Who knows." Chuck Will, coach, was speaking, but only for a moment.

"All right, Bamberger," the director said, "I'll see you tomorrow."

The mighty shadows of a Sawgrass dusk had fallen across the golf course, and reminded me of my wooziness. Less than twenty-fours hours earlier I had been playing blackjack in Las Vegas. The night and day since had been spent flying to Orlando and then making the three-hour drive north, to Ponte Vedra. I hadn't eaten, except for what the flight and the Houston airport offered. I needed a shave. I needed a shower. I needed to eat. I needed to sleep. I had spent most of the day worrying. What would I do for work; where would I stay? I found work; I still needed a place to stay. I needed sleep.

I went to the tournament hospitality desk, which arranges housing for players. They list nearby hotels, some usually offering discounts for golfers. They also have lists of people who live near the golf course and who have an extra bedroom in their house and would like nothing more than the opportunity to put up a (sometimes moody) golfer for the week. Once in a great while a caddie can fall into one of these rooms, I learned on the flight to Florida. The caddies call these arrangements *freebies.* Knowing that in this, my fourth week on the Tour, I was going to spend, again, more money than I'd make, I decided to try for a freebie.

"Did anybody," I asked at the hospitality desk, "volunteer to put up caddies, by any chance?"

The hospitality man looked down the list. "Most of these people," he said, "specified that they wanted a player." He hummed as he went down the list with a pencil. "I might have one person that I can give a call. Give me just one second here." He dialed a telephone number and, while he was waiting for someone to answer, he said to me, "You're not going to trash the joint, are you?"

"No," I said. It was true; I had no plans to trash the joint.

"That's great. Hello, Mrs. Shepard?" the hospitality man said, spinning his chair away from me, the way a managing editor does in a newsroom when he wants to keep a conversation away from ever-listening reporters. "I've got a young man here, a *caddie.* . . ."

I drove over to Mr. and Mrs. Stanley J. Shepard's home on La Vista Drive, a short ride from the golf course. I feared the disappointment I would bring. I was sure they were hoping for a player.

I found their house, and Mrs. Shepard, a gracious woman in her late sixties, answered the door.

"It's awfully kind of you to put me up," I said, bringing in my lone bag. A golfer would have come in with an impressive display of luggage, and a few dozen balls as a gift.

"Well, we were going to put up Brett Upper and his wife. We have the girls' room back there, with its own bathroom, and we thought it would be perfect for them," Mrs. Shepard said. "We don't know them, but they, or rather he, looks like a nice fellow on television. And he hasn't exactly won a pot of money out there."

Brett Upper was number 125 on the 1984 money list, earning $37,782. He was the last man to qualify for exempt status.

"At least not until last week, when he won $13,000. So my husband," said Mrs. Shepard, now pointing to Mr. Shepard, a bald, intelligent-looking man reading a book while smoking a pipe and sitting on the couch, "says, 'Mr. Upper doesn't need a place to stay now.' We're happy to have somebody who needs the bed."

"I know you fellas probably like to go out at night and have a good time," Mrs. Shepard said. "You feel free to come and go as you please. We go to sleep around eleven, so if you come in after that please use the side door." She gave me a key. "We want you to enjoy your week here."

"I won't disappoint you if I go to sleep now, will I?" I asked. It was 9:00 P.M. and there was not a carousing bone in my body. The Shepards had wanted a golfer, and had been sent a neo-caddie instead. I didn't want to cause any more disappointment. If Mrs. Shepard wanted me to carouse, I would carouse.

"Not at all," Mrs. Shepard said, ever gracious.

II

For CBS, the network that broadcasts the most golf tournaments, the Tournament Players Championship is one huge practice session; the Masters arrives a few weeks after the T.P.C., and that is the showpiece of CBS golf, heralded even by other networks as the paragon of the well-televised sporting event.

Not that CBS is trying to please the other networks. Keeping the Masters' czars content is enough of a task. Generally, though, by pleasing the tournament officials, CBS in turn pleases the golfing public. The Masters officials shrewdly understand, and revere, the rarefied atmosphere of their tournament, and by insisting that CBS reflect that atmosphere, CBS provides its viewers with an event that is genuinely unique. The Masters officials monitor such minute details as the number of times announcers may refer to the size of the purse. The Masters is beyond money, they argue, and from their perspective that is true. Jack Whitaker, the veteran sports announcer, was dethroned from his Masters perch for referring to a large gallery concentrated in a single area, all craning their necks for a better view, as a "mob." There are no mobs in Augusta, at least not within the tree-lined confines of the Augusta National. A mob, after all, implies disorder.

CBS seems to thrive on disorder, on ranting, on raving, on peals of laughter, on overworked workers with eyes sagging like water balloons.

"I just flew in from Chicago, from the N.C.A.A.s," a technician reporting for work told Will. "I slept for an hour in an airport lobby, the flight took all night, I haven't eaten in a day, I haven't shaved, I'm sick. . . ."

"At least," said Will, "you slept."

Frank Chirkinian, the executive producer for CBS golf, barreled through the little trailer door. He wore pants with a Masters emblem on them and a "CBS Masters '84" shirt; he was in the spirit of the season.

"Frank, where do we get these people?" Will asked, complaining about a man who dared to complain about his lack of food or sleep.

"I don't know, Chuck," said Chirkinian. "I do not know." He entered the trailer with a large smile, which broadened with Will's deadpan rage.

Chirkinian grabbed a Styrofoam cup and headed for the door. Before he exited a look of sobriety came

to his face as he asked Will, "Is Trevino playing?"
Trevino's presence, or lack of it, can single-handedly
affect the ratings by whole percentage points.

"Yes," said Will.

Chirkinian nodded and walked out, relieved.

Nielsen ratings are deceptive when it comes to golf.
The percentage of ignited television sets turned to
golf on a Saturday or Sunday afternoon is seldom
more than fifteen percent, a small share in the
television business. But it is an influential fifteen
percent. Advertisers know that through golf telecasts
they can reach people in a position to be bullish with
Merrill Lynch, or to fly the friendly skies of United.

In 1985 CBS televised seventeen tournaments,
NBC televised seven, and ABC televised five (including three big ones: the U.S. and British Opens and the
P.G.A. Championship). ESPN televised eight tournaments. The climax of the CBS golf season—the Masters—comes early; it is their sixth event for the
season. The success of CBS golf is dependent on how
it fares at the Masters.

III

Chuck Will explained the job: "You're a spotter,
Bamberger. You know what that is, and if you don't,
ask Barbara; she'll show you what's going on."

A spotter, Barbara further explained, is in a booth
with a *talent*—that's the word they use to describe the
announcers: Steve Melnyk, Ken Venturi, Ben Wright,
Pat Summerall are all *talents*. The booth spotter,
hooked up to headphones, listens to a fairway spotter
and finds out which player is away, how many yards
he has to the green, and what club he is using. The
booth spotter then relays this information to the
talent. When a group approaches the green, the booth
spotter must know which player is away and what
number shot he is playing. The director must be

precisely aware of what sixty or so different players are doing at an exact moment. During a live broadcast he has only one chance to decide which shot to televise. When Maltbie, in the final group of the day on the final hole, needs a three-foot putt to win a tournament, the live camera will, obviously, be focused on him. But when Nicklaus is getting a standing ovation on the eighteeth green, Watson is making a birdie bid from eight feet away on number sixteen to tie for the lead, and Wadkins has a birdie putt from twenty feet to go one ahead, the decision is not so easy. The director must know exactly who is about to hit and when. Although he is watching nine different monitors, the director relies on the spotters in the booth, who collectively can give him information he would otherwise not have.

Spotting, Barbara said, is what makes CBS as good as it is. Spotting, Barbara said, was an important job. Spotting, Barbara said, was an art. "And if you're no good at it you'll find out quick enough," she said. "Chuck will let you know."

The Chuck Will show began in earnest on Saturday at 11:00 A.M. Twenty-five of us comprised Chuckles's merry band of spotters. We were each handed a color sheet, a list of the players, by their playing group, with descriptions of their pants, shirts, sweaters, and headwear. This information had been gathered earlier that morning. As the players took to the practice range and putting green, a CBS man made the rounds and took notes on their dress. These notes become the color chart:

Player: Chen. Group Number: 10. Pants: light blue. Shirt: white with blue. Sweater: dark blue. Other: white cap.

Player: Nicklaus. Group Number: 7. Pants: burgundy. Shirt: burgundy striped.

Player: Mize. Group Number: 15. Pants: tan. Shirt: aqua with pink stripes.

Will positioned his boys like a Little League coach setting the field.

"Gypsy," he said to "Gypsy" Joe Grillo, "I want you in the fourteenth fairway. I want yardages and as many clubs as you can get. Bamberger, I want you in the booth at fourteen, with Steve Melnyk. Australian Brian. Has anyone seen Australian Brian? Look, Brian, if you want to keep your job you're going to have to be more attentive. Now I know you Aussies are damn charming, and I'm damn happy for it, but we've got a golf telecast to put on. 'Nough said? Okay, Brian, I want you at. . . ."

After getting our positions, we were allowed to eat in the CBS mess tent, which for many of the caddies was the best meal they had seen since their last tour of duty with CBS. There were trays and trays of curried chicken, fried rice, green beans, salad, fruit, and pudding. Seconds and thirds were the rule. Fourths were not uncommon.

I ate with Gypsy, who is Brad Faxon's favorite caddie and one of the most respected caddies on the Tour. Gypsy, short, strong, earringed, was the co-chairman of the Professional Tour Caddies' Association, which is the closest thing the caddies have to a union. The association, which is run by Gypsy and Mike Carrick, Tom Kite's caddie, works at getting parking passes at tournaments and discounts on motel rooms. It does not, however, negotiate the rates at which caddies are paid and has no influence over the hiring and firing of caddies. The feeling among caddies is that a real union would not work, anyway. Caddies are too independent to want the terms of their employment dictated by an organization. Perhaps the most important thing the association does is to run the caddie dinner, the caddie tournament, and the caddie-player softball game.

Gypsy, who, like many of his colleagues, came to be a Tour caddie after working in the restaurant business, had been on the Tour for ten years, He was working for Jim Simons, when Simons played. In recent years Simons has been making more money as a financial consultant than as a golfer and is spending less time on the Tour. Gypsy also has an outside business. He is a caddie consultant. For a fee, he sets up players with caddies. Brad Faxon subscribes to Gypsy's service. On the day before the first round of the T.P.C., Brad's caddie fell through, and he asked for me if I was available. Before I could answer, Brad said that first he'd have to check with Gypsy; if Gypsy had somebody else lined up for him he would have to take him. Gypsy did. If you believe that a caddie can have a political personality, and I do, then Gypsy was a politician. As one caddie said, "Gypsy's for Gypsy." But, like a good politician, he was hard not to like.

At 1:00 P.M. we went to our positions, put on our headphones, and listened to the Chuck Will Show. Here's a sample:

CHUCK WILL: Canadian Dave on fifteen, who's away?

WILL: Canadian Dave, fifteen green, who's away?

WILL: Oh, Christ. What's going on here? Telephone company, did you check that problem at fifteen yesterday?

[No immediate response.]

WILL: Telephone company, telephone company, hello?

TELEPHONE COMPANY MAN: Yes, Chuck, fifteen is OK.

WILL: Well, then, why the hell. . . ?

VOICE: Chuck?

WILL: Who is this?

VOICE: Canadian Dave on fifteen.

WILL: Where the hell have you been?

CANADIAN DAVE: I didn't know. . . .

WILL: Obviously, you didn't know. [Then, more to himself than to the thirty others listening:] Christ Almighty, I'm surrounded by friggin' idiots. Idiots everywhere.

VOICE: Chuck?

WILL: Yes?

VOICE: Peete's putting for birdie here.

WILL: I can see that on my monitor. And I'll ask you
    when I need information.

Steve Melnyk, tall, somewhat rotund, and friendly, climbed into the booth overlooking the fourteenth green. He introduced himself and asked, "Who do you have working with you in the fairway?"

"Gypsy," I said.

"Good," said Melnyk. "Tell Gypsy that we need yardages and clubs as soon as he knows them, then you write them down and hand them to me."

As Melnyk was speaking to me in one ear, Chuckles was giving me an order on the headphones. But I didn't catch what he said.

ME: I'm sorry, Chuck, but I didn't hear you.

WILL: Bamberger, do your ears work? 'Cause if they
    don't you're going to find this job very difficult.
    What's happening on the fourteenth green?

ME: Wayne Levi's got a tricky chip for a three. Burns
    has a twenty-footer for bird. Haas has a ten-footer
    to save par.

WILL: No. Levi, third shot. Burns, birdie putt. Haas
    par putt. "Tricky chips and saves"—we don't have
    time for that, right, Bamberger?

ME: Right.

WILL: You're a fast learner, Bamberger; knew that
    when I hired you.

WILL: Gypsy?

GYPSY: Yes, Chuck.

WILL: What's happening on fourteenth tee?

GYPSY: The order will be Miller, Black, Gilder.

WILL: Good. If everybody was as good as Gypsy we
    might actually be able to get a broadcast out,
    know what I mean, Jimmy? I mean, basically, I
    think I'm a good judge of character. But where do

I get these guys? How could I possibly have this much bad luck in one week? Scott on thirteenth tee, what's going on?

[No answer.]

WILL: Scott on thirteen, do you hear me? Oh, shit, where the hell is he?

[Two minutes pass.]

VOICE: You call, Chuck?

WILL: Who is that?

VOICE: Scott.

WILL: Where the hell were you?

SCOTT: I was on break, I thought we was on break.

WILL: Did I call for a break? Does anybody remember me calling for a break?

[There was no answer; Chuck had not called for a break.]

WILL: Scott, take off your headphone, place it down gently, walk to the trailer, and pick up your check. You're fired.

SCOTT: Come on, Chuck.

WILL: You're fired, Scott. Stewart, can you work the mouthpiece on the headset?

STEWART: I think so, Chuck.

WILL: "I think so, Chuck; I think so, Chuck." Well, then go over to thirteen and fill in there. [Pause] Idiots, Jimmy, I'm surrounded by idiots.

And on it went, part air traffic control dialogue, part Marx Brothers. Everybody laughed with Chuckles, until it was their turn to be butchered.

Although Steve Melnyk did not accomplish much as a player in his fourteen years on the Tour—he never won a tournament and never finished better than forty-six on the money list—he is well-respected by players and well-liked by viewers. In the late 1960s and early 1970s, playing for the University of Florida, Melnyk was one of the best amateur golfers in the country, winning the U.S. Amateur in 1969 and the British Amateur two years later. Over the years on the Tour he lost his hair and his golf game (there is dispute over which was lost first) but not his geniality. He serves as CBS's knowledgeable, not-too-intrusive, understated announcer.

Melnyk takes his job seriously, although not over-bearingly so. For each player who played through fourteen, Melnyk mentioned something in the booth that demonstrated that he had done his announcer's homework. One player was distracted from his game because of marital problems. Another was hitting the longest drives of his career after changing to a metal-headed driver. One just started playing with the Wilson ProStaff because he wants to hit the ball higher. And another is going to miss the U.S. Open to attend his daughter's college graduation. Melnyk shares this information in small doses and with few words. In golf, Melnyk well understands, the picture tells the most important story, as long as the right picture is being shown. And that is up to Chuck Will and his team of spotters.

"Bamberger, what's going on at fourteen green?" Chuck demanded.

"Fergus, third shot. Bean, birdie putt. Cook, par putt," I said.

"Good, Bamberger, good," Chuckles said. "There may be hope for you yet."

6
NOT THE MASTERS

I

IN THE MISSISSIPPI TOWN of Hattiesburg, which is separated from New Augusta by Palmers Crossing, the locals run a tournament called the Magnolia during Masters week. If you're not from Mississippi you probably haven't heard of it. But the golfers have. Before Craig Stadler was a Masters champion, he was a Magnolia champion. Before Payne Stewart was a runner-up in the British Open, he won the Magnolia. Before Johnny Miller was a U.S. Open champion, he was a Magnolia contestant. Before Hal Sutton was a P.G.A. Championship champion, he played the Magnolia. Before Tom Watson was Tom Watson, he was another face at the Magnolia. Some consider the Magnolia a rite of passage to the Masters. Billy Britton is among them.

At 6:30 in the morning, several hours and several states away from the opening ceremonies for the Masters, Billy Britton was at the first tee of the Hattiesburg Country Club preparing for the Magnolia. I was on his bag. We had to play at 6:30, before the pro-am, in which Billy was not a contestant. There were many other players who weren't contestants in the pro-am, but they weren't at the golf course at 6:30 A.M. Few players have Billy's sense of the work ethic. Billy believes in preparing himself as best he can for any tournament; he is an exceptionally disciplined player. "The way I see it," he said, "practice is part of my job."

We played the front nine of the Hattiesburg Coun- try Club, a short, well-groomed course whose fair- ways are defined by groves of tall, thin, densely growing pine trees. On some holes you can barely see the adjoining fairways, there are so many trees. Billy played with Larry Rentz, a twenty-five-year-old as- sistant pro from Lanham, Maryland, who was a freshman at the University of Florida when Billy was a senior. Larry, like most of the Magnolia field, was a Tournament Players Series player, the minor leagues of the Tour. Larry is a long hitter and a gifted athlete; on the Tour he would be among the longest hitters. He took up the game at sixteen. The next year he won the *Golf Digest* National Junior Long Drive Contest. The next year he played in the U.S. Open.

We finished playing the front nine by 8:30 A.M. and couldn't play the back nine because of the pro-am. We went to Shoney's for breakfast, which Larry liked because it had an all-you-can-eat buffet. Larry's a big eater.

Three people sat in the booth next to us, two businessmen and Charley Pride. Pride was playing in the pro-am, his tenth of the year.

Pride recognized Larry and Billy as professional golfers (tanned arms coupled with a pale left hand, where a right-handed golfer wears his glove, are the telltale signs) and began a conversation with them.

They discussed golf technique for ten minutes until Pride, before leaving for the course, said, "As you can tell, I'm fairly well addicted. Some people are doing drugs. Some people are drinking. I don't need any of that stuff. I just play golf."

II

After breakfast, Billy went back to the golf course to putt. I took a drive through Hattiesburg, a Southern town that appeared to be still recovering from the Civil War.

The population of Hattiesburg is 41,000, but that figure is deceivingly large, for there are no apartment buildings in this sprawling town. It has a Main Street, lined with once-sturdy, two-story brick buildings, but the street, when I toured it, was nearly deserted. Half the stores were boarded up. On the outskirts of town there is the University of Southern Mississippi, a hospital, and several malls. Beyond that is agrarian Hattiesburg, where cattle are raised, cotton and soybeans grown, and timber cut. The malls, by the nature of malls, are indistinct: You can see similar ones in Ohio, or Texas, or Rhode Island. In Hattiesburg, though, waitresses at Chi-Chi's speak with a Mississippi accent, the only quality that lends the joint a sense of place.

Back at my room at the Days Inn, I dipped into a map of Mississippi and created a thematic tour of the state. I created a These Golfers Should Have Been Born There Tour, featuring the Mississippi towns of (Larry) Mize; (Bob) Murphy; (Chris) Perry; (John) Adams; (Johnny) Miller; (Lon) Hinkle; (Andy) Magee; (George) Burns; and (Jack) Newton.

Half a year earlier I had only slight familiarity with those names. Now they were part of my daily conversations, and the personalities behind them were beginning to emerge.

III

Billy Britton had started playing golf with his older brothers and neighborhood friends on the public courses of Staten Island, sneaking on late in the day. He loved the game from the beginning and developed at it quickly. His lessons, informal free instruction from Jim Albus, gave Billy the basics. When they got older, Billy and his buddies, all Irish, all Catholic, all middle class, got in cars and drove off Staten Island in search of golf. They peaked at Winged Foot. They sneaked onto Baltusrol. They ferried to Fishers Island and sneaked onto the course there. They played in junior tournaments. They putted for Cokes and quarters into the darkness of long summer days.

When Billy was eighteen he won the Metropolitan Amateur, an esteemed amateur tournament. The next year he won the National Junior College title, playing for Miami Dade North Community College. He defended the Metropolitan Amateur title. He went to the University of Florida and made the starting team (which is nearly tantamount to making the Tour: Andy Bean played for Florida, as did Tour players Phil Hancock, Gary Koch, Pat Lindsey, Bob Murphy, Andy North, Larry Rinker, Mike Sullivan, Woody Blackburn, Mark Calcavecchia, John DeForrest, and Ken Green).

Billy was a good, steady player. He turned professional in 1979 and won the Metropolitan Open, a non-Tour event, but a professional golf tournament all the same. His career was off to a good start. He qualified for the Tour in the spring of 1980.

After spending the first half of the year playing in

Australia—between expenses and his winnings there
Billy broke even, which he considered a small accomplishment—he took on the U.S. Tour in the late
summer and fall of 1980. He won $9,022 for 171st
place on the money list. It was not a bad half-year, not
bad at all. He had never seen the courses before. He
was playing without a sponsor, and he was driving
himself from tournament to tournament in a Comet
he'd borrowed from his parents. Some of the drives
took the better part of a day, but Billy did not want to
be burdened with the expense of flying. He was a
Tour player on a budget and determined to make it
on his own. The next year, 1981, Billy learned to play
the Tour. He earned $39,358 for ninety-seventh place.
Nothing spectacular, but a decent first full year.
Billy knew he wasn't among the most talented players on the Tour, but he also knew that he could make
a living out there.

He made friends. He and Mike Donald, Jim Booros,
Freddy Couples, Lance Ten Broeck, David Thore,
Ronnie Black, and Jon Chaffee were all close. They
gave each other nicknames. Billy was Brit, the Toy
Cannon, Otis, the Bulldog, and occasionally, the
Grinder. He and his friends were all making decent
money. They were having fun. Billy won $75,328 in
1982, finishing in fifty-seventh place on the money
list. Freddy finished four ahead of Brit.

At the end of 1982 Billy started changing his
swing. He felt he had swung more purely in 1981
than in 1982, even if he had made less money. Bad
habits had crept in. He wanted to have the best swing
he could. Money was secondary. Swinging well was
everything.

The next season, 1983, did not begin well, and it got
worse. Billy's swing had deteriorated and he did not
know why. The old swing keys that had worked for
him failed him. Meanwhile, Freddy Couples won a

tournament and had an outstanding year. He won
$209,733 and seldom practiced. Lance didn't practice
too much, either. Booros's game was either on or off.
Donald and Billy beat balls more than ever. They
practiced all the time. Because of his good year in
1982, Billy was in all the tournaments—the T.P.C.,
the Memorial, the Open. Friends, and even people
Billy scarcely knew, could not understand what happened to his game in a single year. Many offered
suggestions. Others made standing offers to help if
Billy wanted it, which is not common on the Tour. He
finished the year in 148th place on the money list,
earning $20,492. After having a decent year and a
good year in his first two years on the Tour, he had
plummeted, badly, in his third.

Billy spent 1984 working on his game, working
with Peter Kostis, a leading teacher. He made progress. At the end of the year he made seven of eight
cuts. He finished 142nd on the money list, earning
$28,149. After the season he went back to the Tour
Qualifying School. His 142nd position was not going
to get him in a lot of tournaments for 1985. A good
finish at the school would. For five days he played
well, shooting 71, 70, 71, 73, 72. He was near the top
of the field. But on the final day he shot a 78, and
finished only a few ahead of the middle of the field. In
1985, with a season fourteen tournaments old, Billy
had been in three tournaments and had missed three
cuts.

IV

At the Magnolia, Billy drew as playing partners
Tom Costello (who some golf observers think could
play the Tour if he didn't insist on quenching his golf-
course thirst with cranberry juice and vodka from
plastic containers) and Bradley Dub Bryant, a reli-

gious, chatty man who had finished second in tournaments three times in seven years on the Tour but had never won.

"Play good, guys," Brad said on the first tee.

By the ninth hole the group's play was not especially good.

"Let's make some birdies, guys," Brad said on the tenth tee. He started making some bogeys. His wife, Sue, followed every shot, dipping into a book between shots, using a scorecard as a bookmark. As the round progressed, she read more and watched less. She was reading the Bible.

"How 'bout some room, guys?" Brad said on the fourteenth tee, feeling that the caddies were crowding him in on the tee. There was no one within five feet of him.

"He's just a little jumpy," Brian, Bryant's Australian caddie, said to Tom Costello's caddie, named Butch, and me. "Chomping on the bit," Brian said.

On the seventeenth tee, with all the warning of a glass that suddenly falls and shatters in the middle of a quiet dinner, the skies blackened and the rain began to fall. Hastily, umbrellas were popped open, bag covers were snapped on, rain gear came out.

A caddie's job becomes especially important in the rain. Realistically or not, the professional golfer expects to play as well in the rain as he does in the sunshine, and he expects to be as comfortable, too. The caddie holds the umbrella over him while he is contemplating a shot or lining up a putt. The caddie inserts one towel in the umbrella's spokes and uses it to keep the grips dry. A golfer can do nothing without a dry grip. If a caddie can create a sense of order during the rain, and keep things dry, he will save his man shots.

Mississippi had suffered a dry spell and the fairways were hard. Pools of water filled every valley. By the time our group putted out on the seventeenth, the siren sounded, marking the postponement of play. The timing was unfortunate for us, since we had only one hole left to play, and since Billy had been playing better as the round progressed (although he was not playing terribly well).

We walked back to the clubhouse. The caddies congregated in dry overhangs and waited for the rain to stop. The players went into the clubhouse, coming out periodically to give a caddie a sandwich, the latest news from the Masters, or an update on the rain delay.

The rain never stopped, and after two hours the officials postponed play for the rest of Friday. They canceled Saturday's round, reducing the fifty-four-hole tournament to thirty-six holes. Saturday would be used to conclude Friday's play (some of the field was just beginning their round). There would be no cut, and the tournament would conclude on Sunday. The top half of the field would get checks.

We returned to the golf course Saturday morning needing to play one hole. Billy went through his preround warm-up. He putted for twenty minutes, hit a bucket of balls, hit some chips, some sand shots, some pitches. We walked out to the eighteenth, a 425-yard par four which rolls slightly downhill and leads to a pond 300 yards off the tee. To hit a driver off the tee would be an unduly risky shot. Billy hit a three wood and hit it well, with a gentle draw. It landed hard, though, kicked left and ended a yard into the rough. We had 162 yards to the pin. Billy chose a six iron, which was more than enough club. He played the ball forward in his stance to promote a high shot. He took a nice swing at the ball and the ball began to soar, and directly on line with the pin. But then, at the height of its trajectory, the ball started drifting right. The ball landed in a greenside bunker on the right, whose sand had the consistency of flour before the rain but, since the downpour, had become a pool of heavy mud.

Billy's ball was buried deep: We could see maybe thirty of its dimples. The bunker had a severe lip on it. Billy was looking at a treacherous shot, one that requires as much physical strength as technique. He dug in, the face of the club closed to about a forty-five degree angle. He swung so hard at it that a small grunt escaped from his lips as he hit the ball. The ball smashed into the bottom lip of the bunker and lodged itself there. His first bunker shot was nearly impossible, but his second harder yet. There was almost no chance of him getting it out. This time he opened the face as widely as he could. He swung hard and the ball smashed into the bunker's lip and rolled backwards a foot. Finally, he had a playable lie. He was also playing his fifth shot. He blasted out to twenty feet from the pin.

Bryant made a putt for birdie. Costello did, too. Billy missed the twenty-footer. He took a seven. It was 9:15 A.M., and Billy had nothing but that triple bogey staring at him for the rest of the day.

"Think I'll go back to the room," Billy said, "and zone out for a while."

Billy was relaxed for Sunday's round. The triple bogey had taken him out of the possibility of finishing at all in the money. Still, Billy gave every shot all his effort. He was one under par for the day, finishing the round in the warm, pleasant Mississippi dusk. The week had not been good. In five days in Mississippi he was able to play only one eighteen-hole round. He lost $800 on the week, between air travel, a rented car, the hotel room, meals, the registration fee, and $200 for his caddie. Still, at the end he had played a decent round of golf, and his spirits were lifted.

7
MR. GEORGE ARCHER

I

ONE DAY on the practice tee of the Hattiesburg
Country Club, while watching Billy Britton beat
balls, a short, strongly built, Oriental caddie came up
to me. He pointed his stringy beard at me, peered
through red-tinted, horned-rimmed glasses, and
said, "Do you know Beelee's brother?" He curled the
right side of his upper lip. His pants were rolled up to
his knees and his socks were pushed down to his
ankles.

"No," I said, "I don't know Billy's brother."

"Neither do I," he said. He walked back to his spot,
behind Jim Dent's golf bag.

Later, when Kim Armstrong and I became friends,
of sorts, I came to understand his unusual method of
introduction.

By asking if I knew "Beelee's brother," Kim
learned all he wanted from me. If I knew Billy's
brother, then I was friend of Billy's from home, and

113

Hattiesburg was a one-week stint as a caddie, just for fun. But if I didn't know Billy's brother, then I was an aspiring Tour caddie, and he would have to watch me closely: Kim had worked for Billy in half a dozen tournaments in 1984, and we could be competitive for his bag somewhere down the road. During the week of the Magnolia, Kim and I played at the University of Southern Mississippi golf course. Kim was a good, but not humble player: "I tell Beelee Britton that he give me three shots on long, hilly golf course on hot day, and Beelee have to carry own heavy bag, I can beat Beelee," said Kim, who had perfected Hemingway's mock-Indian accent.

I lost our match and had to pay for dinner, which we had at a place called the Catfish Shack. We colored the catfish on the paper placemats with crayons provided by the restaurant while Kim talked about the social structure of the Tour. He spoke of things that I had never considered.

As Kim saw it, there were three groups of caddies: young, white, college-educated caddies; middle-aged, white caddies, not college-educated; and middle-aged and older black caddies, most of them from the South, some of them illiterate. The existence of these groups, Kim said, was not evident at the golf course, but the groupings defined the rules by which caddies traveled and shared motel rooms, ate and hung out. Within each group there was a class structure. "If you have a big bag [a player winning tournaments], you're a big man," Kim said. Years on the Tour, curiously, played little role in determining a caddie's status. Caddies, as Kim saw it, were not bound by history. Three weeks was the typical perspective: how much you made last week; how you're playing this week; and what you have lined up for next week.

"You going to Hilton Head?" Kim asked.

"I'll go if I can line up a bag here," I said, meaning the Magnolia.

"You can't," Kim said. "Only six players here play Hilton Head, and they're all set for caddies.

"Make you a deal," Kim said. "Keep rent-a-car another week. I pay you seventy-five dollars for ride to Hilton Head, and I set you up with bag there."

There's no five-year plan for Tour caddies—hell, there's no five-week plan—and Kim's plan sounded as good as anything I had thought of. So, on Sunday night after the Magnolia, at about 9:00 P.M., I began my first big caddie drive, with Kim Armstrong. We had Mississippi, Alabama, Georgia, and South Carolina ahead of us, and an AM radio.

"I meet Big Boy [Jim Dent] at ten in Hilton Head," Kim said. "Slow and steady, we get there." We had thirteen hours to make it.

II

"What are you?" Kim asked. We were on U.S. Highway 84, a winding two-lane road that runs through the heart of the rural Deep South.

"What do you mean?" I asked.

"You're not Chinese, you're not black—so what are you?"

"I'm Jewish, if that answers your question."

"Oh, a Jew boy," Kim said. "Now there two Jewish caddies. Andy Davidson, he a Jew. He get picked on a lot. And three Jewish players. Corey Pavin, he the other type of Jew. Body of a lamb, but the heart of a lion. He gonna win big. Tom Watson, he sort of a Jew—his wife Jewish. And Morris Hatalsky. He was a Jew, but now he something *different*."

"What are you?" I asked Kim.

He paused, and looked outside the car window at the passing highway signs.

"Just a caddie," he said.

We drove on for several miles in silence.

"Why didn't the Jews fight back when the Nazis

were taking them away to the concentration camps?" Kim asked.

I began an answer: the resistance movements, the overwhelming numbers against the Jews, the refusal to believe what was happening. But I soon realized I was talking to the radio. Kim Armstrong, more interested in his question than an answer, had fallen soundly asleep. Just then, Kim's chief interest was sleep, and he was good at it. I stopped for gas; Kim remained asleep. I stopped for coffee; Kim remained asleep. I stopped for a red light in Phenix City, Alabama; Kim remained asleep. I drove all through the night. Kim slept all through the night.

In Macon, Georgia, the sun rose and, finally, we reached a four-lane interstate highway. We were well behind schedule, if Kim was to meet Big Boy at the first tee at ten in Hilton Head. I began to drive fast on Interstate 16, Savannah bound. Somewhere around Dudley, Georgia, eastbound, the interstate becomes a downsloping hill, and one cannot help but do seventy miles per hour without even touching the accelerator.

The state trooper was not impressed with that reasoning; neither was he impressed with Kim. "What's with your partner there?" the trooper asked. He eyed Kim suspiciously.

"Oh, he's just a good sleeper, that's all," I said.

The big trooper nodded, unconvinced, and wrote me up. I owed the Laurens County Probate Court ninety dollars. I stashed the citation in the glove compartment and resumed the drive. I was angry at myself, driving too quickly to make Kim's tee time while he slept through the entire ride, ticket and all.

"Told you not to drive so fast," Kim said. His mouth moved, but his body didn't, and before I could respond he was asleep again.

We arrived on Hilton Head at 11:00 A.M.; the drive had been thirteen hours, excluding a nap I took in a Piggly Wiggly parking lot somewhere in Alabama.

We pulled into the golf course and Kim saw a caddie known as the Hippie. The Hippie and Kim were friends.

"Hey, Hippie, you see Big Boy?" Kim asked.

"He just landed," the Hippie said. "He's waiting on you on the putting green."

"You see Pancho [Victor Regalado, a Mexican-born professional]?" Kim asked.

"Pancho's out on the course, probably making the turn now," the Hippie said. "What you want with Pancho?"

"New York here lookin' for a bag," Kim said, pointing his chin in my direction.

"He don't want Pancho," the Hippie said. The caddies consider Regalado among the most difficult golfers to work for. Only two others go through caddies as quickly: Mac O'Grady and John Fought.

"New York not fussy New Yorker. He want work," Kim said.

"Pancho's set anyhow," the Hippie said.

"You see Akron Trash?" Kim asked. "He supposed to have condo for you, me, and him. Buck each for the week."

Akron Trash caddied for Mike Smith. Smith had finished second in Las Vegas, earning $100,000, more than he had won in his four previous years on the Tour combined. Akron Trash picked up $5,000 for the week, and had been living opulently since. Five grand goes a long way in the caddie world.

"He's here," the Hippie said. "He's got a girl with him. You got any cash for him?"

Kim handed two fifty-dollar bills to the Hippie.

"Can he put up New York?" Kim asked.

"Can he sleep in the bathtub?" the Hippie asked.

"Can you sleep in the bathtub?" Kim asked me. He curled the right side of his upper lip. This was a joke. Caddies may sleep in cars, they may sleep in hedgerows, but they do not sleep in bathtubs.

"New York's got a credit card, man," Kim said to the Hippie. "No bathtub for him."

We walked over to the putting green. Kim picked up Jim Dent's bag. He was going right to work.

"See George Archer? Go ask George," Kim said to me.

George Archer, twenty-two-year Tour veteran, winner of thirteen tournaments including the 1969 Masters and the 1984 Bank of Boston Classic, twenty-first on the all-time career earnings list (at the start of the 1985 season), was putting. His tall and lanky frame was curled over the ball, working on his much-imitated pendulum putting stroke, the stroke that has made him one of golf's best putters. He rolled in putt after putt after putt.

The Tour caddies respect Archer, who competes successfully with players half his age. But they seldom ask him for jobs, for reasons I discovered later in the week. Archer's oldest daughter, Elizabeth Taylor Archer (his younger daughter is Marilyn Monroe Archer), often caddies for him. When she doesn't Archer typically takes local caddies.

"George, how would you like to break in a guy who'll be working for Al Geiberger next week?" I asked him with the sort of caddie assertiveness I was fast learning.

"Who's that?" Archer asked.

"Me," I said.

He looked me over, not a careful study, just a glance.

"All right," he said. He returned to his putting. "I'll see you tomorrow at ten."

"Are you set for a yardage book?" I asked.

"Yes, I am," Archer said, continuing to putt. "You needn't bother getting one. I don't want yardages from caddies anymore. I find when they give me the yardages I stop thinking and when I stop thinking I can't play. We're going to do this the old-fashioned

way. Just carry the bag and keep the clubs and the
ball clean. Best caddie I know is my daughter. She
doesn't know a thing about golf."

"OK," I said, "see you tomorrow." It occurred to me
that it might be useful for Archer to know my name.
"My name's Mike, by the way," I said.

"OK, Mark, see you tomorrow," said Archer.

Calling me Mark, it came to pass in the week
ahead, was the closest Archer ever came to using my
name.

At the moment, I didn't care whether Archer knew
my name or not. I had a bag, and a good one. It was
my birthday. I had turned twenty-five and had
landed the first big bag of my new career.

III

Hilton Head Island, a peninsula that dips into Port
Royal Sound in South Carolina's extreme southern
tip, was in full bloom in mid-April, with flowers and
gardens and shrubs and seas of golf courses and acres
of tennis courts all bursting with life.

Hotels are few and expensive on Hilton Head Island; villas, town houses, and condominiums predom-
inate. Some of the caddies went off the island to find
accommodations, a twenty-five-mile drive from the
Sea Pines Plantation, site of the Harbour Town Golf
Links, home of the Sea Pines Heritage Classic.
Twenty-five Hilton Head miles in spring can mean
two hours of driving, allowing for the lines to get into
the Sea Pines Plantation, a privately owned real-
estate development the size of a small town.

Kim Armstrong thought the tournament officials
might know of discounted motels for caddies. I was
ready for an afternoon of sleep after the all-night
drive and went into the pro shop, behind Archer and
the putting green, to find out about such accommodations. When I asked a woman on the other side of a

counter of Hilton Head sweaters about cheap motels, a man behind me answered.

"Are you looking for a place to stay for the week?" he asked.

"Yes," I said.

"Well, I've got a villa off the sixth hole, where we've got an extra bedroom, and you're welcome to stay with us," he said. He introduced his son, Larry, and himself: Bill Gruttemeyer of New City, New York, and, for the week of the Heritage Classic, Hilton Head, South Carolina.

One factor prompted William R. Gruttemeyer, president of James Talcott, Inc., bankers to the garment industry, to invite me, a total stranger, into his home. His love of golf, and for the Sea Pines Heritage Classic, linked us inextricably: I was not a stranger; I was part of the tournament.

Larry and Bill were off to play golf: Did I want to join them? Exhausted from the all-night drive, I declined.

Bill Gruttemeyer pulled a key out of his pocket and directed me to 2550 Gleneagle Drive. "My wife, Cathryn, and Larry's wife, Monica, are there. I'll call and tell them you're coming. You get yourself some sleep."

Cathryn Gruttemeyer, a sprightly woman in her late fifties, with no interest in golf and a keen interest in people, greeted me at the door. Did I want anything before going to sleep? A glass of milk, perhaps?

I commented on my great birthday fortune: I came to the island when caddie jobs were scarce and rooms scarcer yet, and within an hour I stumbled into a good job and a family of New Yorkers who gave new meaning to the phrase southern hospitality.

When I woke up, it was 11:00 P.M. From downstairs, in the living room, the dancing sounds of late-night television bounced quietly against dark walls. Mrs. Gruttemeyer was still awake.

"I'm so glad you woke up," she said. She motioned

me toward the kitchen. There, on the breakfast table, sat a coconut-vanilla fudge cake. She lit the twenty-five skinny, pink candles and sang the Happy Birthday song.

The next morning Bill Gruttemeyer and I had breakfast on the back deck overlooking the sixth green.

"Have you ever met Craig Stadler?" Bill asked. "He stays two houses down from us and, frankly, I don't particularly care for him. That gruff manner, and throwing those clubs all over the golf course. That's not right.

"We had Hale Irwin come for one of our corporate outings. He was fairly expensive. I think five, six thousand for the day, but worth every penny of it. There is a gentleman. A patient teacher. Not overbearing.

"You know what I don't like about most of these teachers? They want to make you swing like the pros do. I've had surgery; I've had a heart attack. I'm happy to be playing the game. Sure, I'd like to play a little better. But I'm not gonna become a scratch golfer. If I break 90, I'm happy. But some of these guys just want to completely tear your swing right apart. Not a guy like Irwin; he'll work with what you've got. He's not expecting miracles."

Just then Brad Faxon, playing an early morning round, reached the sixth green. He looked up and saw me having breakfast on the sun-drenched deck.

"Bamberger, how come your accommodations are always three times nicer than mine?" Brad asked. Bill Gruttemeyer beamed.

"Missed a great tournament in Hattiesburg last week," I said.

"Heard you all had a great time," Brad said. "Never rains in Hattiesburg, huh?" Brad kept up on everything.

"What did you do last week?" I asked.

"Went to Atlanta, to my girlfriend's," Brad said. "Didn't touch a club for eight days. Spent the whole week horizontal.

"Who you got this week?" he asked.

"Archer," I said.

Brad nodded, impressed. It was the same nod Angelo Argea had given me when I told him I was working for Brad.

"Movin' up in the world," Brad said. "Soon I won't even be able to get you to work for me."

"I got a couple weeks open, Brad; I think I can squeeze you in," I said.

"How come you guys aren't playing?" Brad asked.

"We're playing at ten."

"What a life," Brad said, referring to the late time. He went back to work. Bill Gruttemeyer put down his orange juice with a flourish and a smile and said, "What a nice young man. Seems like a terrific fellow. Is he a terrific fellow? What a nice young man." Bill Gruttemeyer was an enthusiast, a golf enthusiast.

Bill intimated, in a subtle way, that he would be very pleased if I would invite George Archer over to the Gruttemeyer villa for drinks after one of the rounds. I was, of course, in no position to do this. But I was also careful not to say anything that might diminish Bill Gruttemeyer's high opinion of George Archer in any way.

Archer is especially popular with older golf fans, like Bill Gruttemeyer, who remember when the pros did not wear bracelets and did wear Amana hats. Archer still has the Amana hat, a throwback to the sixties when the Radarange people offered free life insurance to any of the pros who would wear one of their hats. The business of athlete endorsements has exploded since then, and there are not too many players left with the Amana hats. There are not too many players left wearing flared plaid pants several inches too short, for that matter, either. His too-short pants distinguish Archer, and accentuate his height, which is six feet, five inches. His distinctive appearance goes hand-in-hand with his opinionated manner. George Archer is no namby-pamby, a fact that attracts some golf fans to him and repels others. In the June 1985 issue of *Golf Magazine*, Archer argued in a column called "Head-to-Head" over whether the great golf courses should be open to the public. He said they should not, that heavy traffic from the public could ruin the great golf courses. A reader responded with a letter urging the magazine to "write an article entitled 'The Fifty Snobbiest Golfers in America.' George Archer would qualify for the top ten."

Snob or not, Archer is a member of one of golf's most elite societies, the fraternity of Masters champions. Having just returned from Augusta, the scene of his greatest golf accomplishment, it occurred to me that Archer might be feeling sentimental. I asked him what it's like to be in the Champion's locker room at Augusta. I imagined it as one of golf's sacred temples.

"It's a room, just like any other room," he said. "The only thing that's good about it is that the press isn't allowed in there. They let 'em in the clubhouse now and, Christ, you can't even get a bite to eat without questions thrown out at you every which way. It's ridiculous.

"It's not the same since Clifford Roberts died," said Archer. Roberts was the Masters' chairman for nearly five decades. "The guy after him, he was pretty much all right, but he died before we got to know him. But this new guy—I don't know—he's something else. He doesn't ask the people their opinions. At one point he says at the Champion's dinner, 'This is the way Clifford Roberts would have wanted it.' How would he know? Roberts used to ask the players all sorts of things, from the way the dinner was run to golf course changes."

If the trip to Augusta was not sentimental for

Archer, maybe it's because he's still a good enough player to live in the present.

He is a very good player. In 1984 he had the best year of his career, financially, winning $207,000 and placing at number twenty-eight on the money list. He had a higher money position in only six seasons. He remains good because he is a brilliant putter, and has long been. In 1984 he averaged 28.73 putts per round, the third best figure on the Tour. In 1980 he set an all-time Tour record by playing the four rounds of the Sea Pines Heritage Classic with only ninety-four putts. That's an average of 23.5 putts per round, a formidable record. Second best is ninety-nine. Any time a professional takes fewer than 116 putts for a seventy-two-hole tournament, he is pleased. Archer improved on that by twenty!

When Archer won a tournament in 1984, it was the first time he had won since 1976 and the second time since 1972. Archer lost four years on the Tour to injury. In 1974 and 1975, a torn tendon in his left wrist resulted in surgery, and in 1978 and 1979, when two of his disks fused, he needed surgery again.

A healthy George Archer plays a dazzling game of golf, but there was nothing dazzling about Archer's game in our practice round. The aches and pains of two decades of professional golf all seemed to be catching up with him in this one round. He didn't like the golf course. He didn't like the recent changes made to it. He didn't like the heat. He didn't like the way he was hitting the ball. I was taken by his candid, complaining way, as if he were taking me in as a confidant. This illusion of mine did not last long.

"I'm gonna tell you what I tell all my caddies," Archer began in a short conversation from which I never recovered. We had come in from the practice round. "You can't help me, but you sure can hurt me.

"Years ago I had a caddie, a big high school football player, who was looking for my ball in the rough. He found the ball, all right. Kicked it right out of bounds. Terrible scene. The kid was crying. Cost me two shots. So just one word of advice: Be careful."

George Archer, I figured, had never heard of the school of positive reinforcement.

IV

Mrs. Gruttemeyer—I could not bring myself to call a woman older than my mother by her first name no matter how much she insisted—explained to me how golf kept the Gruttemeyers together.

"Before Larry went to Viet Nam, he was the most shy, quiet guy you could imagine. Everything his father or anybody else asked him to do, he did immediately, no questions asked, no fuss. He worked very hard, did very well in school. The studious type. When he came back from Viet Nam, everything had changed. He was Mr. Outgoing. Party all the time. Didn't listen to his father anymore. Didn't listen to anyone. His father and he used to be very close, but all of a sudden they had nothing to talk about anymore. And then Larry discovered golf. And then they started playing golf together. Now everything's golf between them. What they shot this day and that day, who won this tournament and that tournament, what the golf magazines are saying for this problem and that problem. It's really brought them together.

"That's why this tournament has become so important to us. The way we've arranged the financing on this villa, it's rented almost every week of the year except this one. Bill loves the tournament with a passion, and so does Larry. This Sea Pines Half Wedge, whatever it's called, it brings us together."

V

Over the next five days, the Wednesday pro-am and

the four rounds of the tournament, I learned why the Tour caddies don't bother asking George Archer for jobs.

"You can't do anything to help me, but you sure can hurt me."

His inspired message ran through my head all week.

I didn't cost George Archer any strokes in the 1985 Sea Pines Herritage Classic. I didn't kick any balls out of bounds. I didn't leave the pin in the hole while he was putting and cause him a two-shot penalty. I didn't step in his line. I didn't lose his scorecard. But I didn't do much right, either.

Before the Wednesday pro-am, George asked me to help him with an elastic bandage he wears around his left forearm. He held it in place and told me to pull. I pulled it.

"Pull it hard," he said.

I pulled it hard.

"Pull it harder," he said.

I pulled it harder.

"Pull it as hard as you can," he said.

I pulled it as hard as I could.

"Here," he said. We switched positions. I held the bandage in place; George pulled and breathed audibly through his nose, which, I had learned quickly, was one of his signs of irritation. He spent a lot of that week breathing audibly through his nose.

On the day of the pro-am, George's back ached. He didn't have much to say to his amateur partners. He didn't have much to say to anyone. He would hit his shot and head for the woods while the amateurs hacked their shots about. He would emerge from the woods to play his shot and then dart back to them immediately afterward for their shaded protection. He offered not a single golf tip to any of his partners.

Yet when the round was over, and George had shot a 77 and the group was about twenty-five shots out of the pro-am tournament, Harry, one of the amateurs, said, "I've played in a dozen of these pro-ams, and not one pro can hold a candle to George." Harry had learned not to expect much from the pros in the pro-ams.

Once, in a pro-am, Harry was grouped with a young golfer who was playing poorly. Morose about his own game, the young pro gave no advice to his amateur partners, who, by their standards, were playing even more miserably. Harry approached the young player.

"Say," he said, "I realize you're not playing all that great, but you could give us a couple of words, couldn't you? I mean, this is a big thing for us."

The pro looked at Harry.

"You want a couple words?" he asked.

"Yeah, you know, just a tip here and there," said Harry, a good-natured sort. "Little conversation couldn't hurt."

"Here's two," the young pro said. "Fuck you."

I could not, as the players say about their games, get anything going. At one point the towel fell off the bag and into a muddy puddle.

"That's why I tell caddies to wear the towel over their shoulders," George said. There it remained for the rest of the week.

In Friday's round, I left George standing on the seventh green for several seconds without his putter. It was only a moment, but a moment is an eternity to a pro standing on the green without his putter when he wants it, and he let me know it.

Several times I wanted to crawl into a bunker and bury my head in the soft Hilton Head sand. For instance, on the fifteenth tee in Saturday's round, with a sizable gallery within earshot, George informed me that my fly was open; the other caddies roared with laughter. Two holes later, before a bigger gallery, George gave me a public lesson in how to tend a pin.

When the tournament was over Sunday afternoon, I brought the clubs to Archer's borrowed Cadillac, a courtesy car from the tournament, and put them in the trunk.

"Thank you, sir," Archer said gratuitously. He had shot 79, the worst round of the day. His back was hurting him. He was not in a good mood and having to part with $250 for shoddy caddie job didn't help any.

That night I began the long trip to New Orleans to return the rental car. From there I would fly to Houston for the next tournament. I drove to Chaires, Florida, an eight-hour drive, and for the eight hours I was troubled by thoughts of George Archer. I had blown my chance with a big bag.

When I woke up the next morning, I looked at the sports section of the *Tallahassee Democrat*; they carried a two-paragraph Associated Press story about the Sea Pines Heritage Classic, telling how Bernhard Langer, in the wake of his Masters victory, had won his second straight tournament. There was no mention of George Archer's back problems, his caddie's inability to keep the towel on the bag, or even the $824 Archer had earned. My thoughts turned to Al Geiberger and the next tournament, the Byron Nelson Golf Classic. On the pro golf Tour, every week's a fresh start.

8
SKIPPY GEIBERGER

I

AL GEIBERGER AND GEORGE ARCHER occupy similar
positions in golf history. Geiberger, born in 1937,
joined the Tour in 1960. Archer, born in 1939, joined
the Tour in 1964. Geiberger has won eleven tournaments including one major, the 1966 P.G.A. Championship. Archer has won thirteen tournaments including one major. Both are, for now, well
entrenched in the career earnings list. Both are
superb putters and long hitters, able to keep up with
players twenty years younger. Both are expected to
be dominant forces on the Senior Tour when they
turn fifty.

They are both tall and thin. Geiberger is six feet,
two inches tall, and weighs 185 pounds; Archer has
three inches and fifteen pounds on Geiberger. Both
have had running battles with surgery. Both have a
special interest in photography. Both had daughters

in the class of 1985 at Stanford University. Both were born in California and live in California.

But in every other regard they are totally dissimilar.

I met Geiberger in the same way I met Archer, in the happenstance of Tour life. He had just been through his second divorce, was raising five children from the two marriages, considering a third marriage, trying to sell an expensive house in Santa Barbara, working on his golf game, and restoring his health. Somehow, in the middle of all this, he was still accepting new people into his life. Geiberger and I started as Archer and I did—as caddie and golfer. We moved beyond that most peculiar of relationships to something a great deal more satisfying. We became friends.

Geiberger carries a bright red Spalding golf bag made, I'm sad to report, of kangaroo skin. Fortunately, Spalding makes only four of these bags, for the only four players they keep under contract in the United States: Geiberger, Craig Stadler, Johnny Miller, and Greg Norman. Among the sea of black Titleist bags and the white Wilson bags made of unmalleable plastic and vinyl, the pliable, vibrant Spalding bags command attention. On my first day in Houston, while carrying Geiberger's bag from the practice tee to the putting green, an unusual caddie named Lee Lynch followed me, determined to see which Spalding bag I had. Lee, seventy-eight years old, little, firm, always in need of a shave and always looking for a cigarette, had been caddying for seven decades, four of them on the Tour.

Lee used to work for Geiberger steadily—he has worked for many different players steadily going back to Walter Hagen—and still works for him occasionally. Lee manages to get a bag at every tournament but seldom the same one more than one week in

a row. Lee is fired today for the same reason he was
fired twenty years ago: He takes over a player's
game. Lee Lynch long ago transcended the royal use
of *we* that caddies use when their golfer plays well—
"We shot a 68." He, alone, shot 59 at the Colonial
Country Club in Memphis in 1977; Geiberger, like a
good soldier, merely executed the shots. Lee Lynch
did all the planning and set all the strategy.

Lee is an authority on most topics important to
Tour life and, while his authority may be self-appointed, he is, nevertheless, listened to. He gives a
person no choice but to listen. After several weeks on
the Tour you learn that, if you walk away from Lee
Lynch while he is talking to you, he will simply follow
you. Lee Lynch is not shy.

The topics upon which Lee lectures—barks might
be a better verb—are many and varied. They include
putting; chipping; the nation's best golf courses; the
best (cheapest) places to eat; the best (cheapest)
motels; the best (cheapest) means of transportation
between any two points; the exact yardage from any
landmark on any golf course, anywhere, to the front
edge of its corresponding green; the exact break of
any putt, anywhere; the proper shot to hit, under any
circumstance, anywhere; the ranking of the best
golfers in history (none of whom are playing
anymore).

Lee took a look at my bag, which he considered *his*
bag, and grunted. It was Tuesday of the Houston
Open and Lee was looking for work. Lee was always
looking for a bag on Tuesdays.

Lee Lynch was born in East Hampton, Long Island, New York, in 1907, and was, according to his
tradition, the son of the town's chief of police and the
grandson of the sheriff. Some say that Lee once had a
wife, but if he did, he doesn't know what happened to
her. Some say that he has a son, but this is only

speculation. Lee doesn't give much away about himself. Lee and I grew up in the same county, Suffolk, the eastern county of Long Island, and I thought this coincidence might give us an affinity.

"Did you ever caddie at the National?" I asked Lee. I had caddied once at a course called the National Golf Links of America in Southampton, Long Island, just to see it. It is as great and beautiful as its name is presumptuous.

"Caddie at the National," Lynch barked back. "Christ, I grew up on the National."

"I've heard Ben Crenshaw say it's one of his favorite courses in the United States," I said.

"Sure," Lynch said. "Crenshaw says that now. He never even heard of the goddamn golf course until I told him about it." So much for affinity. Lee marched off to give Brad Faxon a putting lesson.

"You got to stub it, know what I mean?" he said to Brad, his cigarette dancing as he talked. "Break your wrists coming back, pop it, and then stop. That's how Bobby Locke putted, last good putter there was."

Brad listened. When Lynch was through, Brad resumed his graceful, rhythmic stroke. He was doing his three-foot drill, dropping putt after putt after putt with a stroke that in no way resembled Lee's method.

"That's it," Lee said, "that's the way to do it."

Although the players tolerate Lee, he is not the darling of P.G.A. Tour officials. Lee hasn't much use for them, either.

A decade ago, Lee Lynch would get to the golf course at sunrise on tournament days and walk the course, marking that day's pin placements. He would then make a sheet, noting how far back each pin was from the front edge of the green. He made copies and distributed these sheets as he pleased. He gave them to the (few) players he liked and sold them to a few of

Randy Erskine gave the author his first caddie break.

Brad Faxon on caddying:
"It's not as easy as it looks.
Carrying the bag, that's
the least of it."

Golf Digest

Fred Vance, *Golf Magazine*

Chuck Will, CBS Sports' satiric, funny golf director
on the quality of the caddies he hired as spotters at
the 1985 Tournament Players Championship: "How
could I possibly have this much bad luck in one
week? Idiots, I'm surrounded by idiots."

Killer is among the Tour's most respected, soft-spoken, and famous caddies. His nickname derives from his skill with women, as in the expression "Lady Killer."

Bill Britton in the position that characterizes all his shot making: lips pursed, hands firm, stare intense.

Stephen Szurlej, *Golf Digest*

"Gypsy" Joe Grillo is co-chairman of the Professional Tour Caddie Association, paid caddie consultant to a score of players, and manager of the caddie softball team. He's the pitcher, too.

Steve Coleman, *Hattiesburg American*

Kim Armstrong, the author's all-night driving partner, is as much a sociologist as he is a caddie. He shares the bag with his player, Jim Dent, in Hattiesburg, Mississippi.

Nina Bramhall

The author tries doggedly to impress George Archer with his caddie skills at the tenth hole of the Harbour Town Golf Links.

Bill and Cathryn Gruttemeyer of Hilton Head Island, South Carolina, took in a stray caddie (the author) for the week of the Sea Pines Heritage Classic.

Al Geiberger is also known as "Skippy," for his old peanut butter advertisements, and as "Mr. 59." He is the only player to have broken 60 in a P.G.A. Tour event.

Gary McCord, a Tour player and CBS announcer, on Lee Lynch, the Tour's seventy-eight-year-old caddie: "Lee Lynch will never die. He's just gonna crystallize one day while tending the pin."

Larry Rentz, U.S. Open contestant, is one of the longest hitters in the game.

Golf Digest

Jeff McBride, P.G.A. of America

Mac O'Grady, the only player to list "modern times" as a special interest in the Tour media guide, is an advocate of yoga, marathon running, and natural fruit juices.

For some players, the Tour is a never-ending quest to determine what made Jack Nicklaus great. He is still held in awe.

Nina Bramhall

Tom Watson practices and plays with an obsessiveness that inspires and intimidates his colleagues. Bruce Edwards, who has caddied Watson to more than two dozen Tour victories, is also a Dallas real estate broker.

Steve Elkington, an Australian who lives in Houston, was in a position to win the 1985 Dutch Open until he played with Masters champion Bernhard Langer.

Bernhard Langer, a West German who lives in Florida, won tournaments on three continents in 1985, the year he emerged as a dominant force in international golf.

Two New York club pros who played in the 1985 P.G.A. Championship: Kevin Morris, left, and Jim Albus. Morris was one of four club pros to make the cut in the tournament; Albus taught Bill Britton how to play.

George J. Zahringer III, noted amateur golfer and stockbroker, won the 1985 Metropolitan Open, a tournament earlier won by Walter Hagen, Gene Sarazen, Jim Albus, and Bill Britton.

Brad Faxon hitting against "Gypsy" Joe Grillo in the 1985 Caddie–Player Softball Classic at the B.C. Open.

A relaxed Bill Britton at home on Staten Island at the end of the 1985 golf season.

The author at work.

the others. But to most he would not sell them at any price.

Players on good terms with Lee Lynch, or with ambitious caddies, were, equipped with the pin placement sheets, at a decided advantage, to the ire, naturally, of the disadvantaged. Tour officials responded by making it illegal for caddies to walk on a green before a round to check hole positions, and began to make the pin placement sheets themselves. Now the players pick them up each day, free, from a neat stack at the first tee. This democratic system sets well with just about everybody except Lee. Lee Lynch figures the Tour owes him about eighty dollars a week.

Lee Lynch may be the only caddie in the United States with a truly Scottish caddie philosophy. The caddies in Scotland develop their profession to such an art that they consider giving yardages an insult. They give clubs. One seldom sees this in the United States, and never on the Tour. Except in the case of Lee Lynch.

In 1980 Geiberger was playing very well in the Tournament Players Championship when he fell victim to Lee.

Standing over a fairway shot, he asked Lee for a yardage.

"Seven iron," Lee responded.

"How far, though?" Geiberger asked again.

"Seven iron," Lynch said.

Geiberger knocked the seven iron thirty yards over the green and, in so doing, knocked himself out of a chance to win the T.P.C. for the second time.

Lee can be equally menacing on the greens, where he talks about "overhaul breaks," grains "that run underneath" the ground and mysterious slopes that only he sees due to "optional illusions."

Dan Halldorson, a Tour player from Canada, told a

story about Lee's mastery of the greens at the Houston Open.

"We're on the sixth hole at Atlanta one year, and Lee's been reading putts for Al all day. He looks at the putt on number six and says that the putt should be played six inches outside on the right and firm. Al gives the putt a look—it's a tricky putt, a twenty-footer—and plays the putt a foot and a half outside on the left and real soft. It coasts right into the hole, a perfect read, a perfect putt. Lee takes the putter from Al, puts it back in the bag and says, 'I told you so, I told you so.'"

Gary McCord, who is making the transition from Tour player to CBS color man, has a theory about Lee: "Lee Lynch will never die," McCord declared one day on the practice tee. "He's just gonna crystallize one day while tending the pin."

II

For the first two rounds of the Houston Open, Geiberger was paired with Chi Chi Rodriguez and Tom Jenkins. Chi Chi, who lists his height at five feet, seven and a half inches, and his weight at 132 pounds, is better known for his antics and chatter than his playing record, although he's won eight tournaments. Chi Chi played with the fierce competitiveness one might not expect from a forty-nine-year-old man in his twenty-sixth year on the Tour.

Going into the Houston Open, Chi Chi had career earnings of $996,000. For twenty years he had been talking about winning one million dollars on the Tour, and for the past three years the mark had been within his grasp. A good finish in Houston would put him, finally, over. Chi Chi was deadly serious about achieving that plateau, which, going into the 1985 season, only forty-eight golfers had reached. No television cameras were aimed at Chi Chi; the galleries were small and there were no antics from him. Just serious golf.

At the start of the second round, Chi Chi, on the edge of making the cut, was upset. Jenkins had pulled out of the tournament and the group was now a twosome.

"I don't like that, Skippy, I don't like that," Chi Chi said to Al. "Now we're gonna be waitin' on every shot and on every tee. I can't play like that. And then on the par threes, you lose on the par threes, on club selection."

Some players peer into the bags of their playing partners, which is perfectly legal, to see what club they are using and gauge their own club selection accordingly. "It can cost you at least two shots, not having a third in your group," Chi Chi said.

Golfers are often talking about things that "can cost you two shots." A bad tee time, a hairline crack in your driver, a mediocre caddie—they can all "cost you two shots." And Chi Chi Rodriguez was definitely counting shots.

So was Al. On the ninth green in the second round, Al was at even par. We needed to get to at least one under to make the cut. Looking at a seven-footer to save par, Al suddenly asked, "What do you think?"

I took a look at the putt, the first time I had read a putt for a professional, and said, "Just outside the left lip."

"That's what I think, too," Geiberger said. He rolled the putt into the hole.

On the next hole, after a good drive, we had 158 yards to the pin, hitting into a slight breeze. Al, between clubs, ran his fingers over three of them in the bag.

"What do you think?" he asked.

"A six iron's too much. And an eight iron's not

enough. Just a smooth seven iron," I said, imitating the deductive process of club selection I had heard Al use.

"A soft seven or a regular seven?" Al asked. Some players—Brad Faxon is a good example of one—can hit a single club in a variety of ways, affecting the distance they will hit a shot as much as thirty yards. There are situations where you must hit a club harder than it is meant to be hit—when a nine iron is the only club with enough loft to clear a tree, for example, but is not enough, normally, to reach a green. So you smash it. When playing into the wind, a player might hit a less lofted club than the distance requires, to keep it low, and diminish the effect of the wind. The player must hit such a shot softly.

"Just a good, regular seven," I said, surprising myself by actually sounding like a caddie.

The good, regular seven was the right club. Al knocked the ball to fifteen feet from the hole.

"If you want, you can work for me at Dallas," Geiberger said as we walked to the green. *Dallas* is what the players call the Byron Nelson Classic, two weeks away. Al Geiberger had casually conferred upon me my new status. I was a real caddie.

On the surface, Al Geiberger seems easygoing, the prototype Southern Californian. On occasion, he will refer to a fairway as a *thruway*. His relaxed, conversational manner with galleries has made him extremely popular. Dozens of spectators at Houston walked up to Geiberger to wish him well or to ask for an autograph.

"You're my guy, Al," one said.

"Did you really shoot a 59?" asked another.

"Al, do you remember me? I saw you win the Caracas Open in 1963," said a third.

And Al had time for all of them.

"Are you sure it wasn't 1962? That's the year I won the Caracas. It's one of the few dates I remember, because it was the first tournament I won as a professional."

"That's right, 1962, that's the year it was," the man said.

"That was fun. Not a big tournament, wasn't even a Tour event. In fact, I wouldn't even have known about the tournament except that one of the caddies, Lee Lynch, told me about it."

Certain golf fans appreciate the amount of modern golf history Geiberger spans. Al has many admirers, and on a crowded golf course the walk from the eighteenth green to the clubhouse often takes an hour for him. The fans who stop for a chat—and Geiberger loves a good chat—also appreciate Al's personal history: They appreciate that simply playing the Tour is a courageous act for Geiberger, considering what he has been through. A nervous stomach disorder contributed to four years of mediocre golf, from 1969 through 1973. He overcame that and won a tournament in 1974, two in 1975, two in 1976, and one in 1977. He lost the 1978 season to the operating table when he required intestinal surgery. But he came back the next year and won in 1979. Later in the year he had knee surgery, and the following year, 1980, he needed emergency surgery to remove his colon. Along the way he had two unsuccessful marriages, and his father, with whom he had a close relationship, died in the Canary Islands plane crash. There is no telling how great Geiberger might have been had he been healthy throughout his career, and knowledgeable fans appreciate that, too.

The injuries and heartaches have given Al the sort of perspective that makes some people angry and others easygoing. In Al's case, he is clearly among the latter. But easygoing has its limits with someone of his talent. When Al made a sloppy bogey on the seventeenth hole of the second round, he was irritated. When he hacked a basic bunker shot on the eighteenth and eliminated his chance of making the cut, he smashed his wedge into the sand. His anger was momentary; ten minutes later, walking back to the clubhouse, his good cheer was restored. But at the moment he was frustrated. There was a time in Al Geiberger's life when it would have been virtually impossible for him to blow a shot like that.

9
YOU HAVE TO KNOW JACKIE NICKLAUS

EN ROUTE TO COLUMBUS, OHIO, which gave the world Jack Nicklaus, I felt good. I had a good bag, Al Geiberger, for an important tournament, the Memorial. My caddie skills, and my caddie career, were making significant strides.

I had just come off three successful, confidence-boosting weeks. After the Houston Open I drove to Florida for the Tallahassee Open and worked there for Larry Rentz, the twenty-five-year-old assistant pro from Lanham, Maryland, I had met in Hattiesburg. Larry was so eager, inexperienced, and talented that he could be talked into anything. I did the talking; Larry made the shots. In constant need of coaching, Larry looked to me, older, wiser in the ways of tournament golf (if you can believe that), to keep the reins in on him. He needed a caddie and I responded by being one. Larry played beautifully.

"Yeah, yeah, yeah, I see it," he'd say after every pep

talk. Even after he knocked a tee shot out-of-bounds on a short par five.

"Larry, we can still make a par here," I said.

"Yeah, yeah, yeah, I see it," Larry said.

"Let's put the *good* Rentz drive on it."

He smashed a driver 290 yards and the ball sat nicely in the center of the fairway. Lying three, with the penalty, he knocked a four iron 230 yards. Then he deftly nailed a thirty-footer and saved par. He had to make an eagle on his second ball to do it, but he saved par.

Tallahassee was Rentz's best finish in a professional tournament. At one point we were only a couple of shots off the lead, and we were not nervous. We were brimming with (probably unfounded) confidence. In the end we finished just out of the top ten. Larry made $3,600 and I made $475 for the week and actually managed a $100 profit. It was the first time I had made more money than I had spent in a week since taking up my new profession.

After Tallahassee I drove back to Texas, to Irving, outside of Dallas, for the Byron Nelson Golf Classic, to work for Geiberger. For sixty-three holes, seven-eighths of the tournament, Geiberger played wonderful, bogey-free golf. He made several birdies; we were several under par. And while we weren't going to win the tournament, we were looking at a big check. Geiberger's gallery was sizable and adoring, and Al, back in the hunt after a long absence, was enjoying himself. He consulted me on club selection and I gave good advice. Occasionally he asked my opinion on a putt. We were golfer and caddie the way golfer and caddie are supposed to work. After the rounds Geiberger and I had long, interesting conversations about women and marriage and family and education. We were becoming friends. On the day of the fourth round the heat was oppressive and Al showed signs of fatigue on the final nine holes. He made a series of costly bogeys, $6,000 worth, but still managed to make $3,000 for the week. He paid me $300, my salary, and said he'd give me the rest at the Memorial.

I went home for a week—after five straight weeks on the road I was pooped. I also needed to tend to other aspects of my life. My rise as a Tour caddie, and the weeks on end it required away from anything resembling what I once called a normal life, was not without its costs. Spring was in full bloom, but a romance whose seeds were planted in the pre-Tour winter had not blossomed as I had hoped. My living on the road contributed to its stunted growth. What was good for my caddie career was bad for the relationship. My ability to read putts could not compensate for the sadness I felt at the demise of something never given a proper start. There was a moment in Tallahassee, in a Motel 6 room without a television or telephone, where the lights from the highway never allowed the room to become dark, when I wondered just what I was doing. I resisted measuring myself by moments, and that was my only salvation at times. Seasons, I reasoned, mark progress.

I had come a long way since Brad Faxon. In the thick of battle I showed good nerves. I was actually contributing to my golfers' games now. This success does not translate well in the world at large, and I did not care. Deep within me I felt enormous satisfaction. One day at the Bellport Golf Club, during my week off, I ran into the club's bartender whom I had not seen in several years.

"You graduate yet?" he asked.

"Oh, yeah, long out," I said

"Going to college?"

"Finished that, too."

"Get your degree?"

"Yep."

"Then you're all set," he said, not even knowing that I had bags set up for four of the next five weeks.

I had no telephone answering machine, I was building no equity. I was a career placement officer's nightmare, but I was living my dream, and would as long as the money held out.

Dublin, Ohio, in the days before Jack Nicklaus built the Muirfield Village Golf Club and the surrounding Muirfield Village, was a farm town. It is still attractive, separated by twenty-five miles from the hustle and bustle of downtown Columbus.

I hitched a ride to the golf course from the airport with Steve Golliher, a stockbroker and a former Tour player. We began talking about Billy Britton.

"I used to play against him in college. He still wear that white stuff all over his nose? Damnedest stuff. Nice guy, Billy Britton. Quiet. Polite. But competitive. A real competitor. Not a great player, but a good player. Not a real big hitter, but straight. And a good, good putter. Have I got the right guy?"

"You've got him," I said, "except for the white stuff on the nose."

"That's good.

"You know Russ Cochran? [Cochran is the Tour's best lefthanded golfer and a fine golfer from either side of the ball.] He's a good friend of mine. He made it. I didn't. Tried for two years, until I busted myself."

"Guess you didn't have a sponsor."

"No, actually I did," Steve said. "Busted him, too. I was going through six, seven, eight hundred dollars a week. That'll do it."

"Are you still playing?" I asked. Some golfers who try the Tour unsuccessfully stop playing completely.

"Yeah, I am, now. Just got my amateur standing back. It's very helpful in my business; I play in a lot of these amateur events. But it was hell getting it back. You've got to apply to the U.S.G.A. It's a common enough thing, but they make it tough. Usually they'll put you in limbo for a year, where you can't play in professional or amateur events. But for some reason they slapped me with two years."

"Why?"

"Because they're a bunch of tight-lipped stuffed shirts basically," Steve said with a smile and relaxed southern charm. "Who you working for here?" he asked me.

"Geiberger," I said, with a certain smug satisfaction. I was caddying for a star. Faded, yes, but a star.

When I arrived at the golf course, I went to the registration desk to see if Geiberger had signed in yet.

"No, he hasn't," a man behind the desk told me. "And he won't. This is the complete list, 101 players. If Geiberger's name is not on it, then he's not playing. And it's not. So he's not."

"How can Geiberger not be playing? I'm his caddie. He sent me up here," I asked.

Bewildered and upset, I went to the P.G.A. Tour trailer to see what the mix-up was. This is Al Geiberger, I said to myself, Mr. 59. All right, he is a decade past his prime. But he's still an important player. He *has* to be in the tournament. He sent me up here.

Frank Kavanaugh, a P.G.A. tournament official, was sitting in the trailer. I asked him if he knew of Geiberger's status in the tournament.

"He's not in," said Kavanaugh. "This question came up last week. Al thought he was exempt because of his 1975 T.P.C. title, which gives you a ten-year exemption. But we only count going back until 1976. He's not in."

I called up Geiberger. Collect.

"Oh, no, don't tell me you're in Columbus," he said.

"I'm in Columbus," I said.

"I feel terrible," he said.

"And you owe me 150 bucks," I said.

"I'll mail you a check," he said. "And I tried to reach you."

"What happened?" I asked.

"Well, you're not the only one upset by this thing: I never got my full ten-year exemption on the T.P.C. victory. But anyway, they've got their rules, and they told me I wasn't in a couple of days ago. So I called up the Memorial office. I tried to get Jack [Nicklaus], but he wasn't around. [He was in North Carolina watching his son win the North and South Amateur Golf Championship.] So I spoke to some assistant of his. Tried to see about getting an exemption. Obviously, it didn't happen."

Suddenly, I was back in New Orleans, Las Vegas, Ponte Vedra, and Hilton Head—in town for the tournament, but without a bag. Just when I thought my scrounging days were over, I'd have to be hustling again for work. I was being punished for my smugness. I needed work.

II

The Chuck Will identification system had expanded in the seven weeks since I had last seen it. The sign for "CHUCK WILL'S DESK" remained, but now "CHUCK WILL'S CHAIR" was so marked and, draped over the chair, "CHUCK WILL'S TROUSERS." This Chuck Will, tanned, relaxed, wearing shorts, was not the same Chuck Will I had seen in Florida. This seemed to be the post-Masters Chuck Will.

"I'd love to help you out, Bamberger, but look at this list," Chuck said. The Memorial, with a field only two-thirds the size of a regular tournament, left many caddies without a bag for the week. They sought employment, as I did, from CBS. "I've already got twenty-five guys on this list, and that's more than

I could possibly use. And then Jack Nicklaus calls
and says, 'Chuck, can you get jobs for three more
boys?' Nicklaus, Bamberger, Jack Nicklaus. And one
of the jobs is for the son of the tournament chairman.
What am I going to say, 'No, Jack, sorry, but I can't
help you out?' Sorry, Bamberger."

I went to the caddie shack to see if I could learn
anything there. It was a caddie shack unlike any I
had ever seen.

The caddie shack at Dallas, at the Las Colinas
Sports Club, was a real caddie shack, a wood and
canvas tent crowded inside with long, thin metal
folding tables and folding chairs. In it a middle-aged
black woman named Denise, overweight, friendly,
smiling, cooked pork chops and fried chicken for
sandwiches, which she sold for two dollars each. On a
table in front of her there were heads of lettuce,
tomatoes, loaves of bread, and jars of ketchup. A feast
for the flies. Killer had taken a shining to Denise and
was giving her instructions on how to best fry
chicken.

"Hey, Killer, where's your woman this week?" a
caddie called Bebop asked, interrupting Killer's
serenade.

"I don't know just yet," Killer said. "Might be
lookin' at her right now."

Denise tended her pork chops and smiled shyly.
She was the only woman within fifty yards of the
place.

Behind her, Denise had a cooler filled with luke-
warm beer and soda. Beers were a dollar, sodas fifty
cents. The craps table cost five dollars to get on, and
the poker game cost five dollars to get into. The talk
was of last night's horse-racing results and yesterday's lottery numbers. Because the tournament ran
two pro-ams there was ample opportunity for work,
and there were two dozen local caddies in the shack,
mostly old, black men wearing T-shirts from tourna-

ments long passed. The caddie master, a man called Cryin' Jake—that's what it said on his name tag—presided over the caddie shack. The atmosphere was vibrant, spirited, and half-drunk.

Coming out of that caddie shack one day, I saw Karen Knox, who caddies for her husband, Kenny. They had finished second at Tallahassee, earning a check that was twice as much as Kenny had earned the entire previous year.

"Nice playing last week," I said to her. Caddies say that to one another after a good finish.

"Thanks," she said, "but I wanted it to be better." She eyed my Coke on what was a steamy day. "Can you get those sodas in the caddie shack?"

"Yes," I said.

"How much are they?" Caddies always make certain to get the best possible price before they buy *anything*. The sodas in the caddie shack were one-third the price they were at the concession stands.

"Fifty cents," I said, "and for five dollars you can get into a good craps game."

Karen Knox walked over to the concession stand and bought her soda there.

She might have been more at home at the Muirfield Village Golf Club's caddie shack. It had the feel of a locker room at a stylish prep school; the caddie master, Don Claypool, seemed to be at least part headmaster. Many of Muirfield's caddies are the sons of members and one could easily imagine them asking Don Claypool for a college recommendation.

D.C., as he is called, ran a tight ship, and a good one. He not only developed caddies, he developed character.

"If you want to work for me, your hair must be fashionably short. Ears must be shown," read one of his posted signs.

"No chin-ups on this bar. If you feel hyper, do twenty-five quick push-ups," read another.

He also showed an unusual amount of respect for caddies, both his own and those on the Tour. He set up a message board for the caddies. "Mr. Edwards," said one message, referring to Bruce Edwards, Tom Watson's caddie, "call your Dallas real estate office."

D.C. managed to get jobs for most of his boys, although not as caddies. They ran the bag room, distributed uniforms, and ran the caddie lunch room. I wanted to see D.C. about getting a job, and waited for him at his desk.

D.C. came in with the brusque, rushed manner of a football coach late for his own meeting but wanting to demonstrate his control of the situation. He was a short, gray, lined man.

"What's going on here, fellas?" he asked two of his boys who were trying on caddie shirts. "A fashion show?" His voice was growling but friendly.

D.C. took sympathy to my plight. He had an idea, he said.

We walked through the clubhouse and up a flight of stairs, passed a wall lined with twenty *Sports Illustrated* covers with Jack Nicklaus on them, and wandered about until we found Jeff Parsons. Parsons, the director of marketing for Muirfield Village, was in charge of intravillage transportation for the tournament. Sprawling Muirfield Village had a *club*, the Muirfield Village Golf Club, site of the Memorial, and a *country club*, another, less demanding, less exclusive course. Village residents were entitled to park at the country club and ride in a van to the club's front door, a half-mile away. My job was to drive the van.

My first day on the job was the day before the tournament, and there wasn't much to do. I sat in the country club parking lot, reading the tournament program, or *Golf Digest*, or the *Columbus Dispatch*. Every half-hour or so a couple of people would stumble upon the van, discover that they didn't have

to walk to the club, and take a ride. Then I'd wait at
the club. The job was slow and dull. Frustrated by
my exclusion from the tournament—as a caddie, one
feels to be a real part of a golf event—I quickly grew
restless.

At one point three men came to the van and asked
if I could take them to the Scioto Country Club,
where Nicklaus, essentially, grew up.

"I'm not supposed to leave Muirfield Village," I
said. The job was turning me into a bureaucrat.

This was important, they said; they were late for a
golf game there.

At that moment there was nothing that excited me
more than the idea of driving that van out of Muirfield Village.

"I should check with somebody before I do that," I
said.

"I'm sure it's all right," one of the men said. "After
all, we're friends of Jack's."

"Jack?" I asked. If they thought they were talking
to an idiot, I didn't want to disappoint them.

"Mr. Nicklaus," said another.

"Oh," I said. "Jack *Nicklaus*. Well, you better get in
the van."

We had to go by their hotel to pick up their golf
clubs. We made another stop at a dry cleaner. Then
we got lost. The trip there took nearly an hour.

As I took the clubs out of the back of the van, neatly
and gingerly, one of the men dug into his wallet and
put a twenty-dollar bill in my palm.

"Well, thank *you*, sir," I said. The overstated
manner of those who rely on tips for a living is
instinctive, I suddenly realized; twenty was what I
figured. These fellows were corporate sharpies, after
all.

I snuck back to the Muirfield Village, waving to
the policeman at the fenced-in community's gates,

trying to conceal my guilt: I had been away for an
hour and a half. I waited in front of the club, hoping
for passengers. Jeff Parsons came out of the clubhouse and signaled for me to roll down my window.

My goose, I said to myself, is cooked.

"How's it going?" Jeff asked kindly.

"Pretty good." I said. "Little on the slow side,"

"Did you get yourself lunch yet?" Jeff asked.

"No, I haven't," I said.

"It's half past one," Jeff said, looking at his watch.
"You must be starved. We've made an arrangement
with Holly Farms [one of the corporations taking a
tent to entertain clients]. Just tell them that I sent
you over; they'll give you lunch."

I had a turkey sandwich on a bun, potato chips, and
an orange juice, but I did not enjoy it. It's hard to eat
on a bothered conscience.

After lunch I was determined to start doing my job
properly. I went to the country club in search of
passengers. After fifteen minutes one arrived, a frail
woman who sat in the very rear. I brought her to the
club. There I waited again. Traffic was sporadic but
legitimate until late in the afternoon, when four
people came into the van, two middle-aged couples
from New York. They had recently bought into a real
estate–golf complex in New York called the St. Andrews Golf Club, another of Nicklaus's enterprises.
They had been watching the practice round and
needed to go back to their hotel to change for a party
being thrown by Barbara Nicklaus. Did I know
where the Hilton was?

The Hilton was fifteen miles away.

"I'm not supposed to go off the village property," I
said. "I go only from the club to the country club, and
back again."

"Maybe we didn't make ourselves clear," one of the
New York men said. "We don't want to go the country

club. We want to go to the Hilton." I could not tell if
he was genuinely baffled, or if acting baffled was his
style.

"Barry," said his wife, "the driver said he's not
supposed to leave the village development here."

"What do you mean, 'He's not supposed to leave the
development.' First off, this is not a development, it's
a real estate complex and, second, our invitation said
that transportation would be provided between the
hotel and the golf course, so I don't know what you're
talking about, 'He's not supposed to leave the
development.'"

"Is there another transportation service?" asked
Larry, the man next to Barry.

"I don't know; you have to ask inside about that," I
said, learning how to speak officiously.

"I'm not leaving this van," said Barry. "It's been
one big headache since we got here, and I've had
enough headaches for one day, thank you. Will you
take us to the Hilton or not?"

Forty silent minutes later, we arrived at the hotel.

"Don't mind Barry," Barry's wife said to me in a
whispered voice as she got out of the van, handing me
a one-dollar bill. I got out to open the door, one of
those tricky sliding doors that vans have.

Larry popped out. "Appreciate it," he said softly,
handing me a five-dollar bill. His wife followed,
smiling.

Finally Barry came out. "Don't mind me," he said,
slipping me a ten-dollar bill. I'm just a crotchety old
fart."

When I rolled in from that trip, it was 6:00 P.M. Jeff
Parsons was at the clubhouse door, clipboard in
hand. I pulled up next to him, with the radio blaring,
and watched him as he slid his finger across his
throat, a mock slitting.

I was petrified.

Jeff Parsons walked around the back of the van

slowly. I watched him in the side-view mirror as he strolled up the length of the van looking, I thought, like a state trooper. He came to the window and made the slitting motion again. I turned off the radio and rolled down the window.

"Cut the engine," he said. I looked at him blankly; is that all he had meant with this throat-slitting business? Cut the engine? The queasiness I had felt when I was unable to find Brad Faxon's scorecard returned.

"How'd it go?" he asked.

"OK," I said. Maybe he knew everything and was waiting for me to confess. Confession would have felt very good just then.

"Terrific. Let's call it a day. You've been behind that wheel nine hours. You must be bushed."

"Jeff, you know," I began, "some of the people, well, on two occasions, they've been tipping me, and I think I should give the money over. The tournament's, you know, a charity, after all."

"Oh, no," Jeff said, "you keep that money. Go ahead. You've earned it."

Why did Jeff Parsons have to be so, so midwestern. Why did Jeff Parsons have to be so *nice*?

On my way back to the motel, I stopped at a 7-Eleven and stuffed twenty dollars into a jar for Jerry's Kids. And I enjoyed dinner much more than lunch.

III

Fortunately, as the week progressed, my shuttle service job became more demanding. I didn't have time for tempting road trips. Every time I pulled up to the club, there were people who wanted to go to the country club. Every time I pulled up to the country club, there were people who wanted to go to the club. The system was working as it was supposed to. Down

the clubhouse driveway, a right onto Memorial
Drive, past Strathmore Lane and a neat cluster of
condominiums and town houses, and a sign: "Weath-
erstone—Another Bob Webb Community." Past the
Mid-American Expositions, Inc., trailer and their
red, white, and blue sign ("Convention Service Con-
tractors Since 1955"), past a staff parking lot, past a
lemonade stand. A right onto Muirfield Drive, past
the Corporate Hospitality Tents and to the country
club gates. There I was greeted with a salute by a
Pinkerton guard, Philip Drayea ("It's only three-
forty an hour, but I get to wear a uniform"), a junior
at Ohio State, enrolled in the Naval R.O.T.C.
program.

If the route became old and familiar quickly, and it
did, the talk of the passengers never ceased to be
interesting. Particularly when my job was expanded
to bringing tournament volunteers to the staff parking lot. (Interlopers were easily identified: The bona
fide volunteers had uniforms of green pants and
white shirts or green skirts and white blouses.)

"I *know*, Doris, that the canvas on this chair is red.
I looked everywhere for one Muirfield green, or *any*
shade of green, and I could not find one *anywhere*,"
said a woman boarding the van at seven in the
morning.

"Jesus, was Lanny Wadkins hotter than a fire-
cracker today," said a man boarding the van at seven
in the evening.

For some, simply being at the tournament was not
enough. They watched on the clubhouse television.
"Did you see Hale Irwin on TV?" one man asked
anyone in the van who would listen. "They asked him
how his round was. You know what he said? He said,
'It stank.' "

And another man said, "They had Jim Simons on
the TV saying that it was a good thing the hole got in
the way of his ball on that putt on fifteen, or it would

have run clear off the green. Can you imagine? The hole got in the way of the ball. I just thought that was so terrific."

"Guess he hit it solider [sic] than he wanted to," another man said in response.

Information, or anything that passed for it, flowed from the lips of my passengers.

"You know what I was told yesterday?" said one volunteer, a courtesy car driver. "I was told that Rex Caldwell, Ben Crenshaw, and Ronnie Black aren't allowed to get courtesy cars anymore. They abuse the privilege."

"I heard that Jack Nicklaus, personally, insisted that none of the women drivers drive J. C. Snead. That boy's supposed to have quite a tongue on him," said another woman.

"I've driven him," a third said. "He's not too bad. I'd say he's *interesting*. He says exactly what's on his mind."

"Johnny Miller came to the desk today," another courtesy car driver said, this one a man. "He wanted *another* car. He said there was something faulty with the car he had. I drove that car to the airport before he got it, and I can tell you there was *nothing* wrong with that car."

"I heard he was letting his caddie drive it," the second woman said in a hushed tone.

"I don't know, but there was mud all *over* that car when we picked it up," said the man. "You don't get mud on the top of the windshield by driving through a little puddle at thirty, that's for sure," he said.

"That's for sure," said the first woman.

Later in the week a man named C. D. Myers rode the van with his wife, Tou Tou. C.D. was a fit man in his early sixties who, like most of Columbus, had some personal connection to Jack Nicklaus, or at least claimed one.

"See, when Jackie was just a boy, his father, Charlie, used to come into Walkers' Clothing, where I was a sales clerk. This is the original store I'm talking now, the one on North High Street. Charlie used to come in to buy his trousers, Hart Schaffner & Marx. Then when Jackie was eighteen, and getting ready for college, Charlie brought Jackie in to be fitted. I remember it well. Jackie weighed two and a quarter, easy, and he had thighs like this," C.D. said, shaping his arms as if they were arched around a gigantic oak. "I watched Jackie grow up, and of course I knew Charlie very well, because he came in regularly. And I always fitted him.

"Once I made a bet with Charlie. I bet him a Titleist, as a matter of fact. Right there in the store I told him, 'All right, you know the rules of golf. Tell me what's wrong with this.' " At this point C.D. jumped out of the van and started kicking his feet back and forth like a dog about to go on a rampage. "I says to Charlie, 'If I was in a trap and doing this, what's wrong with it?'

"And he says, 'Nothing.'

"I figured he should know, what with Jackie just starting on the Tour and all.

"And I say, 'Oh yes there is, it's building a stance in the sand trap, and that's illegal. Two stroke penalty in medal play and automatic loss of hole in match.'

"But he wanted proof before he'd pay me the golf ball. So when they had the tournament over at Scioto Country Club, this is going back years now, I went over to one of the rules officials and I say, 'I got a bet with Charlie Nicklaus,' and I went through the whole thing, and I wind up by saying, 'Would you mind telling him the next time you see him that it's illegal to do that, that it's building a stance in a trap?'

"And the rule man looks at me as if I'm crazy and he says, 'Far as I know, there's nothing wrong with it.'

"Well, that sank my ship, if you know what I mean. So the next time Charlie comes into the shop for a fitting, I give him a golf ball. I say, 'You're right, Charlie, I'm wrong. There's nothing wrong with it.' And he takes the ball.

"Then about ten years later I'm at Scioto Country Club for the tournament again, and a man comes up to me and says, 'Do you remember me?' It was the rules official. And he says, 'I'm glad I ran into you, because you were right about that building the stance business. It *is* illegal!'

"So Charlie Nicklaus owes me two Titleists. The one I gave him, and the one he owes me from the bet. But unfortunately he's no longer with us by this point. And I don't say that just because I won the bet. I say that because he was a prince of a man. But I can say that Charlie Nicklaus went to his grave owing me two Titleists. Not too many guys can say that!

"Now, Jackie, he doesn't come in anymore. I'm a Jackie fan, of course; how could I not be? But there's something that's different about him than Charlie. Jackie's shy in a way Charlie never was. If we see one another in a crowd, and our eyes meet, he'll just turn away. He recognizes me, but he'd never say anything."

"Is Jack aloof?" I asked.

"You have to know Jackie Nicklaus," C. D. Myers said, his wife Tou Tou nodding enthusiastically and silently all through the story. "That's just the way Jackie is."

10
AN EASTERN
ATTITUDE

I

ON THE BACK COVER of the May 27, 1985, issue of
Sports Illustrated, which included a profile of Peter
Jacobsen, I wrote down the names of the players who
were on the same flight I was on as the Tour lurched
forward from Columbus, Ohio, to Washington, D.C.:
Peter Jacobsen, George Burns, Mac O'Grady, Dan
Forsman, Pat McGowan, Ronnie Black, and Larry
Mize. Sandra Black, Bonnie Mize, Fumiko Aoyagi
(Mrs. Mac O'Grady), and Paul Simpson, a caddie who
had been working for Mike Reid, were also on the
flight.

Mize, who was twenty-six years old, threw spit-
balls at Black, who was celebrating his twenty-
seventh birthday on the flight, while Sandra Black
and Bonnie Mize discussed Florida real estate values.
Forsman, a midwesterner by birth, a Californian by
upbringing, and one of the few players to list reading
as a special interest in the P.G.A. media guide, talked

157

about golf theory with O'Grady, who is a midwesterner by birth, a Californian by upbringing, and the only player to list "modern times" as a special interest in the P.G.A. guide. Fumiko Aoyagi read a book that was not written in English. Jacobsen moved from seat to seat as conversation and impulse moved him. George Burns slept wearing his sunglasses. Pat McGowan read *Time*. Mike Reid sat in the back of the plane and read *Reader's Digest*. Simpson, the caddie, sat in the first row of the plane and read *GQ*.

Both Simpson and Reid attended Brigham Young, the university of the Mormon Church. Reid, ever dedicated to his alma mater, gave Simpson a caddie job in response to a letter Simpson had written Reid at Christmas. Simpson became a prominent caddie quickly, and not only because Reid was playing consistently well. In the ragtag world of caddies, Simpson cut an impressive figure. A blond, muscular Californian, Paul Simpson looked and acted like a high school football star, circa 1958. He caddied wearing a pith helmet and too-short khaki trousers. Several times he was seen drinking half-quarts of whole milk straight from the carton after a round. He was also seen with the right people, which is important in the career development of the young Tour caddie. Before long he had become buddies with Pete Bender, one of the most respected caddies, who works for Greg Norman and, sometimes, Jack Nicklaus. Although his caddie skills were considered average, at best, Paul Simpson quickly gained stature as a caddie.

At the Memorial, Simpson was hired away from Mike Reid by Andy Bean, who was a decidedly big bag. Although Reid is a fine player and a good bag—he won $135,000 in 1984—Bean represents another level altogether. He won $423,000 in 1984. Simpson went for the money and left Reid in search of a caddie.

But Bean and Simpson did not work out at the Memorial—someone in Don Claypool's caddie shack said his lack of knowledge about golf had finally caught up with him. As fast as his rise had been, Paul Simpson's caddie decline was faster yet. The last word out of Columbus was that both Reid and Bean were looking for caddies and that Simpson was looking for work off the Tour. There was not, the reports said, much conversation between Simpson and Bean, Simpson and Reid, or Reid and Bean. Simpson was flying to Washington en route home. Reid and the other players were Kemper Open-bound.

They were greeted at the airport by middle-aged, over-enthusiastic courtesy car drivers not dissimilar to the volunteer crowd I had been driving in Muirfield Village, except that the green and white uniforms were now red and white and bore the emblem of a different tournament.

"Hello, Peter, how are you?"

"Mac, good to see you."

"Nice playing last week, George, nice playing."

The players were carted off to Bethesda, Maryland. Most would see nothing of the nation's capital in their week of playing at the Congressional Country Club. Airport, golf course, motel—these are the vertices of the triangle that define the Tour player's life. Worn out from several days of climbing up and down the hills of Muirfield Village, with a week climbing up and down the hills of Congressional ahead of them, the players boarded the diesel-powered station wagons with weary legs and faded smiles.

I got in a cab (the subways in Washington don't run on Sundays) and headed for downtown Washington, to Foggy Bottom, and an apartment building called the Statesman. A friend of mine named Scott Heller lived there.

Scott, a reporter on the *Chronicle of Higher Education*, has the acute sense of time and place critical to

success in his profession. During dinner he looked at
his watch and saw that it was past midnight; Memorial Day had begun. Ever the reporter, ever curious,
he suggested a walk over to the Viet Nam Memorial.

At the memorial, a woman wept uncontrollably as
she searched for her husband's name, etched somewhere in the memorial's shiny black granite. One
veteran slept at the memorial, body curled in the
fetal position, the ends of his long hair linking him to
the wall. Another veteran, in combat fatigues, paced
up and down the wall, a self-appointed guard. He
stopped six inches away from my face.

"Ask me what it was like," he demanded. His eyes
were clear and very small.

"What was it like?" I asked.

"It was hell," he said, staring me in the face, his
own face trembling as he waited for a reaction.

II

On the Tour, every week begins with hope. Also
promise, enthusiasm, and confidence. In the 1985
Kemper Open there were fifty players—one-third of
the starting field—with enough game to shoot 280 for
the four rounds. In 1984, 280 would have won the
tournament by five shots. The rest of the field had
enough game to shoot even par for the four days, 288,
and win $10,000.

Billy Britton could do that. I thoroughly believed
that. Billy Britton was a good enough player to shoot
four rounds of even par and make $10,000; Billy
Britton was a good enough player to shoot four
rounds of 70 and win the whole thing. One might
argue, later in the week, against the logic of such a
proposition. He hadn't, after all, ever won a Tour
event. He hadn't made a cut in 1985. He was struggling with his game, and had been for a while. As a
caddie, though, these bouts of realism wouldn't cross

your mind on a Monday. Your only thought would be: My man has as good a chance to win this as anybody. And you would believe it.

Billy, realistic, practical, and not particularly lofty, had probably set a more modest goal: to make the cut, and to play decently on the weekend.

We played a practice round with Mac O'Grady, Dan Forsman, and a non-Tour player named Dan Goodman, who hoped to get into the tournament in an open qualifying round. O'Grady was giving Goodman a lesson. Forsman, wearing sneakers, hit only an occasional shot. His chief interest seemed to be to continue the conversation he and O'Grady had had on the flight to Washington. O'Grady is quite a conversationalist.

Mac O'Grady, short for Phillip McClelland O'Grady, is, from what I could observe, the most unusual player on the Tour. He is also one of the most intelligent, fit, determined, hard-working, difficult, liked, and disliked players on the Tour. His colleagues are in awe of his length and admire the grace of his swing, which is considered one of the best on the Tour. His teaching is not limited to the Dan Goodmans of the golf world; at the Honda Classic he worked for hours with Seve Ballesteros. Despite O'Grady's awesome length—in 1984 his average drive traveled 273 yards, the tenth longest on the Tour—and his picturesque swing, his record is less than distinguished. Yet he is nearly famous. He may be the best known nonwinner on the Tour. His fame is attributed, chiefly, to a *Sports Illustrated* profile of him that appeared in the April 16, 1984, issue, and his steadfast refusal to speak to any member of the press since then. This refusal does not, of course, stop the press from writing about him. It encourages it. And sometimes as a news subject, not a feature subject, he must be written about. For instance, he led the 1985 Byron Nelson Golf Classic for each of the first three rounds. He was news even if he wasn't speaking to reporters. His silence simply tempted reporters to rehash the stuff in the *Sports Illustrated* profile. Because he won't talk to the press, the same overreported facts continue to be overreported: He went to the Qualifying School seventeen times before he made the Tour, which is a record; he plays righthanded but putts lefthanded; he reads Oriental philosphy; his surname at birth was McGleno.

O'Grady's colleagues don't understand why he disliked the *Sports Illustrated* story. Some think it was the best thing ever to happen to him. Others think it was good for golf, an example to the general public that all golfers are not blond, bland, and decked out in pink polyester. But none were able to convince O'Grady of the story's attributes, and probably not many tried. No one goes to the Tour Qualifying School seventeen times listening to other people.

Caddies, not generally known for having a collective opinion, are universal in their view of O'Grady: He is a pleasant guy to talk to but the last guy, with the exception of Victor Regalado and John Fought, you would want to work for. O'Grady has, in some tournaments, gone through caddies like others go through socks; in one tournament he fired four caddies. Former caddies, like O'Grady, and Ballesteros, are often hard on caddies. If a caddie doesn't voluntarily mark down the scenario and results of each shot O'Grady takes in a practice round, he may be well on his way to being fired.

On the first tee, O'Grady stepped up to the ball sitting on a tee two inches off the ground and took a mighty cut at it. The ball soared and sailed far away. This was O'Grady in full power and, for curiosity's sake, I paced off that drive. It was 330 yards. Billy hit a good drive and was eighty yards behind him.

We had 190 yards to the pin, and Billy hit a lovely five iron that bounced once, softly, and stopped fif-

teen feet from the hole. It was a terrific golf shot, and
Billy was pleased.

"You should mark that down in your yardage
book," O'Grady said to Billy. "Your short-term memory recall will store that in your brain for three days.
If you bring it out of your passive memory and into
your active memory when it's time to play that same
shot in the tournament, you'll be able to duplicate it
exactly—your brain will instruct your muscles to do
again precisely the same thing."

Billy nodded, but I doubt he was paying much
attention. Knowing his own game well, he doesn't like
unsolicited advice.

We walked up to the green.

"When I look at a green like this," O'Grady said,
answering no one's question, "I divide it into four
quadrants, each with its own break. Now, in this
quadrant, Billy, where your ball is, there's a ridge
that runs right through the middle of it, eight yards
up from the bottom. So I mark that in the yardage
book." He grabbed Billy's yardage book from him
and began drawing in it.

"I don't know, Mac, I think you're confusing me,"
Billy said.

O'Grady paid no attention.

"Now, once you know where the ridge is in that first
quadrant, and you know they'll put the pin in either
the first or the second quadrant, then you know. . . ."

Billy putted his ball. He seemed to be making a
conscious effort to block out Mac. Mac, oblivious,
went on and on and on.

We played only the front nine with Mac. On the
back nine Billy's game came truly alive; he played it
in four under. He then hit balls until the stifling,
muggy day softened into a graceful eastern dusk. The
whole world seemed perfect. As I waited for Billy to
come out of the locker room—we were going to get
dinner—I stood on the putting green with Brad

Faxon, Jeff Sluman, and Peter Jacobsen, and we
talked about the Bruce Springsteen tour. Jacobsen,
using his putter as a guitar, began singing a song
that was then the most popular in the country.
Summer was on the horizon, and the start of summer
always offers promise. Billy was playing well; anything seemed possible. Congressional's ancient ever-
greens made the sweet dusk even sweeter.

"Born in the U.S.A.," Jacobsen sang, imitating
Bruce Springsteen with considerable authenticity.
"Born in the U.S.A. Born in the U.S.A. I'm a cool
rocking daddy in the U.S.A."

III

At the time of the Kemper Open, Billy was dating
a woman named Isabelle Farrell, who was also from
Staten Island. Isabelle, a registered nurse with ten
years of experience, was then in her third year at the
University of Bridgeport Law School. She had as
much Irish good sense as Billy, if not more. Billy and
Isabelle knew each other from Staten Island, but
their courtship began in Williamsburg, Virginia, in
July 1984, on the day Isabelle brought Billy an iced
tea after a round in the Anheuser-Busch Golf Classic
on an especially hot and steamy day. Billy was won
over, right then and there, but their relationship had
been progressing steadily and carefully since then.

Billy is a careful, planned—and exceedingly honest—person. These attributes revealed themselves
continually.

I never saw Billy carry wads of cash, or use a credit
card, or drive over the speed limit, or steal sandwiches from the clubhouse, or leave a tournament
with a borrowed locker-room towel still on his golf
bag. Growing up on Staten Island, Billy went to
Catholic schools, and learned their lessons well. Billy
Britton's sense of decency is uncommon, and I found

myself greatly admiring him. And wishing that he
would play better.

En route to the first tee for the first round, Billy
ran into Fred Couples, one of the longest-hitting,
freewheeling, and easy-spending players on the Tour.

"Hey, Billy, what's up?" Fred asked.

Billy told him what was up.

"When's that Staten Island tournament of yours?"
Fred asked.

Billy runs a tournament on Staten Island in memory of one of his childhood friends who died just as he
was beginning a career in law.

Fred started chatting and Billy started to walk to
the first tee. Suddenly it occurred to Fred that they
were not headed in the same direction.

"Hey, where you going, Billy?" Fred asked.

"I gotta go play," said Billy.

"Oh," said Fred, wandering off with no apparent
direction. "Hey," Fred called out as an afterthought,
"good luck."

"Freddy Couples," Billy said to me a moment later.
"If he's leading a tournament, or if he's just missed a
cut, he's exactly the same. It always seems like he
doesn't have a care in the world."

Seeing Billy and Fred standing there, I was reminded of something that Davis Love of Sea Island,
Georgia, one of the game's leading teachers and a
former Tour player, once told me:

"In my years in golf I've found that the guy who
makes sure his home is locked before he leaves,
makes sure his oil level is right before he goes on a
trip in the car, makes sure all the patio furniture is
moved in if heavy winds are predicted, this guy
seldom, if ever, hits a long ball.

"And the guy who doesn't have a care in the world,"
Love continued, using the same phrase Billy had,
"he's the one who can crush it."

Billy was not a crusher. But the week began with

promise. In all his practice rounds, and in his hours on end on the practice tee, Billy was hitting the ball wonderfully. I sensed the week would be good for us. So did Billy. So why he pushed that first tee shot nearly out of bounds, leaving himself no shot to the first green and an opening bogey, I do not know. Clinically, there's always an answer: He swung too fast, his body got in front of his arms, the ball was struck with an open face. But the real reason was surely more complex than that.

When a golf ball is hit sufficiently wild so that it is in danger of being picked up by a spectator, a caddie has a responsibility to literally run after the ball and serve as its guardian until the player gets there. I ran to Billy's first tee shot. Seconds later, a tournament marshall came over to clear the few spectators who gathered around that opening blow.

"Not an especially distinguished way to begin a round, is it?" the marshall said in a burst of insight.

Yet there was no denying the accuracy of that observation. A pushed tee shot nearly out of bounds was an inauspicious start. And inauspicious starts usually lead to inauspicious rounds. I was not too surprised when we made the turn at four over and finished the day with a 76. The next day Billy shot an 81 and there was not much to say. Billy's game had bottomed out, and there was only one way for it go.

IV

Four days later, at the U.S. Open regional qualifying rounds at the Montclair Country Club in Montclair, New Jersey, Billy looked refreshed, as if he had had a ten-hour sleep.

"Today, Mike, I'm gonna see if I can talk to you all through the round," Billy said when we met. His reference was to the silence that descended upon us during the 81: Neither of us could think of anything appropriate to say to the other, with one exception.

That was when Billy, deep within the bowels of the back nine, chipped in to save par.

"That's a great golf shot, Billy," I said. (Caddies differentiate between mere *shots* and *golf shots*. The latter, used sparingly, denotes emphasis.)

"Thanks," Billy said, in a tone heartfelt and sincere.

Through most of that final round Billy glowered. But he gave every shot complete concentration and total effort, a demand of his heroic sense of the work ethic. Billy takes enormous pride in his profession and, in shooting an 81, that pride had taken a beating. But like the best of the old-time prizefighters (and Billy has more than a little boxer in him), if he was going to go down, it would be swinging. Billy was determined to diminish the stinging as best he could. When he chipped in and saved himself a stroke, it meant more to Billy than a single stroke saved.

After that round Billy spoke briefly about the importance of being your own best friend on the golf course, a wisdom so imbedded in the mind of every golfer it would seem hardly worth repeating. But just then the old, sensible idea suddenly had fresh meaning for Billy.

"If you were playing golf with your best friend, and he started playing badly, you wouldn't start kicking him," Billy said. "I'm going to try to adopt that attitude."

Attitude is, the players say, the most elusive quality that separates the professional golfer making a living from the professional golfer winning tournaments. Brad Faxon believed in himself, all right; he could say to reporters and his parents and his friends and himself that he knew he belonged on the Tour, that he could win tournaments. But somewhere within the depths of his soul, in the dark places where not even a one iron can reach, he doesn't wholly believe his own words, I think. He has the game but, not yet, the attitude. Corey Pavin, who joined the

Tour in the same year Brad did, is visually a less impressive player than Brad, but he has the attitude. The players see astrologists, hypnotists, and psychologists in search of it, whatever it is. But they must suspect that those who really have it were born with it.

When Nicklaus won the U.S. Open in his first year on the Tour, 1962, he was twenty-two years old. He had already won the U.S. Amateur twice. He had mastered golf skills other players didn't know existed. But pure skill only partly explains his precocious start and his utter domination of the sport for most of the two decades that followed. His thorough belief in his ability to win golf tournaments can be seen in his staggering accomplishments. We don't know how it happened; we just know that it did.

Judging accomplishment in golf is far more pure and neat than judging the accomplishment of a musician, an actor, a statesman, or even an athlete who plays a team sport. The external influences in golf are less; the emphasis on one man's ability all-consuming. If someone could explain what made Nicklaus great, that person would be making a genuine scientific breakthrough, for that person would be explaining a great deal more than an individual golfer.

Billy and I were struggling with a smaller problem at the Montclair Country Club. We were trying to qualify for the U.S. Open. There were 120 golfers competing for eighteen spots. At the end of thirty-six holes, Billy had taken 142 strokes. Fifteen players had shot 141 or better and were guaranteed spots in the Open. Larry Rentz, for whom I worked at the Tallahassee Open, was among them. He shot a 74 before lunch and a 67 after lunch for 141. Seven others, including Billy, remained for three more spots. There would be a playoff, and a sizable gallery for it.

The glories of Billy's golf career, the 1974 and 1975 Metropolitan Amateur and the 1979 Metropolitan Open titles, occurred in tournaments close enough to home that he could return there at night. Billy spoke of the comfort that comes with playing in familiar surroundings. His thirty-six-hole score at Montclair, a tricky course from which he could return home to Staten Island after each round, was fifteen strokes better than his thirty-six-hole score at Congressional the week before.

After thirty-six holes on a sultry, humid day, with sunlight quickly fading, Billy was faced with more golf: a sudden-death play-off to get into the U.S. Open. Two of the seven players birdied the first of the playoff holes. Five players were left for one spot. A birdie on the second hole by a New York club pro named Robert Wenz, Jr., put him in the Open, and Billy out. Ten days later Robert Wenz, Jr., made Pete Bender, the caddie, $200 richer by having the worst thirty-six-hole score in the U.S. Open. In the caddie High Pool, Bender picked Wenz to finish at twenty-three over par for the two days, and he was right.

Billy had played thirty-eight good holes of golf in this twelve-hour golf day and had nothing but a sunburn to show for it. As I put the clubs in the back of his car, Billy looked up at the orange-pink dusk sky.

"Beat me, beat me," he cried, and he was only half in jest.

"You know what the crazy thing is?" Billy asked. "I'd come out tomorrow and do the whole thing again.

"Sick, isn't it?"

V

The Westchester Classic, played at the Westchester Country Club in Harrison, New York, was a two-day event for Al Geiberger and me.

Geiberger, who had just come from a string of corporate outings, was slightly tired, and more than slightly distracted: He was considering a third marriage. We missed the cut by a shot, and did it in the most inexcusable fashion. We were one under par after twenty-eight holes, a stroke away from the leader board. We then played the final eight holes in five over par. Our collective will was not there.

I was distracted, too. The U.S. Open, the granddaddy of them all, was next week, and I had a bag, Larry Rentz. I was excited. Among the golfers and the caddies most of the talk at Westchester was about the U.S. Open. The players talked about the Open course, Oakland Hills, and tried to guess the severity of the rough. The caddies talked about their picks for the High Pool. The anticipation reminded me of schoolchildren before summer vacation.

For the week, the Tour was in New York. I was home; the sites were familiar. But it was not a return home, as the train rides through an autumn countryside at Thanksgiving are. Staying at my brother David's apartment in Manhattan, the setting of my nightly dreams was Michigan, where the U.S. Open would be played. In the early morning, staring at David's law school diploma hanging on the wall, I wondered what I might possibly trade for my bag at the U.S. Open. I could come up with no answer.

11
OPEN HOUSE

I

CADDIES, LIKE COOKS, stockbrokers, and cabbies, treat their profession in one of two ways: either as a job or as a way of life. There is an English caddie on the American Tour, Andy Podger, who is a wonderful example of the latter way. Short—he is nearly a foot shorter than Peter Oosterhuis, for whom he often caddies—and hunched from his years of carrying bags that weigh nearly as much as he does, Andy looks classically caddie, like another person might look classically Greek. His dark eyes bulge from underneath a white-brimmed baseball cap, and he carries the bag nearly vertical to the ground. The bottoms of his too-long corduroy pants (even on the hottest of days he wears corduroy pants) are tattered from their frequent dragging through dew and mud. I worked with Andy at the Byron Nelson, when Oosterhuis and Geiberger, who are close friends, were paired. Andy, being an old-school, old-world

171

caddie, spoke only when spoken to. In our two days together, he made only one unsolicited comment. But that comment revealed his deep love for the game and his abiding respect for players.

Geiberger was telling stories about Lee Lynch, the seventy-eight-year-old caddie, making specific reference to Lee's use of the word *overhaul*, as in, "The overhaul break is to the right."

"Whenever Lee is reading a green and says that word *overhaul*," Geiberger told the group as we waited to play tee shots on a par three, "I always look at the putt and imagine an engine transmission being hauled out from underneath the line of my putt. Happens every time."

While Oosterhuis and I laughed, Andy considered Geiberger's problem and said, to no one in particular, "Ah, it's great to know the stuff that goes through a golfer's mind."

Andy Podger was one of the first people I saw when I arrived at the Oakland Hills Country Club South Course in Birmingham, Michigan, outside Detroit, for the United States Open. Andy, who normally exudes an air of supreme confidence, looked anxious and worried. He was working for Bernhard Langer, who the press had unofficially declared as the Open favorite. Langer had won the Masters and the Sea Pines and was playing highly charged golf. Andy had never won a major, and he now had the opportunity to do so. Andy was, however, in the disadvantaged position of knowing that he was not Langer's first choice. Langer wanted Peter Coleman, an Englishman who generally works only in Europe, where he drives his Porsche from tournament to tournament, to work for him at the Open. Coleman was on Langer's bag when they won the Masters and Sea Pines back to back, and although Langer offered to pay for Coleman's flight over and take care of all his expenses, Coleman, who dislikes flying, could not be

enticed to leave England for a one-week jaunt, even
for the U.S. Open. Andy Podger, in his own way,
probably loves the game as much as Bobby Jones
did—and if you don't know how much that is, I
recommend to you Jones's book, *Down the Fairway.*
But sitting on Langer's bag on the side of the practice
green at the Oakland Hills Country Club, waiting for
Langer to come out of a press interview, Andy probably had, in his own way, the same kind of tournament jitters that finally made Hogan give up competitive play.

Andy Podger taught me that intense love for and
sophisticated understanding of the game of golf re-
veal themselves in subtle ways. I learned that again
from a Michigan club pro named Lynn Jansen, with
whom Larry Rentz played a practice round on the
Monday before the Open.

"Now be careful on these next two holes," Jansen
told Rentz and Freddy Funk, the coach of the University of Maryland golf team, who had qualified for the
Open. The three players stood on the seventh tee.
"The greens are not the original ones. They were
rebuilt in the past ten years, and the undersoil is not
nearly as settled. They're much less porous than the
other greens, and harder, and they will not hold shots
like the other greens will."

When Larry hit a soft, high wedge into number
seven, it bounced thirty feet high and thirty feet over
the back of the green. On the other greens it would
have been an ideal shot.

Jansen hit the proper shot, a British-style bump-
and-run. He might have said, "See" to Larry, but he
did not. He was far too gracious and too knowledgeable for that.

Larry is a different sort of golfing animal, and
animal is not an inappropriate word to use. He
crushes golf balls off the tee with apelike strength.
The longest drivers on the Tour average 275 yards.

Rentz consistently hits drives more than 285 yards
and is quite capable of hitting them thirty yards
farther than that (although he will as often as not be
playing his tee shot from the wrong fairway after
such a shot). Still, when Rentz's driving is straight,
and it sometimes is, he can make a mockery out of
golf course architecture, reducing substantial par
fours to driver–pitching wedge holes, and reaching
formidable par fives with a driver and a five iron. He
is also—and this is why I believe he will become an
outstanding player—a deft putter who seldom misses
from five feet and in and who makes more than his
share of thirty- and forty-footers. Or, as he puts it, "I
can drain those long suckers." He is happy-go-lucky
and plays bon vivant golf. He also has a smugness
about him that will no doubt mature into confidence
and serve him well as his game develops. Now it gets
him in trouble. The smugness showed up after playing a practice round with Larry Mize and Don
Pooley, both of whom have won Tour events, both of
whom are successful, consistent Tour players. Said
Larry of the round with his two more accomplished
partners, "You know something? They didn't show me
anything."

But those qualities worked to Rentz's advantage on
Tuesday, when we played a practice round with Mr.
Tom Watson, who, if you haven't been watching, has
dominated the game without parallel for the past
eight years. Mr. Rentz was at total ease.

It happened in unspectacular fashion that the man
who has won the British Open five times, the Masters
twice, and the U.S. Open once, along with twenty-
eight other Tour victories, decided to play golf with
Larry Rentz, the 1985 Club Pro Series champion.
Ben Crenshaw, Seve Ballesteros, Hale Irwin, and
Bernhard Langer had teed off for a practice round,
sweeping a huge gallery away from the clubhouse
with them. Ronnie Black, Danny Mijovic, and Larry

stood on the first tee waiting for their practice round
to begin. From behind them came a voice.

"Mind if I join you?" the voice, which belonged to
Watson, said.

"Yeah, I guess so," said Ronnie Black.

While Larry calmly shook hands with Watson, I
quivered in the back of the tee. And it was not just
because the temperature was forty-nine degrees, the
wind was blowing at thirty knots, and a cold, steady
drizzle was falling. It was because of Tom Watson. He
is only five feet, nine inches tall. But his presence is
enormous.

Geiberger once told me that when Watson first
came on to the Tour in 1971 without much fanfare or
public expectation—there was nothing especially distinguished about his amateur record—he was struck
by the intellectual concentration with which Watson
practiced. Geiberger had never seen anything like it.
Watson outpracticed even Hogan, who frightened
other players into submission with his six- and eight-
hour sessions on the practice tee. Geiberger said he
was struck not only by the length of time Watson
spent on the practice tee, but by the intensity of his
purpose, as if hitting golf balls was a religious
exercise.

I had two clear memories of Watson in my term on
the Tour through the Open. The first was from Las
Vegas, on the eighteenth green in the final round of
the Panasonic–Las Vegas Invitational. Going into the
round Watson was in a position to win the tournament and get his first victory of the season. After
nine holes on Sunday he was still in a position to do so.
But in the stretch he made a few bogeys when he
needed to make birdies and took himself out of
contention. Watson plays golf tournaments only to
win them; any other finish is, essentially, unimportant. Standing on the eighteenth green over a not
especially meaningful putt, one could see, in his

dripping shirt and lined face, Watson's disappointment in himself.

Watson was in the second to last group, and, by the
time they made it to the eighteenth green, the marshalls had permitted the score of press photographers to come to the edge of the green to get pictures
of the tournament's final putts. As Watson stood over
a twenty-foot putt, one could almost hear the photographers picking up their zoom lenses and pointing
them at Watson, waiting to snap away the moment he
made contact with the putt. Watson stood over the
putt and one of the photographers jumped the gun.
The too-soon click set off a whirl of shutters in false
start. The whirring sound of automatic advances
filled the thin Las Vegas air. Watson stood up and
turned away from his putt. Perspiration now dripping down his arms, he said, "C'mon, fellas, how 'bout
a break." When he turned back to his putt, every lens
was pointed down. An embarrassed look came over
the photographers, collectively. Many of them may
not have known who and what Tom Watson was, but
they felt his presence.

The other clear image I had of Tom Watson was at
the practice tee at the Byron Nelson Golf Classic.
Watson, dissatisfied with his play in that day's round
(he is almost always dissatisfied with his play), was
on the practice range. A boy working on the range
gingerly placed a bucket of balls two feet away from
where Watson was taking divots. He stood there for
half a minute, gawking, hoping to catch Watson's
attention. He might have hoped for a thank you from
him. Watson was oblivious to the boy and just kept
pounding out the balls. When his first pile of balls
was finished, Watson went to the new batch by
flipping over the bucket in one decisive motion. Even
this action was unusual; players generally lean the
basket of balls on its side and take out each ball
individually. With the toe of the club they will caress

the ball out of the bucket, taking a short rest between shots. No breathers for Watson. After each shot he would chip another ball toward him with the club head in one decisive motion.

Watson seemed to be enjoying the severe conditions at Oakland Hills. The more severe the conditions, the more fun he has. On that miserable Tuesday before the Open, in the cold rain and wind, with the golfers and caddies and gallery complaining about the Detroit weather as the first order of business, Watson did not mention the weather once.

I found myself feeling like that boy with the bucket of balls on the practice tee at the Byron Nelson, wanting, somehow, to get some small measure of recognition from Watson. He seemed friendly, talking about the prospects for the Kansas City Royals with Larry, asking Ronnie Black how he got his start in golf, discussing Yugoslavian politics with Danny Mijovic and real estate with Bruce Edwards, his caddie. Larry, with admirable grace, was carrying on with Tom as if he were another Dick or Harry. Not I: My shirt was soaked, my mouth dry.

On a short par four on the front, Larry popped up his drive. Watson hit a good three-wood shot and they were about the same distance from the hole, both in the middle of the fairway. Larry selected his club and I wandered to my right, in the direction of Watson. He glanced over at me, and it occurred to me he might want to know what club Larry was hitting.

"Nine iron," I volunteered.

Watson raised his eyebrows, smiled thinly, and pointed his chin toward me. He hadn't heard me in the howling wind.

"It's a nine iron," I said. Now he had heard me, but his expression did not change. I suddenly realized my naïveté.

Tom Watson might talk about baseball, he might talk about real estate, he might talk about politics, but he could not have cared less what Larry Rentz, assistant pro at the Newbridge Country Club, was hitting into the sixth green of the Oakland Hills Country Club in the Tuesday practice round before the U.S. Open.

As it turned out, Tom Watson did not make the cut in the 1985 U.S. Open, and neither did Jack Nicklaus, Bernhard Langer, Ben Crenshaw, or Larry Rentz. Missing the cut in that most unusual Open will serve as one small lesson, among others, that will, I think, make Larry a winner on the P.G.A. Tour someday.

After winning the 1951 U.S. Open at Oakland Hills, Ben Hogan said, "I am glad that I brought this course, this monster, to its knees." After remodeling Oakland Hills before the 1951 U.S. Open, golf course architect Robert Trent Jones called it "the greatest test of professional tournament championship golf in the world." In 1985 Oakland Hills was more of a golf course than Larry Rentz was a golfer, which is not to discredit Larry. Somewhere down the road the two will be more evenly matched. But a player must have a profound understanding of the game, and his game, to succeed at Oakland Hills, especially at a U.S. Open at Oakland Hills. And that can only come with time.

The subtleties of Oakland Hills, which lie in the shapes and varieties of its holes, the slopes of its fairways, the undulations of its greens, the variety of its grass lengths, and its history, are not easily discernible. One can play the course once or twice or three times and not nearly appreciate it. In tournament play, though, one comes to understand its greatness. And, if it has beaten you in the first round, you will fear it in the second.

Larry and I discovered that birdies are rare at Oakland Hills and that the bogey lurks everywhere. If you do make a birdie—and we did; we made one birdie in thirty-six holes—odds are good you will make a bogey on the next hole. Making a birdie at

Oakland Hills is exhausting and usually promotes giddiness. And that combination—exhaustion and giddiness—is a sure way down the bogey path.

Bogeys at Oakland Hills seem to come with no apparent effort, except for sometimes, when making bogey requires a great deal of effort, as in the last two holes. Golf coaches like to tell their players that all shots count equally, and while this is logistically indisputable, golfers will always talk about what they did on the last few holes, especially the last hole, with greater zeal. They will discuss how closing shots affected their entire score and, sometimes, their entire well-being.

The seventeenth and eighteenth holes, which we played in five over par for the two days—we played the other thirty-two holes in one over par—were our nemesis. They are two of the most difficult holes on a golf course consisting only of difficult holes.

On Friday, standing in the middle of the fourteenth fairway, a formidable par four of 465 yards, we felt sure of ourselves. Larry had made a beautiful birdie on eleven and had avoided bogeys with wonderful, scrambling pars on twelve and thirteen. He smashed a drive off the fourteenth tee, fifty yards ahead of one of his playing partners, Ken Mast, and seventy-five yards in front of the other, Robert Wenz, Jr. Larry had driven the ball 305 yards; we had only 160 yards left to the pin. Weekend play seemed within our grasp.

"Normally it's a seven but I'm gonna take one less for the wind and one more less 'cause I'm so pumped," Larry said. "Think nine is right?"

One hundred sixty yards is considerable distance to hit a nine iron, even for a long-hitting professional. But Larry Rentz is not a typical long-hitting professional.

"I think nine's plenty," I said.

I handed him the nine iron. He addressed the ball.

"You don't think nine's too much, do you?"

"What do you think?" I asked. This was the U.S. Open and we were trying to make the cut. It was no time for caddie heroics.

"I feel like I can hit a pitching wedge there," Larry said.

He took the pitching wedge. If the wind were howling with him, one could easily imagine Larry hitting a 160-yard wedge, but the breeze downhole was little more than a whisper.

Larry stood over the ball with his pitching wedge.

"Who am I kidding?" he said. "Nobody hits 160-yard pitching wedges."

He took back the nine iron and took a beautiful, smooth swing. The ball sailed directly at the hole, landed only a few feet from it, took a big bounce, and rolled gently over the green and into the nasty rough beyond. Larry made a bogey—you're doing well just to get your ball out of the particular patch of rough we ended up in—and our cut cushion was pulled out from under us. We needed to play the final four holes in even par to make the cut.

The fifteenth is a brilliant example of the equality, if not the superiority, of the cleverly designed short hole versus the unimaginative long hole. The fifteenth is only 400 yards, but it plays like a 475-yard hole. In the prime tee shot landing area there is an oval of sand and long grass, thirty-five yards deep and fifteen yards wide, sprawling unkindly in the middle of the narrow fairway. The bunker effectively eliminates the use of a driver off the tee. Although a player of Larry's length could consider blasting a driver over the bunker, such a choice would be unwise, even by his bold standards of play. First, 270 yards of carry is a long way for anyone. Second, even if Larry did drive the ball over the bunker, keeping it in the fairway afterward would be all but impossible. The fairway doglegs sharply to the left immediately after the bunker and becomes quite narrow quite quickly.

On Friday Larry hit a five iron to avoid reaching the bunker and got under it too much. We were left with 200 yards to the pin. We were playing the little par four with proper caution, and the result was that it was playing like a 470-yard hole. We were happy to make a four. We now needed three more pars.

The sixteenth at Oakland Hills, which Arnold Palmer considers among the ten best par fours in the country, is a 409-yard hole that doglegs severely to the right. A pond borders the entire turn of the dogleg and nestles up against a tiny putting green that slopes down to the water. For Larry, the water, which begins 275 yards from the tee, on the right side of the fairway, comes into play off the tee, and it had to be avoided. Avoided it was: Larry hooked his tee shot badly to a grove of trees protected by a jungle of rough with blades of clingy grass five inches long. With sheer strength Larry hacked a seven iron out of that rough and saved par by making an eight-foot putt.

Standing on the seventeenth tee Friday we knew that we had to make two pars coming home to have a chance at making the cut. The seventeenth is a 200-yard par three, which, up a hill and into a prevailing breeze, plays to roughly 225 yards. The green sits on the crown of a hill and errant shots could do much worse than drop into one of the six severe bunkers that protect the green like a moat. Over the green there is a dense grove of trees where you don't want to be. The tendency, therefore, is to underclub, but the sledding is equally rough in front of the green. The grass there is so high that one is delighted to find one's ball, let alone have a shot. Our shot called for a regular full three iron. Unfortunately, Larry did not carry a three iron, sacrificing one of the long iron clubs for a third wedge, which is a practice not

uncommon among professionals. (They may carry
only fourteen clubs.) We were faced with a difficult
decision. A two iron was too much club and a four
iron not enough. An easy two iron, because of the
length and unwieldiness of that club, is a difficult
shot. We were left with the hard four. Larry knocked
the four iron as hard as he could, and it went high,
very high, as a hard-hit shot tends to do, and leaked to
the right, as a hard-hit shot tends to do. The ball,
caught in the wind at the height of its trajectory, fell
straight down and burrowed its way through half an
inch of sand in a well-lipped bunker. Larry had
virtually no chance to make par and, as on fourteen,
did well to make bogey.

We now needed a birdie at eighteen to make the
cut.

The eighteenth is the most challenging hole on the
course, an uphill 453-yard par four dogleg to the
right. The green is shaped like an upside-down yar-
mulke and is about the same size. It is wholly unre-
ceptive to long iron shots. The hole plays as a par five
for club members, and even the pros regarded five as
a not-bad score on the hole. The fairway, in the prime
landing area, is a mere twenty-three yards wide. To
the right there is a grove of trees and a group of
three small bunkers and to the left a large bunker
and much U.S. Open–style rough. A three on this
hole, think of that—to negotiate a tiny ball through
453 yards of that *stuff* in three swings—would
require three ingenious golf strokes and a small act
of God.

On the walk from the seventeenth green to the
eighteenth tee, I said to Larry, "OK, let's just put the
drive in the middle of the fairway; that's the first
step," and Larry said back, "Right, one shot a time;
that's the way to play this game." We both tried to
think positive thoughts, imagining the flight of the
ball soaring away from the tee right down the center.

But in our heart of hearts lived doom. Where, precisely, our earlier confidence had gone I cannot tell
you. We were in the process of choking away our
chance to make the cut, and there didn't seem to be
anything we could do about it. Larry hooked his drive
into the bunker, topped his second shot, left his third
shot on the fringe, chipped, and two-putted for a
double bogey. A quick six. Our bogey, double bogey
finish finished us, and I don't think there was anyone
more disappointed than I, except for Larry.

II

There was, actually, one person more disappointed
than Larry and I were about missing the cut. And
that was a fellow named Scott Uffelman, who in the
course of a week had become Larry's biggest fan.

Scott T. Uffelman (his initials, S.T.U., "are only
halfway to being stupid," he says), and his wife,
Pamela Bacon Uffelman, were our hosts in Birmingham. On Thursday and Friday Scott took off
from work (he is a financial advisor for Merrill
Lynch), and, patchwork sweater draped around his
shoulders, binoculars around his neck, followed
Larry for each of his 149 shots.

"Gosh," he said to Larry in the morbid aftermath of
the second round, "it looked so good after that birdie
on eleven. I just thought for sure that was going to
change the momentum. I couldn't believe the size of
some of those putts you made on the front side. That
one on three must have been seventy feet!"

The putt was about a twenty-five-footer, but there
was no point in dampening Scott Uffelman's
enthusiasm.

The Uffelmans, who needed only to cross a road,
cut through a front yard, a backyard, and hop a fence
to be on the fourth tee of Oakland Hills, had offered,
through the club, their guest room to a player in

need. Larry took the Uffelmans up on their offer and kindly made arrangements for me to stay with him.

Scott and Pam, who were only a couple of years older than Larry and I, were considerably more advanced by, say, the standards of credit-risk rating companies. For instance, they were married. They owned a home (finished basement, large yard). They had a dog (Saucy). They owned a Cadillac (a baby-blue 1977 Seville, which they had bought from Pam's father for $2,000). They were established.

"There's only one thing we want in the way of rent," Scott said as he and Pam showed Larry and me to the room we would be sharing (with one king-sized bed and one five-foot-long cot).

"That's right," Pam said, "just one thing."

"I need to cure my slice," said Scott.

"And I've got to fix my hook," said Pam.

By local standards, those were reasonable rents: thirty-dollars-a-night hotel rooms were going for ninety dollars, and ninety-dollar hotel rooms were going for two hundred dollars. If you hadn't booked a room six months before the Open, you were out of luck, even if you were a contestant.

We woke up Saturday morning with no plans but to watch the tournament on television. But over breakfast Larry and I realized that we had not yet paid our rent. With both Scott and Pam away at their respective offices, our chances to do so were becoming increasingly slim. We discussed the possibility of buying a gift to replace the lessons. But what could you buy the Uffelmans? Matching water and food bowls for Saucy with the dog's name on it? A new set of balls for the bumper pool table in the cellar? A matching patchwork-quilt sweater for Pam? The Uffelmans, as far as we could tell, had everything.

The Uffelmans were at their respective offices, and we were thinking hard: What would Pam and Scott want? Something entrepreneurial, Larry and I decided. Scott was unabashedly entrepreneurial, and that added in great part to his charm. Pam said it was that quality in Scott (she called it "inventiveness") that first attracted her to him. Over long, pleasant dinners earlier in the week, Scott had told endearing, funny stories about his first efforts in the business world, about his inventiveness.

One high school summer, Scott left the comfort and safety of Short Hills, New Jersey, to go to Rolla, Missouri, to sell the Volume Library. He lived in the basement of an old man's house for twenty dollars a month. He had no car. But he sold scores of the Volume Library and saved $6,000. Later, as an undergraduate at Wake Forest, Scott began a company called Fans Are Fun. He bought thousands of small, hand-held, battery-run fans and applied to them decals from ten different major universities. He tried to sell them to the schools, hoping the schools would sell them at football games. But football is played in the fall, when it's cool, and his idea never caught on. Scott sold about as many fans as he did Volume Libraries, at a considerably smaller per-sale profit. But this did not dampen his entrepreneurial instinct, even now, in professional life. In 1981, when the U.S. Senior Open was played at Oakland Hills, Scott realized the demand for pay parking. The course's parking lots for spectators involved walks up to a mile. Responding to the complaints, and the market they implied, he converted his backyard into a pay-parking field.

"Larry, would it be beneath your dignity to park cars on the weekend of the U.S. Open?" I asked at breakfast, thinking of the previous night's dinner conversation with Scott.

"Wasn't beneath my dignity to make a double bogey on eighteen," he answered.

Twenty minutes later I was standing in the traffic jam at the corner of West Maple Road and Red Maple

Road. Larry was at the corner of Red Maple Road and the Uffelman driveway. The cars on West Maple Road were at a standstill, waiting to get into the Oakland Hills parking fields. "Park with the Pros, $5," read my sign. To each driver I made a personal pitch.

"Park with the pros," I said a thousand times that day. "Only five dollars, all day."

Sometimes I'd wait right at a driver's window until they rolled it down. One conversation went this way:

ME: You've heard about our special today, I'm sure.

DRIVER: Special?

ME: Saturday U.S. Open special. Today only. Park with "Park with the Pros" and get a free Larry Rentz autograph after he parks your car.

DRIVER: Larry who?

ME: Larry Rentz.

DRIVER: Who's that?

ME: Only one of the longest hitters in professional golf. He nearly made the cut.

DRIVER: You got a guy who played in the first two rounds parking cars?

YOUNG VOICES IN BACK SEAT: We gotta check it out, Dad. Yeah, let's check it out.

WOMAN'S VOICE FROM PASSENGER SEAT: Honey, this sounds like some kind of prank. Ask if we can take the keys with us.

DRIVER: Can we take the keys with us?

ME: Of course you can, sir. At "Park with the Pros" you're the boss. And, as an extra special today, if you tell the parking attendant, "I carry a three iron," you may be eligible for a special grand prize.

DRIVER: *I* carry a three iron?

ME: That's right.

DRIVER [NOW REASONABLY AMUSED]: What's the prize?

ME: A free Larry Rentz long-drive lesson.

DRIVER [CATCHING ON]: Are there any consolation prizes?

ME: As a matter of fact, there are. Special, today only, a free golf ball.

In about three hours, Larry had expertly converted the backyard lawn, where Scott had been happily cutting away only a few days earlier on his tractor lawn mower, into a professional parking field. He crammed seventy cars onto the property, each with just enough room to get out. We had made a quick $350, about as much as Larry earned for making it to the U.S. Open and not surviving the cut, and $100 more than Larry paid me for the week. At no point were we concerned that Scott or Pam might object to all the cars parked on their neatly manicured lawn. And we were right. Scott came home first. When we handed him an envelope with the money in it, he beamed as if he'd just become a father.

Pam and Scott took Larry and me out to dinner. They argued over whether to invest the money in a special fund, or take a weekend in the Michigan woods with it.

On Sunday, it seemed that all of Michigan, and the better part of the Midwest, had come to Birmingham for the tournament's finale in a cold rain. The four of us were quite content to watch the fate of T. C. Chen on television. (Ultimately, we were not content with T. C. Chen's fate; we were all rooting for him.)

Sunday night, like every other Sunday night when you're living on the Tour, was time to say au revoir. The Tour life is ideal when the week has been bad and you cannot wait to leave and start fresh somewhere else. And it is sad when you've thoroughly enjoyed your week and the people with whom you have been.

Larry summed up the week at the airport terminal.

"Well, it was a good learning experience," Larry said. "There's one thing I can't figure out, though."

"What's that?" I asked.

"Why did all these people come up to me when we were parking cars and say, '*I* carry a three iron,' and then ask if they won a long-drive lesson?

"Do you figure they all saw us struggling on seventeen?"

12
THE BREEZE IS UP

I

THE WORD *CADDIE* was born in seventeenth-century France as *cadet*, a military term describing the young son of a noble family serving in the army without a commissioned rank. The word lost a *t* and gained a vowel or two as it worked its way across the English Channel and then up the English coast to Scotland. It hit the Scottish shores as *caudie* but settled in as *caddie*, except in certain quarters, where the preferred spelling was *caddy*. Both spellings were, and are, considered correct. And so was the position the word described: a young gentleman enlisted in the army. Because of their superior social position, caddies were envied by plebeian soldiers. After their tour of duty, the caddies went on to become generals, landowners, or barons and, by the eighteenth century, club members. Clubs for gentlemen were then becoming fashionable. A certain percentage of the plebeians, ill-equipped for regular work because of their physical or psychological makeup, became freelance, odd-job workers. They formed guilds and clubs in imitation of their social superiors. And they gave themselves a name: caddies. In naming themselves they were probably being both satiric and self-deprecating. They were former soldiers but they were not considered gentlemen. By the end of the eighteenth century, golfers, many of whom were former military caddies and by then established gentry, began to hire these other caddies to carry their golf bags. A term and a profession were born.

Golfers quickly realized that caddies, like others who work at humbling jobs, were shrewd observers. Dr. Alister Mackenzie, the great Scottish-born golf course architect, once asked a caddie what the members of a particular club thought of a stream that ran through several holes. Replied the caddie, "Well, we've got an old Scotch major here, and when he gets over he says, 'Well ower the bonnie wee burn, ma laddie,' but when he gets in he says, 'Pick ma ball oot o' that domned sewer.' "

Caddies watch carefully, but they are watched, too. En route to England for the British Open, I read this letter in *Golf World*, a British magazine. It ran with the title "Untidy Caddies":

At the recent Hennessy Cognac Ladies' Cup match in France, Laura Davies was fined fifty pounds for breaking the W.P.G.A.'s dress code rules. But isn't it about time the P.G.A. did something about the real scruffs of the golf course, the caddies?

Before the spectators and on TV they are as much centre stage as the players yet they seem to care little for their appearances. Torn and dirty anoraks, trousers that look as if they have been slept in, dirty training shoes, shirts hanging out, and cycle clips are just some of the complaints I have.

Some sponsors provide overalls but this is only a

partial solution, even when they fit. I know that
caddies are not reckoned to have much money, but
can't they tidy themselves up a bit?

I rolled down the sleeves of my shirt, neatened the
knot in my tie, and began a conversation with the
Englishwoman next to me, who had loaned me the
Golf World. She also gave me a small but important
lesson.

"When discussing the Open with an Englishman,"
she said, "you need refer to the Open simply as 'the
Open.' There are other 'Opens,' but we take the view
that this is the world's Open."

Although the U.S. Open is widely regarded as
golf's premier event by most players, there is no
tournament that attracts as international a crowd as
the (British) Open. It is, by and large, an elite crowd,
too. Only the best of the American players come over:
In 1985 the American players at the Open included
Fuzzy Zoeller, Payne Stewart, Peter Jacobsen, Gary
Koch, Craig Stadler, David Graham, D. A. Weibring,
Tom Kite, Corey Pavin, Mark O'Meara, Jack Nicklaus, Tom Watson, and Lee Trevino. The rest of the
field comprised golfers from England, Japan, Australia, Spain, France, Germany, Sweden, and South
Africa. Typically, for a caddie to get a bag in the
Open he must be in a superior position. I came over
on the chance that a twenty-two-year-old New Jersey-
ite named Jamie Howell and I could get through the
thirty-six-hole qualifying round and into the Open. I
met Jamie, who is friends with Billy Britton and
Larry Rentz, at the Tallahassee Open; he had come to
England for his honeymoon. He had never qualified
for the U.S. Tour, or even the U.S. Open, in half a
dozen tries. I came to England in the hope that Jamie
Howell's honeymoon would inspire him to great
things.

I caught up with the Howells in accordance with a
plan we made in a New York–New Jersey telephone

conversation, at the Royal Cinque Ports Golf Club, where the Open was played in 1909 and 1920. Cinque Ports, in Deal, on the coast of Kent, was one of the sites for the two-day, thirty-six-hole qualifying. Our meeting date was three days before the qualifying rounds, and Jamie had already been there one day. In giving himself four days of preparation, Jamie had demonstrated wisdom well beyond his twenty-two years.

After a night flight to London and a morning arrival, I rented a car and drove south to Deal. Cinque Ports is on the North Sea, off which the breeze blows steadily. Especially in the afternoon. And especially during a summer storm. Storms there are the norm—either recently arrived, recently departed, or firmly in place. There was always some explanation for the wind, which was blowing at thirty knots when I arrived. My source of weather information was Andrew Reynolds, Cinque Ports' young, ruddy professional.

"Can't quite believe how much the groom is practicing, considering," Reynolds said, looking out on the golf course through the pro shop window. Then, without looking at his watch, "He should be, rather, they should be, on thirteen by now."

Cinque Ports is a small and very British club, and the professional, like the editor of a country newspaper, knows what's going on in his domain. He set me on a direction, into the golf course, into the wind. The club flag flapped so hard I thought it might suddenly snap free from its mast.

"It's really howling, huh," I said.

Reynolds considered the wind and looked over his golf score like a farmer looking at his fields before a harvest. "The breeze," he said, "is up."

Royal Cinque Ports is unlike any golf course in the United States. It is a true links course. The fairways

are unwatered, with sandy soil underneath and wind-
smoothed bumps on top. The nature of the course is
dictated by the wind; only one hole plays with the
prevailing breeze. The wind makes the greens hard
and fast. So does their age. All of the greens but one
are original, meaning they date to 1895. Their grass
is dense and healthy, which enables the greenskeeper
to shave the greens closely. The course has no rough,
as rough is known in the United States; it has hay
fields. Although it measures only 6,744 yards from
the back tees, it plays at least 700 yards longer if one
is playing into the prevailing gale. To master the
course one must play shots one doesn't develop, cus-
tomarily, in the United States. The most important of
these is the bump-and-run—a line-drive shot that
first lands short of the green and skips and rolls to
the hole. The other important shot is the feather
shot—hitting more club than one needs to keep a shot
low, but hitting it with less than regular force to keep
it from being too much. If one had played all of one's
golf in the United States, as Jamie Howell had, one
had much to learn to succeed on this classic links
course. And if one had done all of one's caddying in
the United States, as I had, one also had much to
learn in order to succeed on this classic links course.

"Jamie and I made a bet," Dawn Howell told me
when I caught up with the couple on a spot on the
course called Vardon's Patch. Dawn, redheaded, attractive, and vivacious, was discovering then what it
means to be a golfer's wife. "If Jamie shoots 74 or less
today I buy him one of those cashmere sweaters in the
pro shop. And if he shoots 75 or higher, he doubles my
spending money in London."

"You know, newlywed stuff," said Jamie, whose
serious and mature manner suggest a man twice his
age.

"How's the bet going?" I asked.

"If I get up and down from here," Jamie said,

standing in the thirteenth fairway, "I think it'll be for
74." He needed fours on the remaining six holes to
shoot 98.

"Guess you made the bet before the breeze came
up," I offered.

Dawn laughed; Jamie did not. "The breeze," he
said. "This breeze has been blowing for a week now.
Tell you what: If the breeze doesn't simmer down, you
can shoot 160 [for two rounds] in the qualifying and
you know something? You'll have yourself a spot in
the British Open."

"You mean 'the Open,' Jamie," Dawn said.

"The Open," Jamie said dourly. He hit what looked
like a good shot into number thirteen. The ball
bounced in front of the green, rolled on, and finally
over. "I've never seen anything like this in my life,"
Jamie said. "Have you?"

"Never," I said.

II

The North Sea seaside towns of Deal and Sandwich
are connected by a winding ten-foot-wide path called
Golf Road. The road begins at the Royal Cinque Ports
clubhouse, a simple, elegant, two-story affair of white
stucco, bay windows, and heavy mahogany doors, and
runs alongside the course for a mile. With a few dips
and turns the road passes Prince's Golf Club, another
Open qualifying site. The road finally pours into the
Royal St. George's Golf Club, where the 1985 Open
would be played. There the great course lived, at the
end of Golf Road, two miles away from Cinque Ports:
Tantalizing and mysterious, it stretched before us, a
sort of barren green pasture with pastel tents—a
reward of the Old World.

One lone building was built alongside the Golf
Road, a rambling old house called the Chequers Inn,
containing a pub, a restaurant, and, for fifteen

pounds a night, bedrooms. I took a room there and
was happy I did. The inn's food was hearty and the
bar crowded with players, caddies, and serious spectators of a jovial nature. Conversation was single-
minded and detailed, sustaining and sustained. It
flowed effortlessly, as did the good ale from the old
barrels on the other side of the bar.

The Chequers, lodged between Golf Road and the
fifteenth fairway of Cinque Ports, occupied a splen-
did spot. On the other side of the road there was a
sprawling sheep farm with a square mile of grazing
land. Beyond the golf course the sea shimmered, and
France shimmered beyond that. A train track sliced
through the sheep farm. In the early morning after
my first night's sleep in England, the whole world
dripped with fog, and the smell was sweet. The last
smoke from the final coals in the pub's fireplace was
lodged in the thick air, and that was sweet, too.

III

We had our work cut out for us.

We—Jamie, Dawn (she followed every shot), and
I—had two days to learn to play British-style golf on
this most British of golf courses. We had to learn the
bump-and-run. We had to learn the feather shot. We
had to learn to hit the ball low off the tee into the
wind, a problem exasperated by Jamie's tendency to
hit toweringly high drives. We had to learn to play
bunker shots out of coarse sand. We had to learn to
read greens the breaks of which looked subtle but
were monstrous. We had our work cut out for us.

We did this by playing several hundred different
shots in our practice round two days before the
qualifying rounds began. And we made progress.
Early on I demonstrated a reasonable knack for
reading the Cinque Ports greens, and Jamie placed
his faith in me. Jamie, to be candid in the British

fashion, is not a gifted putter, but is quite good at
following directions. I told him where to put the ball
(in the jargon of the business which was by now
second nature to me: a cup outside on the high side;
half a ball outside on the left; over that white thing
halfway between us and the hole). And he put it
there. Our arrangement was lovely.

The second-day practice round boosted our confidence immeasurably. We played with two players
from the United Kingdom, a Londoner named Roger
Dawson and an Irishman named Jimmy Hegarty.
Hegarty was an unspectacular but steady player on
the European tour. Dawson was a young player
hoping to join the European Tour, roughly the European equivalent, in terms of his golf station in life, of
Jamie.

In the United States the difference between the
average Tour player and the good Tour player is
hardly discernible on the practice tee or in a practice
round; the difference between Jamie and his European colleagues was nearly as obvious as the difference between their accents. Although the Europeans
knew more about playing a British-style game, Jamie
knew far more about making shots. He swung at the
ball with greater authority. He also took a more
cerebral approach to preparation. They would hit a
shot and move on. Jamie would hit a shot and then
wonder about other, better ways to play the same
shot. Then he'd practice them.

One of the recurrent golf debates in 1985 was
whether American or European players were emerging as the leaders of the game. Bernhard Langer, a
German; Seve Ballesteros, a Spaniard; Greg Norman, an Australian; and Sandy Lyle, an Englishman,
were regularly mentioned in these arguments. Since
they were winning tournaments, and important ones,
the argument for the Europeans was not difficult to
make. Many of the players on the U.S. Tour consider

Ballesteros the best player in the game now, and the adjective *awesome* has been used to describe Langer more than once. One would be hard pressed to find a U.S. Tour player to take Mark O'Meara and Curtis Strange over Langer and Ballesteros in a team better-ball match, even though O'Meara and Strange are outstanding players. But in this American versus European debate one important fact is lost. The depth of talent is far greater in the United States than it is in Europe. If you changed the bet, to pit the forty-ninth and fiftieth ranked players from the American Tour against their counterparts from the European Tour, no one, I think, would bet with the Europeans. The approach to the game at its less than highest levels is markedly different in the United States and in Europe. The compulsiveness with which Jamie Howell played his practice rounds was typical by American standards; his golfing brethren overseas thought it highly unusual.

IV

We did nicely, Jamie, Dawn, and I. Jamie made the shots, Dawn did the cheerleading, and I carried the bag and read the putts. In the first round we went a round in 70, two under par, on a day when the breeze was up. Jamie was low man by two shots and bettered the average score by ten. In the clubhouse, and in the pro shop, Jamie was talked about in low tones as an unsmiling American golfing machine. The club's members were rather astonished that a twenty-two-year-old could play their course in two under par with the breeze up, making pars coming home in the teeth of the wind. The *Times* ran an item on Jamie and his newly wedded wife. He was news. As a young man, Michael Bonallack, now secretary of the Royal and Ancient Golf Club, went a round at Cinque Ports in sixty-five strokes. But the breeze was not up that day and the tees were. Jamie had played the course with the tees all the way back and the wind all the way up. The people of Deal were impressed. Jamie's 70 was considered among the best rounds ever played on the course.

Over dinner Jamie grumbled about how the round should have been a 69, or a 68. At one point he had it down to a 67. But behind his moustache, and in the corners of his mouth, Dawn and I could plainly see the satisfaction he felt. We needed to play one more round to make our qualifying official, but the Open seemed within grasp, and the marriage of Jamie and Dawn Howell was off to a good start.

At Cinque Ports, 130 golfers competed for thirty Open spots. Jamie shot 76 in the second round, not a distinguished round, but good enough to earn an Open spot. He was in by two shots.

"Can't really believe it," Jamie said. "I've never qualified for the Open in my own country, and I get into the British Open on my first try."

Dawn kissed him on the cheek.

"You'll play there soon enough," she said, grasping his hand.

V

During Open week, Yankee entrepreneurial spirit thrived through all of Deal and Sandwich, and in great chunks of Canterbury and Dover, too. Based on the signs posted, and the advertisements in newspapers, it seemed that anyone with an extra bed, cot, or hammock was renting out their spare sleeping space by the night. Most included breakfast at no extra charge. These bed-and-breakfast spots, which housed players and officials and spectators and caddies and reporters, typically rented their rooms for twenty pounds a night. Some charged as little as five.

The start of the Open week finished my stay at the

Chequers Inn; the British Broadcasting Company had booked the whole place for the week a year in advance. I had the good fortune of finding a couple who had converted their home into a bed-and-break-fast boardinghouse more as a lark than as a way to make money. They were Mr. and Mrs. R. B. Venables, Raymond and Doris, formerly of London and Deal and now, in their retirement, only Deal.

Ray Venables, a former housemaster at Harrow, the boys' public school, was gray-haired, fit, and lively, qualities shared by Mrs. Venables, who was also a master gardener. The small back lawn of their 250-year-old house was nicely suited to putting or lawn bowling or croquet, which Mrs. Venables pro-nounced *crow-key*, in the style of the country. These were people very much in the style of the country. They were delightfully unstylish. In the United States one sometimes associates such unstylishness among educated people as a snobbery of sorts. The Venables were beyond snobbery. Mr. Venables watched the cricket matches on the television with intense and genuine interest but shared his favorite game with the uninitiated enthusiastically. He was very much in the spirit of old England—he cared deeply about the future of Oxford, his alma mater; less so about Prince Charles—but he was delightfully informal, too. For several decades he had led Ameri-cans on tours of Europe. He has fond memories of the journeys. He returned from those summer trips something of an expert on American sociology.

"I'm especially fond of your Italian-Americans," Mr. Venables said one afternoon. It was warm but he wore wool pants and a long-sleeved shirt. "Sometimes a tour guide is placed in the perplexing position of having to allocate bedrooms. He must determine which couples would be more at ease with twin beds and which would be happier with king-sized beds. In these situations I always placed the Italians in the rooms with the king-sized beds. Never a complaint, and more than once one of the couple, and sometimes both, would come up to me and say, 'Say, Ray, that was terrific last night. See if you can do that again.'"

Mrs. Venables did not demur at this story. But she did dip her head perceptibly closer to the egg she was beating, ostensibly to remove a small piece of broken eggshell.

Also staying at the Venables' was a man named Colum Smith, a golf correspondent for a group of Irish newspapers. Mr. Smith, who had none of the solemnity one often associates with lifelong newspapermen, was made especially merry by the results of the first round of the Open. A fellow countryman, one Christy O'Connor, Jr., shot a 64 to tie the course record. O'Connor led the tournament and Smith had the lead story in newspapers across Ireland.

Colum Smith, like many Englishmen and Irishmen, has an acute sense of golf course architecture. And, as a newspaperman, he was curious. No small talk over breakfast. He wanted to know about the fairway bunker at number four ("Can your man carry it from the back tees and the wind in his face?"). And about putting number twelve ("Is there any way to get a good read there?"). And about playing number fourteen into the teeth of the wind ("What'd the fellows hit into there yesterday?").

Perhaps because we didn't have as much chance to learn Royal St. George's as well as we did Royal Cinque Ports—there were only two days between the qualifying rounds and the beginning of the tournament—our goose was cooked partly before we set the dimpled white egg on the first tee. As it turned out, Jamie and I never did learn how to avoid that fairway bunker at number four, or how to read the green at twelve, or how to play fourteen into the teeth of the wind. Bernard Darwin, who wrote about golf for the London *Times* for forty-six years, once described

Royal St. George's as "nearly my idea of heaven as is to be attained on earthly links." But that description must have been uttered when the golf course appeared under reasonably benign conditions. We played the course only in a gale.

We shot 75 the first round, with problems at our (and most everybody's) trouble spots, holes four, twelve, and fourteen. Although not a good score, 75 was not a bad score, either. Two strokes less and we would have been in the middle of the field. On the second day we made a triple bogey at number four and a bogey at twelve and had to snake in a sizable putt to save par at fourteen. A 77. Only ten strokes separated the entire field after the cut; at 152, the same total as Nicklaus, we were three shots away from that.

We played golf under treacherous conditions. Jamie took on and off his rain pants seven times in the second round. I opened and closed the umbrella sixteen times. On two occasions Jamie added a sweater, wearing, at one point, a total of three. Once we had to stop walking forward; the wind would not permit us a single step.

That was on the dreaded number fourteen, a par five of 500 yards where Peter Jacobsen took a nine in 1985 and Arnold Palmer made a three in 1975. It's a tough, little hole with an out-of-bounds all along the right side and a hayfield all the way down the left, separated by a sliver of fairway. Some 325 yards off the tee, a ten-yard-wide stream called the Suez Canal splits the fairway.

Palmer, playing the hole downwind in the 1975 Penfold P.G.A. Championship, smashed a driver off the tee nearly to the canal, knocked a three iron to six feet, and made the putt for an eagle.

Jamie, playing into the wind, smashed a driver that sneaked onto the beginning of the fairway, 175 yards from the tee. It was while walking to that tee shot that all forward marching came to a halt, in deference to the wind. Our playing partner, Maurice Bembridge, who once shot a 64 at Augusta National in the 1974 Masters, did not reach the fairway with his tee shot. Like Palmer a decade before us, we took a three iron for our second shot. But we did not reach the green. We just cleared the canal, the same canal Palmer nearly drove. A one iron from there (still short), a chip, and a putt, and Jamie had made a feisty, hard-fought, and exhausting par. Bembridge cursed heaven and hell and all in between at the top of his lungs, but with no jeopardy of being fined, for he was virtually inaudible; words became lost as soon as they met with the wind. Mark McNulty, our other playing partner, had given up talking on the fourth hole. But nobody gave up playing. This was, after all, the Open.

VI

Once, not so long ago, in the glory days of O.H.C. Barry & Company, Ltd., Tom Weiskopf, Johnny Miller, Ray Floyd, Hale Irwin, and Jack Nicklaus all wore the company's star product, the Star Grip Golf Glove. The gloves, handmade in a small, family-owned business, were considered the best: The leather was more supple, the fit closer, and the resistance to water better than any other glove on the market. The company was founded in 1965 and produced 20,000 gloves that year. In 1976 the company made 120,000 gloves. And there the Star Grip Golf Glove peaked, for reasons the company's owners are still trying to figure out. Jack Nicklaus may have had something to do with it.

I learned about this during Open week, when seemingly the entire golf world, even those with the most remote of connections to it, was linked. The

Open is almost as much trade show as it is tournament. One night during Open week I found myself having dinner with, among others, Stephen and Roland Wright, who represented two generations of O.H.C Barry & Co., makers of the Star Grip Golf Glove.

"We don't really know what happened after 1976," Stephen Wright, the father, said. "Maybe we grew too quickly, but our quality never suffered, not in the slightest."

Mr. Wright was in charge of Star Grip Golf Glove quality control, a job he treated with thorough professionalism.

"In 1976, Mr. Nicklaus, who had been wearing the glove—and quite happily, I might add, for some years—approached us saying he wanted to buy a majority of the company. We were willing to sell forty-nine percent of it to Mr. Nicklaus but wanted to keep ownership in the family. Mr. Nicklaus said he wanted fifty-one percent of it. We said no. And the next thing we knew he wasn't wearing our glove anymore. Soon after, neither were a great many of the other fellows."

Nine years later, the company's annual glove production was only slightly more than half of what it had been the peak year. But the Star Grip Golf Glove, the Wrights said, was on the rebound.

"The secret to our success, and it's not such a secret—it's a question of effort—is that our leather is from only the finest of Abyssinian-hair sheep," Stephen Wright said. "And then it's table cut in the spring. We then shave the leather until it's feather light. The good golfer appreciates this lightness; it vastly improves feel. And then we tan it in such a way that the glove is tacky but maintains good feel. The tailoring is done by hand. And, as you probably know, we were the first to sew in the Velcro strap at an angle natural to one's knuckles and to use elastic to keep the glove snug around the wrist. This is critical to the Star Grip fit."

The glove was invented by a Baltimore man named Ellis Woodward. Ellis Woodward did not have access to the good leathers or the equipment needed to produce the gloves on a large scale, so he brought the glove to a friend, a New York man named John Whitimuir. Whitimuir brought the glove to England, where he found Owen Barry and Stephen Wright, co-owners of a leather-goods manufacturing concern. (Mr. Wright married Mr. Barry's sister, so the company was, essentially, all in one family.) When Whitimuir found Owen and Wright, glove manufacturing was a small part of their small business. Soon, though, it became their chief interest. And the business not so small.

"We're trying to get the top players to wear the glove again, but now we're concentrating on the European players," said Roland Wright, the son. Roland is the company's director of sales. "The problem is that even though most everybody acknowledges that the Star Grip glove is the best glove made, some of the players are paid quite large sums of money to wear gloves made by mass manufacturers, sports companies that deal, primarily, in things other than golf gloves for their income. We can't compete with these companies. We can't afford to make the kinds of offers they make. All we can offer is the glove.

"The best of the players are, of course, above financial considerations when choosing a glove, and this is our salvation. It's quite interesting, really; I've learned a great deal about the personalities of the top players.

"For instance, I made the mistake of approaching Ballesteros after a not especially good round at a tournament earlier in the year. His score wasn't bad—level par, I think—and I knew, after he signed his scorecard and was walking toward the locker room, that that would be my only chance to see him. I got as far as, 'Seve,'—he has no idea who I am—and he said, 'Not now,' and stormed into the locker room. Then, at a tournament some weeks later, I had a few moments with him, and he took the twelve gloves we had picked for him. He grabbed them, stuffed them in his locker, said, 'Thanks,' and was off to play. But he's been wearing them, and I understand from his caddie that he's pleased with them. I don't dare ask him directly.

"Bernhard Langer is quite a different matter. I sat down with him in that same locker room and he tried on gloves for over an hour, scores of them, until he found twelve that he liked. Not a word. He examined each glove, put it on, opened and closed his fist, stretched out his fingers, clapped a few times. The gloves he liked he placed neatly in one pile. He handed back to me those he didn't like. It was quite a procedure. But he found twelve that he liked. He's using them, too, and from the looks of things, he's pleased with them."

"Langer's just the same way in choosing his umbrella," said Steve Harris, our other dinner companion. He was the director of sales of Sol Schaverian & Sons, Ltd., makers of golf umbrellas. And in the next hour we all learned something about the subtleties that separate the good golf umbrella from the merely passable one.

13
A DUTCH TREAT

I

THE STORM THAT PLAGUED the British Open all
week followed the European Tour across the North
Sea to Holland the next week, the week of the KLM
Dutch Open. From Sheerness, England, I took an
overnight ferry to Vlissingen, Holland; when I
boarded the boat (several hours after Sandy Lyle
became the first Englishman to win the British Open
since 1969), it was dark, and when I awoke in Holland
the next morning it was raining. Rain is a semiper-
manent condition on the European Tour.

In concept the European Tour and the U.S. Tour
are identical: professional golfers congregating in a
different place every week to play golf for money.
Instead of going from Orlando to New Orleans to Las
Vegas, the European Tour jumps from France to
Germany to England. In many of the places where
the European Tour goes, such as Holland and the stop
after it, Sweden, golf is starting to boom as it did in
the United States during the 1960s. But, for now,

galleries and purses in Europe are half the size of
what they are in the United States. To entice the
world's best golfers to their tournaments, sponsors of
European events offer large sums of money to the top
players. There is hardly a week in which either Seve
Ballesteros or Bernhard Langer, or both, is offered as
much as $30,000 to play in a tournament. And once
they show up for a tournament, it is not unlikely that
they will win it. Langer and Ballesteros have won
more than fifty European tournaments between
them.

But American players have dominated international golf for so long now that Europeans seem to
half expect their golfing white knight to come from
the other side of the Atlantic. In the past three
decades Europe's greatest golfing heroes have been
American: Palmer, Nicklaus, Trevino, Watson. Now
there is a search for a successor. As part of the
search, leading American players are extended lav-
ish invitations to European tournaments by their
sponsors.

"Burginvest B.V. Welcomes Curtis Strange," read
a large sign at the entrance to the Noordwijk Golf
Club, site of the 1985 Dutch Open. Strange, the
leading money winner in the United States, who
raised the ire of the international golfing press a
week earlier by skipping the British Open, was paid
$25,000 by the tournament sponsors to play in the
Dutch Open. They also paid for his airfare and (first
class) accommodations. They procured a car for him
and, had he asked for it, they would have procured
the moon, too, or at least tried. The terms of Strange's
appearance were negotiated between the tournament's sponsors and the International Management
Group, which represents Strange.

To the general public, I.M.G. is not very well
known, but in a quiet way the company is one of the
most influential forces in golf. It is run by Mark H.

McCormack, who became a multimillionaire by joining his old college golf rival, Arnold Palmer, with
what was then a relatively new invention, the television. When Nicklaus, Palmer, and Gary Player were
arguably the three best golfers in the world, McCormack managed them all. That made McCormack a
powerful golf man. He could make or break tournaments by assuring or denying the presence of his
three stars. He made good deals, and his company
grew. There are now three dozen Tour players under
the standard I.M.G. contract, in which the company
receives ten percent of what a golfer earns in tournament play, while the player receives seventy-five
percent of what I.M.G. arranges for the player in
nontournament income. These include exhibitions,
corporate outings, and special pro-ams. I.M.G. manages many fine players, among them Andy Bean,
Bobby Clampett, Ben Crenshaw, Nick Faldo, Keith
Fergus, Raymond Floyd, David Graham, Hale Irwin,
Peter Jacobsen, Bernhard Langer, Bruce Lietzke,
Sandy Lyle, Johnny Miller, Greg Norman, Mark
O'Meara, Arnold Palmer, Jerry Pate, Corey Pavin,
Calvin Peete, Gary Player, and Hal Sutton. Having so
many good golfers in one stable lends I.M.G. a political golf leverage—some of which they use to get
their younger, experience-eager players into tournaments that might otherwise be shut to them. I.M.G.
got Steve Elkington, who had recently turned pro
after a distinguished amateur record at the University of Houston, into the Dutch Open.

Elkington, considered a bright prospect in golf,
became a professional in May 1985, signed with
I.M.G. in July, and was in the Dutch Open later that
month. For a young player, signing with I.M.G.—an
option available only to the most promising of players—is not unlike going to Harvard; I.M.G. opens
doors. Once they're opened, the golfer is on his own to
perform or to fail. Most perform; I.M.G. picks its

team with great care. Players who start with I.M.G. tend to stay with I.M.G.; the company is like a successful brokerage house—while making money for itself, it makes money for its clients.

Some do leave. Nicklaus left I.M.G. because he reached an indomitable position in the golf market-place where he could make more money managing himself, or so he believed. Maurice Bembridge left I.M.G. when his game deserted him; there came a point when I.M.G. could no longer arrange anything for Bembridge off the golf course, so Bembridge saw no point in giving the company ten percent of the little he made on it.

To combat the influence of I.M.G. and companies like it, the U.S. Tour made the use of appearance money illegal. But before golf became the highly regulated sport it is today, Mark McCormack invented a market, nurtured it, and became rich by it.

Steve Elkington, an Australian who speaks with a Houston accent from his four years there, was not rich, but he was not without advantage. He was beginning his life as a professional golfer with extreme confidence. As a junior golfer in Australia he broke dozens of junior golf records, most of which had been held by Bruce Devlin, David Graham, and Greg Norman. His early successes led to an invitation to play golf at the University of Houston, where collegiate life, for members of the golf team, approximates Tour life. His solid record at Houston, his classic swing, and his contact with Keith Fergus, an I.M.G. man who had also attended the University of Houston, helped secure for Elkington his I.M.G. contract. In the summer and fall of 1985, before Elkington went to the Tour Qualifying School, I.M.G. arranged spots for him to play in a dozen tournaments in Europe and the United States. (If Jamie Howell or Larry Rentz were I.M.G. men, they, too, might have

been playing in a dozen tournaments in the United
States and Europe; although a player's scores ultimately determine his success, connections do lead to
opportunities. The golf world, like the world at large,
is not wholly equitable.) Steve Elkington also had the
advantage of financial security. He was bankrolled
by some well-heeled Houston friends who set him up
with a checking account with $20,000 in it. The
money is a loan, and Steve has to pay it back. But the
terms are decidedly more favorable than the terms
you or I would get if we wanted to borrow $20,000 to
open, say, a delicatessen.

Steve Elkington and I met on the putting green of
the Noordwijk Golf Club. He had already been
through two local caddies when we met, and was
happy to find a caddie who spoke English. English
was my chief attribute.

Because the purses are much smaller in Europe
than they are in the United States, and the distances
between stops much greater, there is only a small
band of caddies that follows the European Tour.
Some of the caddies at the Dutch Open were Noordwijk boys as young as twelve years old. Too thin to
keep the heavy bags on their underdeveloped
shoulders, they wheeled the bags around the course
on trolleys. In the United States they are called pull
carts and it is impossible to imagine one being used
in a U.S. Tour event. The European Tour has an
informality to it that doesn't exist on the U.S. Tour.
The players in Europe are chummy with one another;
such chumminess is absent in the United States.
They also play in conditions American players would
not tolerate. At the Dutch Open the driving-range
balls had covers of syrlyn, not balata. And the driving range was too short to hit anything other than a
nine iron. The U.S. Tour would never pick a tournament site that didn't allow a player to hit drivers on

the practice tee. At Noordwijk a few players launched drivers into the grassy dunes beyond the driving range and off the golf course property. They were all American players.

Two distinct categories of American golfers play the European Tour. The first comprises young, talented players developing their competitive skills and gaining experience while waiting to try to qualify for the U.S. Tour. Corey Pavin played the European Tour briefly before he joined the U.S. Tour. Mac O'Grady played the European Tour for years until he finally qualified for the U.S. Tour. Rick Hartman is a young, promising American playing on the European Tour. When he's ready he'll try the U.S. Tour. So will Nathaniel Crosby, if his game progresses.

The other sort of American player in Europe goes there much the way an American baseball player goes to Japan: He has exhausted the opportunities to play his game professionally in his native land and has left to compete where he can. John Jacobs and Art Russell are expatriate golfers, as is, to a lesser extent, Bob Byman. But unlike baseball player Randy Bass, the American-born home-run king of Japan, these golfers are not stars in Europe.

Europe's golfing idols may be American, but its week-to-week drawing cards are all European. They are not strangers to American golf, and their names are not unfamiliar: Graham Marsh, Nick Faldo, Sam Torrance, Sandy Lyle, Christy O'Connor, Jr., Ian Woosnam, Manual Pinero, and Ian Baker-Finch all win European tournaments periodically. Consequently they get invitations to play in the United States (where most of them are represented by I.M.G.). They are, knowingly and for the most part contentedly, big fish in small ponds. They talk about the U.S. Tour with a certain awe.

Ballesteros and Langer are different. They are beyond week-to-week stardom. They have come West and won, and they are discussed by all of golfing Europe, and all the golfing world, with more than a little awe.

II

Bernhard Langer, 1985 Masters champion, shot 68-72 for 140 in the first two rounds of the Dutch Open. Steve Elkington shot 72-68, also for 140. We were four shots off the lead, and making a bid for the tournament. Our first thought Saturday morning was: What do we have to do to catch Graham Marsh? Our second thought was: What will it be like playing with Langer?

Bernhard Langer's approach to golf, especially tournament preparation, is so distinct one cannot help but take notice. He often plays practice rounds by himself. Using a surveyor's wheel, he gets his own yardages. It's not that he doesn't trust his caddie's figures; it's that he knows humans make errors. His purpose is to diminish human error as best he can. He practices putting for hours at a time, and in total silence. He putts three balls, nods to a point on the green to show his caddie where he wants the balls, and putts them again. Some go in, some lip, some miss the hole altogether. Langer's expression does not change.

Langer is not chatty, but when he does speak his words are well chosen and refreshingly candid, even when talking to the press. At the British Open he told a reporter, "I enjoy being a star." He never makes small talk, for he has no interest in anything small. His chief interest is in winning golf tournaments, preferably important ones. The son of a bricklayer, he finished school at age sixteen, and is thoroughly aristocratic in both manner and appearance. His high cheekbones, broad forehead, and unflappability seem more Kaiserlike than caddielike, although it

was as a caddie that he learned the game. He turned
pro at age fifteen; he caddied at the first tournament
he attended and competed in the second. He plays
golf with an intensity and a single-mindedness of
purpose that reminds older golf observers of young
Jack Nicklaus. Spectators love to follow him. At the
third round of the Dutch Open, there were many
more people following Langer up and down Noordwijk's sandy hills than Marsh, the tournament's
leader. By circumstance, they followed Steve Elkington, too. And that combination—a partisan gallery of
2,000 and playing with Langer, let alone being in
contention for the tournament—was unsettling for
us. It was also thrilling and fun.

We tried to alleviate the pressure. We imitated the
austere style of the starter, who called players to the
first tee by simply announcing their tee time and last
name through cupped hands. We took to calling
Langer "Bernie." We dismissed every player in the
field from contention: Bernie was too depressed by
his weak finish at the British Open; Curtis was not
into it; Graham was threatened by his younger countryman. Elkington's first three shots in that third
round were perfect: Our birdie on the first hole put
us at five under for the tournament, three shots
behind Marsh, one shot ahead of Langer, and three
shots ahead of Strange. We felt momentum and we
felt pressure—and suddenly realized that those
abused words really do have their moment of truth.
We also became aware of our place. The Dutch Open
is not the U.S. Open, or the British Open, or even the
Buick Open, but it *is* a nation's premiere tournament.
Standing on the second tee, on which we had honors,
it felt as if the eyes of every person in the country
were set on us. National television certainly was.
There, on the second tee, trouble began. Steve Elkington's shots, which had sailed arrow-straight all
week, began veering left and right, and on two

occasions stayed in bounds only because they were deflected off Langer's large gallery. After the birdie, our start with Langer was rocky, but I was certain we would settle down. In the first round, perhaps too excited—the state of "too excited" is the blessing and the curse of the too-green pro—Steve opened with a shaky start and made three bogeys on the front side. But he made three birdies on the back side and finished the day at even par. Saturday that never happened. Steve made three bogeys on the front side again, and two more on the back, and finished the day with a fat 76. Langer shot a 72 in a round during which he did not make a putt longer than three feet.

But what extraordinary shots Langer hit! Playing on downwind holes he hit high shots that seemed to ride on a cushion of air. The ball flew remarkably long distances. Playing into the wind he hit low, piercing shots that bore through the air by virtue of their pure velocity. Playing into a right-to-left wind he hit big draws that started well out over the right rough, took the wind for all it could, and finished up on the left side of the fairway. He played the opposite shot in left-to-right winds, where he'd play a fade. No putts fell for Langer on this day—the slow greens were probably difficult for him to get accustomed to—but what a brilliant display of shot making he gave, what mastery of his clubs he demonstrated.

"Tell you what," Steve Elkington said as we doubled up on my rented moped to take a ride to downtown Noordwijk, "ole Bernie can play."

"Think you learned something today?" I asked.

"I know I did," said Steve.

On Sunday Steve got another lesson, this one not from a fellow golfer but from a European Tour official. Through fourteen holes it was clear that we weren't going to win: That battle was being fought by Langer, who had started the day at four under, and Graham Marsh, who had begun the day at minus six.

Curtis Strange had begun the day at one under. He wasn't in the hunt, but he wasn't far off it either. And, at even par, neither were we, until number fifteen.

The fifteenth, a severe dogleg to the right, was a hole very much in the tradition of the Noordwijk Golf Club course: It encouraged courageousness. American professionals usually grumble when they come across such a hole, but in Europe such holes are common. From an elevated tee the player sees 150 yards of fairway, which then begins curving right. To the right of the hole there is a sweeping field of heather and beach grass. If a player is willing to play a big draw over the field and curve the ball back into the fairway he'll have a nine iron or a pitching wedge shot into the green. Using the shape and slope of the hole and the prevailing breeze to his advantage, the daring player can cut the hole's length by one-third. If a player chooses to fade the ball off the tee, a safer shot, he'll be fading it into the wind and up a hill. That will leave him a five or six iron into the green, which is small and well bunkered.

Steve's natural shot is a draw (although he is a skilled enough player so that he can play a fade at will). He is not an especially daring player—he has an unfortunate tendency to leave his birdie putts short— so I was not surprised when he decided to play his natural shot, the draw, over the heather, but not *too* far over. By not going far enough right, each of our tee shots from the first three rounds finished in a gully on the far left side of the fairway. But on Sunday, Elkington hit a perfect tee shot. The shot began 100 yards right of the fairway and finished on a lovely piece of closely-cropped terra firma in the middle of the fairway. It was a long, long drive; Steve used his draw, the wind, and the slope ideally. We had only seventy-five yards to the hole. The shot required a sand wedge, and the one he carried was a new, custom-made one that had been failing him all week. With each poor shot his insecurity with the club grew. Hitting a pull-hook seldom happens with a sand wedge, but that's what Steve did with that second shot at number fifteen. It hit the side of a hill on the left side of a greenside bunker and kicked violently to the left. The ball finished on a work road covered with pebbles.

Although I didn't know it for sure, I had a hunch a rules official was lurking about somewhere in our vicinity around this time. I had seen one standing on his electric cart watching Steve with more than a little disgust when Steve threw his five iron twenty feet in the air after hitting a poor shot on fourteen. Because Steve got into the tournament due to I.M.G.'s clout, and because he has his whole golfing life ahead of him, and it is a promising one, there was more than a little resentment of him by certain players and certain officials. Any action Steve took that was modestly inappropriate—and throwing a club in anger is inappropriate by any standard—would be duly noted, and then some.

Steve walked over to his ball on the pebble road at fifteen and asked his playing partner, a Spaniard named Manuel Calero, if the ball's position on the road granted him a free drop.

"I think so," Calero said, "but you better ask the . . ."

Steve Elkington heard all he needed to after Calero's first three words. He went over to his ball and picked it up, marking the spot with a tee, in accordance with free-lift procedure. He then began to search for a place to take his drop. Calero looked about uneasily. In a moment we knew why.

"Taken an unplayable lie, have you?" came a booming English voice through the Dutch gallery. The voice belonged to a rules official, the same one who had glowered at Steve when he had thrown his club a hole earlier.

"I've taken a free lift off a paved road," said Steve.

"No, you haven't," said the official.

"Huh?"

"You've taken an unplayable lie," the official said. "You will now be playing your fourth shot," he said in a judicial tone.

Steve, badly shaken from this, his first brush with officialdom as a professional, rimmed in a one-foot putt for a double bogey. We finished the tournament at two over par and in a tie for eleventh place, eight behind the winner, Graham Marsh, seven behind Langer, and one behind Strange. Steve made £2,025 ($2,500 or 7,500 Dutch guilders), but he also learned something of the frustrations of professional tournament golf. After thirty-seven holes Steve was five under, which was Langer's score after seventy-two holes. If only Steve could have held that! Being unnerved by Langer's presence Saturday, and acting rashly on Sunday, had cost him. The 1985 Dutch Open was Steve Elkington's best professional finish in a career two months old, but he was more frustrated than pleased. Most professionals recognize frustration as inherent in the nature of the game. Steve Elkington was learning that lesson quickly.

14
PLAYING WITH THE BIG BOYS

I

THE PROFESSIONAL GOLFERS' ASSOCIATION Championship, which is the fourth of the majors played annually, is the most important tournament of the year for fifty or so of the best playing club professionals in the United States. For the club professional, the P.G.A. Championship is a chance to play with the big boys, the touring pros.

From 1916, when the tournament began, to 1957, the P.G.A. Championship was conducted as a match play event, which is a more forgiving game than medal. Since it allows for the occasional botched hole, the less consistent player has a better chance for victory in match play than he would in medal play. Moreover, match play, in which each hole is a separate match, is more subject to the vagaries of a particular day than medal play. Such vagaries include a hot putter in the hands of the underdog or a hangover in the hands of the favorite. The match play

219

format gave a better chance to the club pro in the P.G.A. Championship; since 1958, and the change to medal play, making the cut has been the chief goal of most club pros playing in the P.G.A.

In the past fifteen years the Professional Golfers' Association has made efforts to improve the stature of its tournament—it is clearly a major but just as clearly not the highest ranked of them. They have done this principally by choosing U.S. Open sites for their championships; they have done this eleven times since 1970. In 1985 the P.G.A. was held at one of the finest of the U.S. Open venues, the Cherry Hills Country Club, outside Denver. Cherry Hills is an ingenious course: It compensates for what it lacks in length—in the thin air of Colorado no course plays especially long—by placing strenuous demands on finesse and strategy. A golfer must play for position to succeed at Cherry Hills, and he must be able to putt well on exceptionally fast greens. The importance of length is diminished, and too much length is a hindrance.

At the P.G.A. I worked for Kevin Morris, a New Yorker who is the head pro at the Westchester Hills Country Club. Kevin is a short hitter, but a straight one, a fine putter, and, by club pro standards, a good prospect for the P.G.A.

Kevin Morris played on an exceptionally talented University of Florida golf team, one with Andy Bean, Andy North, Woody Blackburn, Phil Hancock, and Gary Koch. These golfers are all making good livings on the Tour, but Morris demonstrates that the Tour is not the only place where a professional golfer can make a substantial livelihood. His combined income for 1984—his salary, the percentage he makes from the pro shop, the amount he earns giving lessons, and what he wins in small tournaments in New York, Connecticut, and New Jersey—would total to the equivalent of a secure position on the 1984 Tour earnings list, without spending the average $40,000 the Tour player spends annually on expenses.

"I couldn't afford to try the Tour now," Kevin said on the practice tee one day while we hit balls next to Jim Albus, Billy Britton's first teacher, who had arranged for me to work for Morris. "My setup is too good."

Morris, the model of consistency in the practice rounds, broke radically from style once the tournament began. He made a bogey on the easiest hole on the golf course, the first. It is a 390-yard downhill par four that Arnold Palmer drove in the last round of the 1960 U.S. Open. And then on the fourteenth, the most difficult hole on the golf course, he made a birdie. That hole is a 496-yard par four with a narrow fairway, an out-of-bounds to the right, and a creek on the left. There he hit for his second shot a 250-yard three-wood shot to two feet. He made his par on the 423-yard, par-four sixteenth hole by driving it short and into the trees, chipping out, and, from 150 yards, knocking an eight iron to eighteen inches.

Andy Martinez, who caddied for Johnny Miller when Miller won seventeen tournaments in six years and who now works for Gary Hallberg, took Kevin in the caddie High Pool. This worried me, for Martinez has a reputation as a shrewd bettor in the High Pool. But after the first round, when Morris finished with a respectable one over par for the day, placing us in the middle of the field, I knew not only that Martinez was well off the mark, but that we had a chance to make the cut. Kevin had played in four other P.G.A. Championships and one U.S. Open and had never made a cut in any of them. He now had a chance to make his first cut in a major, and so did I.

He certainly had a much better chance than his two playing partners, a Tennessean named Gary Head and a Vermonter named Brien Charter. They were both well represented in the High Pool. Gary Head especially. Last names such as *Head*, or *Ozaki*, or *Funk* are always abundant in the High Pool; caddies love the unusual. Freddy Funk was the most popular choice at the U.S. Open. He fooled everybody by making the cut and finishing only seven shots behind the winner.

II

During the week of the P.G.A. Championship, the University of Denver, where I had taken a dormitory room for five dollars a night, was sponsoring two conventions. One was a program for young actors, a workshop in confidence and assertiveness training. The other meeting was a convention of the Colorado Bagpipers Society. Identifying who belonged to which group was simple. The confident and assertive people would not ride an elevator with a stranger without trying to make conversation. The bagpipers were even easier to identify. They wore kilts around their lower bodies and bagpipes around their upper.

The two groups served to remind me of a vow I had made while in St. Andrews, Scotland, after the Dutch Open. The vow came about after a conversation with Michael F. Bonallack, secretary of the Royal and Ancient Golf Club. I told him I was an American caddie interested in learning about the Scottish tradition of the profession. He showed me into his office, which is in the famous and imposing structure behind the first tee at the Old Course. His office resembled a drawing room, with big chairs, bookshelves, and vast windows which looked out to the course, the town, and the sea. On the shelves were old volumes chronicling the greatness of the Tom Morrises, young and old.

I sat down in a worn leather chair. Mr. Bonallack poured me a room-warm gin and tonic and summed up the difference between Scottish and American caddies.

"There are caddies here," he said, "whom you wouldn't dare ask for a yardage. They consider it their duty to tell a player what club to use, and how to use it."

M. F. Bonallack was speaking of a distinct breed of Scottish caddie—old men, generally, who wear tweed coats through the summer and who have sharp teeth and shiny noses, and who take you around the links not only as your caddie, but as your teaching pro, tour guide, and wet nurse, too.

My St. Andrews vow was this: Upon returning to the United States I promise to be a confident and assertive caddie, in accordance with the situation, in as close to the Scottish tradition as is appropriate for a North American caddie.

Good caddies from any country have one quality in common: They imbue their players with confidence. The caddie must do this with a different approach for each golfer, which is why basic studies in psychology are helpful in the caddying profession. The more secure the player, the more subtle the caddie must be. But if the caddie's work is done properly, and this refers to what Brad Faxon calls the intangibles, not the basics, the caddie truly helps. A caddie's heartfelt, "Knock it in," preferably in a deep voice and slowly spoken, can actually help a player make a putt. A player genuinely caught between a hard six and a smooth five might really need to hear his caddie say, "I *know* the good six will get us there."

Kevin Morris was the first subject on which I could try my caddie vow.

Among the fourteen clubs in his undersized Ram bag, Kevin carried a one iron and a three iron, but not a two. This presented a problem for us in the first round at number fifteen, a clever par three of 220 yards whose green is nestled in among four bunkers, two in front and two more on the left. The green is not deep, only twenty-eight yards, but does slope up and away from the tee and is reasonably receptive to the well-hit shot. We needed a two iron shot, and we didn't have a two iron. A problem. Kevin wanted to hit a hard three; I didn't think that was enough to get us to the green's front edge, let alone up to the hole. Coming up short meant playing out of a bunker, and that was not a Kevin Morris specialty. On the other hand, the one iron, a club Kevin hit with unpredictable length, *was* too much. We needed to determine the lesser of the evils. My choice was the one. Played from the rear of the tee box, choked up slightly, with the tee half an inch higher than normal, the one felt right to me. Even if we ran over the green, chances were with us that we would have a reasonable lie. And Kevin was a good chipper.

"I like the one," I said.

"I think I can get there with a three," Kevin said.

I remembered my vow.

"Wind's pretty swirly," I said.

"Yeah."

"I'd rather see us hit a one," I said again.

"You're sure?"

"I'm sure," I said. And I was.

Kevin hit the one iron, and we were both happy he did. It was the right club.

The obvious problem with being a confident, assertive caddie is that sometimes you will be wrong. And then neither you nor your player will be happy. You, the caddie, will be in the doghouse.

The ninth hole at Cherry Hill is a 440-yard par four. It is a skinny hole that climbs uphill for 250 yards, levels off, and slopes down for the last third of the hole. The hole's rough is death, as the players say, which we discovered after our tee shot in the second round. After punching out of the rough with a six

iron, we were left with ninety downhill yards to a
green harder than the typical outdoor basketball
court. Kevin wanted to hit a three-quarter pitching
wedge. I thought the sand wedge, which imparts
more spin on the ball, was the better choice.

"You're sure?" asked Kevin.

"I'm sure," I said. And I pretty much was.

Kevin hit the sand wedge, and we were both
unhappy he did. The ball didn't reach the green.

"I should have hit the pitching wedge; I wanted to
hit the pitching wedge," Kevin said en route to the
tenth tee after making a double bogey at nine. I was
in the double bogey doghouse. "Why didn't I hit the
pitching wedge?"

My caddie boondoggle was bad enough, but the
worse fear now was that Kevin's black mood, for
which I was responsible, would carry into the back
nine. We were on the verge of making the cut and
urgently needed to change the momentum.

"I blew it, and I'm sorry," I said.

"You sure did," said Kevin. And with that, the air
was cleared and the proper frame of mind restored. I
gave a good read on the twelfth green that went a
long way in the caddie redemption department. So
did a good read at thirteen, and good club advice at
fifteen.

Standing on the eighteenth tee, a par four of 485
yards (that sounds longer than it is; in the Denver air
the ball carries at least ten percent farther), with
water down the left and out of bounds down the right,
we knew we needed only a six to make the cut.

"Think we should play this thing for a five?" Kevin
asked. The suggestion was not a bad one: It is a hole
one could play safely for a five by hitting a cautious
three wood or a one iron off the tee.

"Hell, no," I said without hesitation.

Kevin rose to the occasion. He smoked a drive down
the middle, knocked a five iron to twenty feet, lipped

out his birdie putt, and tapped in for a par. We made the cut by two shots. Only three club pros of the four dozen who started the tournament qualified for the weekend play, and Kevin P. Morris, head pro at the Westchester Hills Country Club, was among them.

The weekend was anticlimactic.

Kevin was clearly a better golfer than the club pros with whom he played Thursday and Friday, and this lent him an assured manner that was reflected in his play. That manner eroded on the weekend playing with the touring pros. On Saturday we played with David Ogrin and Ron Streck, and on Sunday with Bob Murphy and Mark McNulty. They didn't appear to be better players, but they were. Their differences in skill became discernible on shots from 100 yards and in. Streck, Ogrin, Murphy, and McNulty played bunker shots and pitches out of heavy rough that were ordinary by Tour standards but brilliant to the uninitiated. "Oh, great shot," Kevin said to some of these shots, sounding almost as if he were a member of the gallery. Kevin Morris, having made his first cut in a major, was not unlike the good summer stock actor on a first trip to Broadway, the lights of which may be shining and intimidating even if they ought not to be. Kevin Morris is a good player (and a very nice guy), but he is not a Tour player. The difference between the good player and the Tour player is a world made of ten percent skill and ninety percent attitude. Kevin marveled at the games of his playing partners to the point where they were no longer partners at all, to where he no longer belonged in their class.

III

Our poor play Saturday put us in the first three-some of the day for Sunday's round. There were two players with worse scores for fifty-four holes—Mike

Donald and Al Geiberger—and they went off as a twosome ahead of us.

Three significant things had happened to the Geiberger family since I had last seen Al in early June. His daughter, Lee Ann, was graduated from Stanford. Al had won the Colorado Open, with his son John caddying for him. And he and Carolyn Allin, divorced wife of former touring pro Buddy Allin (who is a friend of Al's), had married.

"I told you in Westchester that marriage was under consideration," Al said as we—Al, Carolyn, Bryan (Al's eight-year-old son from his second marriage), and I—drove from Denver to Vail after the P.G.A. Championship. We were headed to the Ninth Annual Jerry Ford Invitational. On the Tour, Al represents the Beaver Creek Resort, which is Vail's backyard and where Jerry Ford has a home. Al plays each year in the Ford tournament. It is limited to fifty professionals.

"Well, it was considered," said Al. "Meet Carolyn Geiberger."

Al pulled the rented car into a Taco Bell for dinner. Carolyn Geiberger urged Bryan Geiberger to try to eat more of his enchilada. And he did. Al was impressed.

"I've been trying to get him to eat more for years," said Al.

Carolyn Geiberger smiled and Bryan Geiberger burped.

"He likes to call this place 'Taco Belch,' " Carolyn explained. Then Bryan Geiberger, pleased with himself, smiled.

The next day it became evident why Al Geiberger invited me along on what was the closest thing he and Carolyn would have to a wedding trip. Bryan Geiberger needed a hunting companion.

Al explained this to me in great detail before he and Carolyn went off to a tournament dinner with

Jerry Ford, Bob Hope, Jack Nicklaus, and the many other representatives of the Vail–California golf crowd.

"Golf ball hunting is one of our favorite activities at Beaver Creek," Al said as Bryan, he, and I descended into the woods and streams of the Beaver Creek golf course wearing long pants and long sleeves and carrying long irons. (They were Spalding Top-Flites.) We also had the kangaroo-skin top to Al's golf bag, for storing the goods.

"Now Bryan has certain secret spots that always produce many balls. But don't worry, you're going to find your own spots, I'm sure. You'll be amazed at how well you can do here. People say they find more golf balls while hunting here than anywhere else. You won't believe how many balls you'll find. And all sorts of colors. Orange, yellow, even an occasional pink. And most of them are brand new!"

While Carolyn and Al were having dinner with Jerry Ford, Bryan and I found eight dozen golf balls hunting in the Colorado dusk. They were under rocks, in the streams, in the high grass, imbedded in the mud. They were everywhere. Bryan was very happy. He stayed up well past his bedtime sorting the balls by color, brand, and quality.

When Al's partners—Dick Herman, who was twice manager of the Republican National Convention; Joe Kern, a Dallas wallcoverings manufacturer ("Wallpaper is the least of it"); and Alfred Swanson, a Michigan hand surgeon—met at the beginning of the Jerry Ford Invitational at the Vail Golf Club, they made the usual get-acquainted conversational stabs.

DICK HERMAN: Nippy morning, isn't it?

ALFRED SWANSON: We're used to this in Michigan. For hunting, though, not for golf.

JOE KERN: Goddamn it, it is cold. When we left Dallas yesterday it was damn near 100.

"There are no types, no plurals," wrote F. Scott
Fitzgerald in a story called " The Rich Boy," and to
reduce these three men to types would be, ultimately,
to make a mockery of them. The too-easy temptation
is to say one was affable, one nervous, and one
competitive. Yet, if you peer in on pro-ams anywhere
in America and examine the conversations and golf
games of the amateurs for a short while, you may
find these three species. Identification is easiest in
the moment after the poorly played important shot.
For instance, when a group is counting on one player
to make a five-foot putt for birdie to bring the group
within the respectable range of, say, twenty under
par. The putt misses.

"Oh, well, it's only a game," says the affable one,
slapping partners on their backs.

"Sorry, fellas, sorry, I don't know where my putting stroke is today. I might as well be putting with a
hockey stick. I feel so bad," says the nervous one,
blabbering on until he realizes that he is the only
person left on the green and that he is talking to
himself.

The aggressive one says nothing at all. He just
emits some sort of guttural, primitive sound and
makes the first motion toward snapping his putter in
two, until he sees the pro watching him.

But along the way friendships develop in these pro-
am groups—friendships, I suspect, that are not unlike friendships that begin in combat. The individual
is revealed for exactly what he is, for these are stress-
filled circumstances. They play, if you can call it that,
in a vulnerable light; the individual is stripped of all
his defenses. But it is also an understanding and
truthful light. Near the end of the pro-am the "affable" one will, after missing yet another five-foot putt,
say, "How'd that thing stay out of the hole? Damn, I
thought I hit a perfect putt." And the "competitive"
sort will allow his primitive growl to come out as a

quite distinct four-letter expletive, after which he will say, "Sorry, fellas; I guess I take these things a little too seriously." And the "nervous" man will say, "Well, you didn't actually expect that I was going to make that putt, did you?" And by the time they hole out on the eighteenth, the group's pro is " 'bout the nicest guy" they have ever met, and business cards have been exchanged every way, and the caddie has been tipped generously, and *he's* " 'bout the best damned caddie" they have ever seen. Everyone's feeling good; vows are made to stay in touch; deep bonds have been formed and Fitzgerald has been proven correct: There are no types. And that's exactly what happened with Dick Herman, Joe Kern, Al Swanson, Al Geiberger, and his caddie at the Ninth Annual Jerry Ford Invitational in Vail, Colorado, in August 1985.

15
THE GREEN
ROAD HOME

I

GOLF IN THE UNITED STATES began on the eastern seaboard, and the golf associations on the East Coast, including the United States Golf Association, revel, quietly, in their sense of history and their manner of conduct. For instance, no rules official at an important tournament on the East Coast would officiate without wearing a necktie. Neckwear and shirts buttoned to their tops are perhaps uncomfortable on days when temperatures and humidity readings well exceed decent golf scores, but respect for tradition is the operative force here. These are the quarters in which one hears long, serious conversations about preserving the integrity of the game.

In this world having a tournament title is not unlike having a royally bestowed title in a European aristocratic life. Money is secondary to title. Some say this preoccupation with title, with having one's name engraved on a cup or a plaque, is how the old golf associations justify the small purses of their tournaments. To me, this view is as naïve as it is cynical. It underestimates what golf is in these certain quarters, here in the Old East. It is life.

In other words, the Metropolitan Open, the open tournament of the Metropolitan (New York) Golf Association, is not the Panasonic–Las Vegas Invitational, nor would it want to be. Although limited to golfers from New York, New Jersey, and Connecticut, and possessing a meager $35,000 purse, the tournament has stature. It has been dominated, particularly in the first half of the century, by formidable players. The tournament's trophy looks like the British Open vase, and the names engraved on it go back to 1905, when Alex Smith won the first Met Open, the year before he won the U.S. Open. The second Met Open was won by George Low, who finished second in the U.S. Open of 1899. Walter Hagen won the Met Open in 1916, 1919, and 1920. Gene Sarazen won it in 1925 and Tommy Armour in 1928. Byron Nelson won it in 1936. Sam Snead was the runner-up in 1938 and Ben Hogan was the runner-up in 1940. Claude Harmon won it in 1951, Doug Ford in 1956, Jim Turnesa in 1959, and Miller Barber in 1962. And Billy Britton won it in 1979, the year he became a professional.

I had come east from Colorado to caddie for Billy in the Met Open.

Billy had not played well on the Tour since I had last worked for him six weeks earlier at the Canadian Open—he missed four cuts—but his spirits were not down. He shot 142 to miss the cut at the Greater Hartford Open and 144 to miss the cut at the Buick Open, both by a shot. But regardless of what he did on the road, he was home now and as much as anybody a pretournament favorite. Our week began with all the early-week hope I had come to know and love. Early-week is when a caddie considers every word his golfer says, and always in a hopeful light.

"I can feel my game coming around a bit," Billy said after we finished a practice round. "I know I'm playing better than I did in New Orleans, or at the Kemper. That was disgraceful. Seventy-one, 72, 73—those are at least not *bad* scores.

"I'm afraid my problem now is as much psychological as anything else. I've got to convince myself that 72 is not an all right score. I'm getting to the point that if I don't make a birdie where I should, I say, 'That's OK—par's a decent score on this hole.' You can't get ahead with that kind of attitude. You're not going to shoot 69 or 68 or 67 if you're satisfied making pars. You're not even going to make cuts that way.

"The big part of the season may be over, but the year's not over by any means. There are still a lot of golf tournaments left. And the way the purses are now, you can get hot in three or four tournaments and make a whole season worthwhile very quickly.

"This tournament means a lot to me because I know this is one where I can and should be in the hunt. It's been a long while since I've been in that position. I want to feel that again: being in the thick of a tournament. To me, that's what it's all about."

The Metropolitan Golf Association conducts its Open championship in much the way the United States Golf Association conducts its Open championship. It begins by choosing courses that are historically rich and architecturally classical, where the roughs can be grown high and the greens mowed short. At a U.S. Open even par for the tournament always proves to be a good score—often it will be a winning score—and this standard holds up for the Met Open as well.

So when Billy made a birdie on the forty-fifth hole of the fifty-four-hole tournament to go even par, I wasn't too surprised that that score put us in a tie for the lead for the tournament. But I was thrilled. So was Billy's father.

"See my father when I made that putt?" Billy asked

as we walked to the tenth tee. "Nearly got a smile out of him."

The birdie tied us with our playing partner, George J. Zahringer III. That much Billy knew. But he did not know that the birdie tied us for the lead for the tournament. The players in the twosome behind us had held a four- and a two-stroke lead when the day began, but they had squandered their leads quickly. (Sudden swings on the leader board is one of the indicators that a purportedly stern test of golf is, in fact, stern. The Met Open site for 1985, the Mountain Ridge Golf Club, in West Caldwell, New Jersey, *is* a stern test of golf.)

George Zahringer, of Manhattan, a stockbroker and, by the looks of him, a successful one, is an amateur of a dying breed. He is a good player and has a distinguished amateur record. Possibly he's good enough to play the game successfully as a professional. But he would not try, for to do so and fail would degrade him and the game. And he has enormous respect for the game. Golf *is* a game for George Zahringer, although it may not seem like one; it's just a serious one.

For George Zahringer, amateur golfer, winning the Met Open would be his greatest moment; he wanted the title with good competitive thirst. For Billy Britton, winning the 1979 Met Open *is* his greatest title, but not his greatest moment in golf. That came in the last tournament of the 1982 season, when he shot a 64 in the last round of the Walt Disney World Classic, with his parents in the gallery, to tie for the lead for the tournament after seventy-two holes. In the end, Hal Sutton beat him with a birdie in the play-off for the title. It was Sutton's first victory. Nevertheless, the second-place finish was a great moment for Billy. Three years later it was diminished, for a moment—inadvertently—by George Zahringer.

"I was talking the other day about putting with a friend of mine who plays on the Tour—maybe you know him—Hal Sutton?" George said to Billy on the putting green before the tournament.

"I know Hal," is all Billy said, but I imagine he was thinking more. Could Billy hear Hal Sutton's name without thinking, consciously or subconsciously, about the 1982 Walt Disney? Could it not churn his heart the way hearing the name of an old flame mentioned casually in conversation does? I suspect not. Moreover, Billy could not be aloof in George's manner. Billy's world has developed certain qualities in him, but aloofness is not among them.

There are borders to Billy Britton's world, to the things he knows most thoroughly—golf and Staten Island—just as there are for all of us. And although he loves them, the two alone cannot satisfy him. Staten Island, especially Billy's middle-class, Catholic, golf-loving Staten Island, is comfortable, but limiting, too. Billy's first big adventure on the mainland came when he won the Met Amateur in 1975. At age nineteen he was the youngest ever to do it. He was also the first golfer without an affiliation with a private club to win the tournament, a fact duly recorded in every newspaper that covered the tournament. The outside world was commenting on something Billy had never considered: his privilege, or lack thereof. Billy was successful despite his lack of privilege, he was told. When you're nineteen, and you love whacking the ball and rolling it into the hole, this lesson is more amusing than anything else. But, given further thought, it might make you curious about the way the world is beyond your world. Four years later, when Billy became a professional, his first order of business was to play the Australian Tour for half a year, even though the U.S. Tour was available to him. Billy wanted to explore other islands.

We were tied for the lead, but Zahringer was playing better golf. He was in a position to make Metropolitan Golf Association history by becoming the first golfer to win the Met Amateur and the Met Open in the same year. Although his putts were not dropping, he was playing outstanding golf. He was playing for keeps.

On the tenth hole of the final round, Zahringer made a birdie while Billy made a par, and Zahringer went up by a stroke. He remained a stroke ahead of Billy through fifteen holes. As we walked off the fifteenth green I asked Billy's brother, Bobby, with Billy out of earshot, what was happening in the twosome behind us.

"George has got the lead by himself. Billy's tied for second with one of the guys from the last group," Bobby said. "But don't tell Billy," Bobby, a past winner of the Staten Island Amateur Championship, said. "He'd rather not know."

Billy knew he was only a stroke behind George but not that he was a stroke off the lead for the tournament.

On the sixteenth tee, a tricky par three of 160 yards, Billy surprised his brother: He asked me if I knew the overall standing in the tournament. It was a departure from his own strategy.

"George has got the lead," I said.

"So we're only a stroke off this thing?" Billy asked.

"That's right," I said. Billy nodded and looked down the hole.

George, with honors, played first. He hit a brilliant shot to ten feet, and the gallery howled, in its genteel way.

"Terrific golf shot, George."

"That's a beauty."

"What a lovely shot, George."

"Well done."

"No mere shot, George. That was art!"

The shot was greeted with a certain frenzy. George Zahringer, sufficiently impressed with himself

and not unjustifiably—it was an outstanding shot by
any standard—was deeply settled into his own world.
He did not acknowledge (he may not have even heard)
any of the hoopla surrounding the shot. But a look of
deep satisfaction came over his face.

Billy had a difficult time selecting a club, and
when he did, finally, he took a constrained swing at
it. The shot hit the embankment that separated the
green from a bunker on the right, and the ball settled
into the bunker. Billy make a bogey and George
made a birdie and suddenly George's lead over us
was three shots. On number seventeen, a par five,
Billy made another bogey, and the difference was
four shots. And then on number eighteen, Billy drove
his tee shot out of bounds and made a double bogey.
Zahringer made another birdie and the difference,
finally, was seven shots. We began and finished the
tournament with double bogeys, and in the end there
were many strokes and many people between us and
George Zahringer, the Metropolitan Golf Association's history-making winner.

Billy, of course, was greatly disappointed. I tried to
say something coachlike about how he had played
forty-five good holes of golf, and how his good ball
striking was a positive omen for next week when the
Tour would be in Endicott, New York, for the B.C.
Open. Jim Albus, Billy's father, and Billy's brother
tried a similar kind of coaching. Several officials
walked by Billy and congratulated him on a well-
played tournament. It must have been obvious to
them that Billy was down. There was no apparent
reason for Billy's game to fall apart when he most
needed it. But then the game of golf doesn't make
much apparent.

Billy went into the locker room to change into his
street shoes, and Bobby Britton and I stood around
his brother's golf bag.

"Well," Bobby said, breaking a silence that one
normally associates with funerals. "At least he had a
chance at it."

II

I went home, got a car, and made the drive upstate to Endicott, for the B.C. Open. I knew this would be my last tournament. For then, at least. When I began I said I would caddie for six months or until my money ran out, whichever came first. They came the same week: The Honda Classic and the B.C. Open were separated by half a year; I began with $5,000 in a special caddie checking account I had opened, and it was now down to $397.65. And I owed $161.50 to Blue Cross/Blue Shield; a Tour caddie receives no health benefits.

Players and caddies face, essentially, the same expenses—travel and food and lodging—the costs of living on the road. The chief difference is that caddies face these expenses with a far greater sense of economy, an economy imposed by necessity. A player will spend anywhere between $30,000 and $90,000 playing the Tour for a year. I spent $12,000 in my education as a Tour caddie, about what a year at an elite private college costs. In addition to the $5,000 in the caddie account, I spent the $2,000 I earned doing assignments for *Golf Digest* and the $5,250 I earned in my various jobs on the road. I worked a total of twenty-two tournaments. I caddied for Billy Britton in seven of them; Al Geiberger in four; Larry Rentz in two; Jamie Howell in two; and Brad Faxon, George Archer, Steve Elkington, and Kevin Morris in one each. I worked for one amateur, Lee Roy Pearson III. I worked for CBS one week, and I drove a van for one week. The most I made in a single week was $450 working for Larry Rentz at the Tallahassee Open, the only week I covered my expenses with a week's salary. The least I made in a week came working for CBS as a spotter, which was $135.

Where did the money go? To rented cars, motels, hotels, food, flights, drinks, books, horse betting, and the occasional souvenir hat. I am not frugal by nature, but for those six months I was downright cheap. A bargain shopper. I found a round-trip airfare to England for $400. I rented cars for as little as sixty-nine dollars a week, some so shabby I wondered if the brakes were extra. I ate more dinners than I care to remember at Dairy Queens and Burger Kings and many less royal establishments. I watched my money dwindle away. At the Westchester Classic each caddie is required to put down a ten dollar deposit for his caddie bib. At the end of the tournament I forgot to return the bib and I forgot to collect my ten dollars and this fact bothers me still.

Once in Endicott, a small shoe-factory town in New York's rural southern tier, north of Pennsylvania, I settled in at Boughton's Rooms for Tourists, where I got a bed and a shared bath for five dollars a night. Stella M. Boughton, the proprietress, had not raised her prices since World War II. She used the same engraved business cards she had inherited from her mother:

Free Parking   **Bath**

BOUGHTON'S
ROOMS FOR TOURISTS
**Half-way Between New York and Buffalo
on Route 17c**

                             2304 E. Main St.
Phone: ST 5-1842   **Endicott, N.Y.**

"In the old days we used to get quite a few of the traveling salesmen," said Miss Boughton, who was in her eighties. "Shoe people from all over comin' to look at E.-J. [Endicott–Johnson]. Now we don't get so

many of the transients like we used to. I've got two
men up there now, and they've been there a while.
The one man, he's got the attic apartment, he's an
I.B.M. man of some sort. Not sure just what he does,
but he's got his family back in Pennsylvania and goes
there every weekend and is on some kind of three-
month project here. I don't know too much about this
computer business stuff, but he's friendly enough.
The other fellow, well, he's 'bout your age. Haven't
the foggiest idea just what he does. One of these quiet
sorts, you know the type. Doesn't say peep. He's out of
the house each morning by 6:30, comes back 'round
seven at night. I'd love to know just what he does all
day. 'Course I'd never ask. Pays right up, though, can
say that for him.

"Now you're here with the golf tournament? You're
a golfer then?" Miss Boughton asked.

"Well, no, I'm a caddie," I said. In the course of my
time on the Tour I had become accustomed to the
disappointment caused by that answer.

"So then you don't actually play," Miss Boughton
said. "Well, that's too bad. Playin' it always seemed to
me to be the best part. 'Course, I don't know much
about golf. Maybe it's the caddying that's best. I
follow the tournament in the paper, and I watch it on
the TV, but I can't say I understand too much of it.

"Now I guess you get to do a pretty goodly amount
of traveling with this job of yours. I see all the places
they play these things on the TV."

"There's a lot of traveling," I said.

"Ever been to California?" Miss Boughton asked.

"Well, no, I haven't," I said.

"I been there," Miss Boughton said. "Nice place.

"Ever been to Arizona?"

"Never been there," I said.

"I have," Miss Boughton said. "Nice place.

"Ever been to Hawaii? I know they got one of those
tournaments in Hawaii, 'cause I watch that one on
the TV every year."

"No, haven't been there, either," I said.

"I like Hawaii. Nice place. I been to all fifty states.
I was in Alaska last year. Me and my girlfriend went,
'cause she likes to travel, too. Alaska was the only one
not on my list. But now I've been to all fifty of 'em.
Ever been to Alaska?"

"No, I haven't," I said.

Miss Boughton gave me a quizzical look. "Thought
you said you did a lot of traveling with that job of
yours."

By some standards—although not Stella Boughton's—I had. My six months on the Tour had brought
me to fifteen different states and three foreign coun-
tries. After spending my first two and a half years
after college on a 100-square-mile island, the travel
was positively expansive.

III

For the Tour elite, the golf season comes to a close
after the Professional Golfers' Association Championship, the last of the year's major tournaments.
But that's by no means the end of the year. There are
tournaments right through mid-December, and some
of them are on television, and some of them are worth
great sums of money, and in some of them the golfing
elite will play. But the Season—the four majors,
which are the very heart of professional tournament
golf—ends with the P.G.A.

For the caddies the 1985 season peaked two weeks
later, at the B.C. Open. Work continues beyond the
B.C., but the B.C. is, for caddies, the pinnacle of each
year. The B.C. hosts the annual caddie–player softball game, the annual caddie dinner, and the annual
caddie tournament. The B.C. Open is an unusually
egalitarian tournament, in part because it is played
on a municipal course in the middle of a middle-class
town; a poorly played shot can wind up on Main
Street.

The En-Joie Golf Club, the tournament's site, was built by the owners of the Endicott–Johnson shoe factory, which, before World War II, employed over three-quarters of the town's citizens. The golf course was a benefit for the employees. When the shoe company became a less dominant force in town, the company sold the course to Endicott. Alex Alexander, an Endicott native who is the tournament's director, caddied at the course during the Depression for eighty cents a round, and he remains a caddie in spirit. He makes the caddies feel special: There are no signs at the En-Joie Golf Club saying, "No Caddies Allowed Here." That is by order of the tournament director.

In my first night in Endicott I went out to dinner with Killer, who takes off a couple weeks after the B.C. each year. He explained to me that if I wanted to play in the Caddie Classic on the day after the tournament, which was Labor Day, I needed to join the Professional Tour Caddie Association. Membership was open to anyone who had caddied in fifteen tournaments during the year, and who paid the seventy-five-dollar dues. (I joined the next day.)

I asked him if he planned on playing.

"No, babe," he said, "I carry the clubs, and that's enough for me."

Killer called all of his friends "Babe." Even those whose names he knew.

"Hey, babe," Killer asked near the end of dinner, "What do you do in the off season?"

IV

"You know what gets me?" Doug Baker, a caddie, asked aloud as we hiked up the ninth fairway in the second round of the B.C. Open.

Doug was working for Tom Lehman, who was paired with Billy Britton and a local club pro named

Stan Lisk. Doug was a junior in college, a native of
Akron, Ohio, and sometimes a full-time caddie.

"It's these young guys who just come on the Tour
with no experience and luck into a big bag. You
know, like Tom, on Mark O'Meara's bag? He's made a
lot of money in the past two years, and where was he
three years ago? Nowhere, just comes up out of the
blue. And Memphis Mike, on Denis Watson's bag?
Parades around like he's God's gift to caddying.
Where was he a couple of years ago? Managing some
restaurant in Memphis. But you know how it is. If the
in group likes you—you know, Mike Carrick and
Gypsy and those guys—and they talk you up, the next
thing you know you've got a really good bag. I've been
out here busting my hump for five, six years now, and
have I ever had a bag like that? Oh, sure, yeah, I've
had good bags. I had Lynn Lott in 1983 when he
damn near won the Pensacola Open. But you know
what I'm saying. A lot of these younger guys haven't
paid their dues, if you know what I mean."

"This is my chance to show 'em," Eric "Zipperhead"
Schwarz, who caddies for Ronnie Black, said as we
ate barbecued chicken at the annual caddie dinner.
"I'm supposed to be a pretty good player; I played the
mini-tours for a while. But I never really play well in
the Caddie Classic. A lot of the players, and the other
caddies, give me a hard time about that. But this year
I really want to show 'em.

"It hasn't been that great a year for me. Getting
held up in Memphis, that was pretty bad. But the
year itself has been a disappointment. After four
years of scraping around out here, I thought I'd have
a good year this year, getting on Ronnie's bag. Last
year he won $175,000 and a tournament, and he won
a tournament the year before, too. So I just thought
that this year he'd improve a little more and that I
could get out from under this constant hole I've been

in. But he's won, what, fifty grand so far this year?
Five percent of that is, what, $2,500? That kind of
money doesn't really get you ahead.

"The year hasn't been a washout. I've been to three
of the majors. Went to the Masters for the first time.
We played in a lot of pro-ams. And we played with a
lot of good players. But I was hoping I might get
ahead enough this year so that I could take some time
off and look for a job. I think maybe I could get a job
as an assistant pro someplace; you can make some
pretty good contacts out here for that sort of thing.
But every week I've got to go to the next tournament
because I don't have enough money not to go."

"This is the highlight of the whole year for me,"
said Gypsy Grillo as we stood on the third-base line
during the caddie–player softball game.

It was a warm, soft, end-of-summer evening. Six
thousand fans filled the Union–Endicott High School
Ty Cobb Stadium, eagerly anticipating the outcome
of the series tie-breaking seventh annual Caddie–Player Softball Classic. (The tie-breaking game
didn't; it ended in a 5–5 tie.) The week of the B.C.
Open is the last hurrah at summer's close for the
people of Broome County, where fall is short and
winter long. And for the caddies, many of whom have
no home, the B.C. is a homecoming of sorts.

On the field, and along the sidelines, I saw my
caddie colleagues. A half year earlier I knew them as
you might now, as vague images walking toward a
pin across a television screen on a Sunday afternoon.
But there they were. People with happy stories and
sad stories, bitter people and hopeful people, people I
liked who liked me back, people I disliked who
disliked me back. As I watched Brad Faxon step in
the batter's box against his caddie, Gypsy, who was
the self-appointed pitcher for the caddie team, I
wondered if the freelance odd-job workers of the

eighteenth century, the first caddies, with their loosely structured convivial guilds, would recognize their twentieth-century equivalents. I wondered if they'd recognize Mike "Fluff" Cowan and "Mr." Bill Tripp; Dolphus "Golf Ball" Hull and Greg "Boats" Rita; "Greasy" Tony Navarro and "Boston" Mike Busfield; "Front Seat" Pete Petrunin and Ed "Sach" Malkus; "Father" Dan Murphy and Ronnie "Priest" McLaughlin; "Big" Jim Medziak and "Big" Lee Trottler; "Memphis" Mike Thurmer and "Canadian" Ken Doig; Russ "Pine" Craver and Mike "Shemp" Boyce; Herman "Mitch" Mitchell and Mike "Hicksey" Hicks; Lonzo "Frog" Wilkerson and Eric "Zipper-head" Schwarz; Don "Donny Wad" Wanstall and Rick "Play-by-Play" Wynn; Jim "Niner" Strickland and Lin "Growler" Strickler; Jerome "Bebop" Douglas and Harry "Hey Bud" Caddell; "Minnesota" Mike Lelos and "Philly" Billy Poore; Jeff "Squeaky" Medlin and Jeff "Boo" Burrell. Would the first caddies recognize their latter-day brethren? I think so. Could I properly count myself among them? I hoped so.

V

Billy Britton came to Endicott with the same spirit with which you might attend a class reunion from the not-too-distant past.

After the Met Open, Billy went to Allentown, Pennsylvania, to play in a one-day tournament sponsored by Jim Booros, an old friend of Billy's. Mike Donald, Fred Couples, and Lance Ten Broeck were there, too, and after the tournament they all drove up to Endicott together.

These days they weren't together that much: Booros had lost his Tour card, and Fred had to deal with the demands of being a Tour star. But the friendships remained, and, given the chance, as they were at the B.C., they hung out together, just like the old days.

Booros, Donald, Ten Broek, and Billy played a practice round and Billy won forty dollars. He played
well—he seems always to play well in practice
rounds—and was relaxed as one can only be in a
familiar environment. He's played in the B.C. every
year he's been on the Tour, and stays each year at the
home of Tony Saraceno, who Billy describes as "just a
regular guy with a regular job, nice house, nice
family," painting a picture I often imagined he
wanted for himself. Wayne Levi, who has won more
than a million dollars on the Tour, and who lives
three counties north of Broome County, and who was
the tournament's defending champion, also stays
with the Saracenos each year, along with his wife and
two children.

"It gets a little tight for space," Billy said, "but
nobody seems to mind."

On Wednesday we met at the golf course at six in
the morning to get in a practice round before the pro-
am. A score of other players had the same idea.

"Few years ago there wouldn't have been anyone
out here this time. Now look at this place," Billy said.
"Tour's getting tougher every year."

In 1983 Billy shot 71-72 at the B.C. to make the cut
on the button, then shot 70-66 on the weekend to
finish in a tie for nineteenth place. He earned $3,385,
his second best finish of the year. In 1984 Billy shot
73-73 to make the cut on the button and 68-70 on the
weekend to finish in a tie for fifteenth. He earned
$5,100, his best finish of that year. Billy was playing
well in the practice rounds, had played well for most
of the Met Open, and had been playing respectably
for a couple of weeks before that, even though he had
not made a dollar in Tour money. Once again a Tour
week began with hope, and it was not unjustified.

On Thursday we shot 73, two over par, which put
us in the middle of the field. It wasn't a bad round;

Billy just didn't make any birdie putts to counteract his two bogeys.

On Friday we knew we had to play even par or better to make the cut. We had a late tee time made later by rain delays. We spent four hours getting ready for the round. I held the umbrella over Billy as he putted. I held the umbrella over the bag as Billy hit balls. When Billy was good and drenched and stiff, our group was finally called to the tee. It was two-thirty in the afternoon. Billy pushed his first tee shot wildly and had to make a ten-foot putt to salvage a bogey, which he did. We were three over. We needed a birdie to get back to two over, to make the cut. Billy made straight pars from number two to number seventeen, many of the scrambling variety. We had one more hole to play and we needed a birdie. We could not play the eighteenth; dusk had descended and the round was called. We would have to come back on Saturday morning to finish.

VI

As I settled into the creaky and comfortable bed at Boughton's Rooms for Tourists that night, stiff and damp from the Friday in the rain, Billy Britton's fate on our single remaining hole on Saturday seemed about the most important question of my life. As I write this, between Christmas and New Year's Eve 1985, the only week of the year in which no major professional golf tournament is played anywhere in the world, the outcome on that hole has diminished in importance. Time, in this case a mere four months, has given perspective, a perspective that was lost in the urgency of the moment. Things change in four months. Here, at home, the green leaves of summer first turned brown and then fell off, as they do every year. The neighborhood kids played football in the road throughout October and November; now the cove is frozen and they're playing hockey. It was the first time I had seen summer turn into fall and fall turn into winter at home in seven years.

Since I saw her last, Carolyn Geiberger has become pregnant. I spoke with her husband on the phone the other day, after seeing him play well on television. After two rounds he and Patty Sheehan were one stroke off the lead in the JCPenney Mixed Team Classic. They finished in a tie for fourth place, and Al earned $13,500 for the week, more than he made in official Tour money all year. Kim Armstrong, my Oriental caddie–driving buddy, fresh from a month of working Florida orange groves, was on Al's bag and picked up $900 for the week, more than I had made in any two weeks combined. Al played in fourteen tournaments in 1985 and won $11,000. That is $489 more than he won in 1960, his first year on the Tour, when he ranked number thirty-seven on the earnings list. In 1985 he came in at number 176. At the time of our conversation, the Senior Tour was two years away for him, and his sixth child five months.

Brad Faxon finished the year at number 124 on the money list, the second to last of the exempt players for 1986. He played in thirty-one tournaments and survived the cut in fifteen of them and earned $46,800 in Tour money. Had he made one less cut he would not have been on the exempt list for 1986. His best tournament of the year was off the Tour: He won the Rhode Island Open, to add nicely to his two Rhode Island amateur titles. We spoke on the phone the other day too. Brad called the year one "where things just didn't click." That he squeezed into the exempt list for 1986, Brad said, "was a good omen for the new year."

George Archer, at forty-six the oldest man to finish in the top 125, played in thirty-one tournaments— only nine golfers played more rounds—and made twenty-five cuts. He earned $109,000, the eighth best year, financially, of his twenty-three-year career. He finished seventy-fourth on the money list, his sixth worst ranking.

Steve Elkington, the young Australian for whom I caddied in the Dutch Open, played in seven Tour events in the United States and made the cut in all of them, earning $9,900. He went to the Tour Qualifying Tournament, also known as the School, in an attempt to earn his Tour card for the 1986 season. He was not successful. He was not even close. He shot 77-74-71-78. One hundred twenty-eight golfers finished better than he did in the school. Larry Rentz won the 1985 Maryland Open but failed to qualify for a Tour card in the 1985 Tour Qualifying School. He missed by eighty-four spots. Jamie Howell missed getting his Tour card by thirty-four spots, which translated to seven strokes for the six-day tournament.

The three young golfers all suffered some temporary damage, but they'll be back. Like a thousand golfers before them, they'll work on their games, play where they can, maybe teach a little, and dream of the Tour. Someday, I think, all three will make it, for they are not of average talent or determination. Roger Kahn cleverly called his book about minor baseball players *Good Enough to Dream*; the title's first word judges the technical skill of these players, the last their ambition. Golf has no minor leagues, but scores of minor leaguers. Elkington, Rentz, and Howell, even though they missed badly in the 1985 Qualifying School, are not among them. They are well beyond Single A ball, or even Double A and Triple A. They have the technical skills of the Tour player. But a more important question about them remains unanswered: Do they have, as the British say, the bottle? Do they have the nerve? Do they have the will? Time will show that they do, I hope.

For the winter of 1986 Larry Rentz will play in the Club Pro Series in Florida, which he won last year. If this year is like last year, he'll take off some time along the way to go scuba diving with his buddy, Randy Erskine—the same Randy Erskine who gave me my Tour caddie start in Charlotte, North Carolina, six years ago. His sole goal that year, before leaving the Tour, was to qualify for the 1979 U.S. Open. He didn't qualify then, or since, until 1985, when the Open was played in his home state, Michigan. He got in off the alternate list two hours before his tee time. He missed the cut at Oakland Hills, a course he played occasionally as a star golfer for the University of Michigan. But like Larry and Brad, he too won his state Open.

Kevin Morris, the Westchester Hills head pro, was named the Met P.G.A. Player of the Year, just as he was in 1984, and not only because he made the cut in the P.G.A. Championship. He finished second in the Met P.G.A. Championship and fourth in the P.G.A. National Club Pro Championship.

Lee Roy Pearson III is planning to play in the 1986 Panasonic-Las Vegas Invitational. We spoke on the phone the other day; he said he's "been kicking around Ranger [Texas], doin' what we do here in Ranger, whatever that is."

Billy Britton won't be at that Las Vegas tournament. He's not likely to be at any Tour events. The year 1985 was his worst as a professional by a long shot. He played in seventeen tournaments and missed the cut in fourteen of them. Of the forty competitive rounds he played, he broke 70 only twice and had a stroke average of 73.60, or 1.2 strokes per round worse than Brad. He ranked number 215 on the earnings list, with $3,245. Arnold Palmer finished immediately ahead of him. Even in 1980, when Billy joined the Tour halfway through the year, he made three times that sum. He failed to qualify to even play in the Tour qualifying tournament.

Billy turned thirty in November. I sent him a birthday card and he wrote back. "I feel a little naked without that Tour card," Billy said, "but like Yogi said, 'There's ten million Chinamen who couldn't care less.' "

We got together on Staten Island the other day. In a bar called Schaeffer's, on Victory Boulevard, Billy told me about his future plans, and he was anything but despondent. His first order of business after Christmas was to ask Isabelle Farrell, who brought him that iced tea on a hot Virginia day at the Anheuser-Busch Classic in 1984, to marry him. She, who was wondering if that day was ever going to come, said yes, and they plan to marry in May of 1986. By then, Isabelle will have been graduated from law school, and Billy will have taken a job as an assistant pro at a club in the Metropolitan Golf Association region. Jim Albus, the Piping Rock Golf Club professional who first gave lessons to Billy on Staten Island fifteen years ago, put out his feelers for Billy and Billy has two offers. As an assistant pro he'll teach, work in the pro shop, work on the carts, and play. He'll be able to play in all the tournaments in the New York area and, in the winter, in Florida.

"I still love the game," Billy said at Schaeffer's, "but right now the Tour seems like the furthest-away thing in the world. I don't even think I'll miss it in the next year.

"In a way, I sort of burned myself out after that 1982 season [when he finished fifty-seventh on the money earnings list]. I had played the Tour well; I sort of satisfied my goal.

"Then, when I started playing poorly, I always tried to *work* my way out of it. I never tried to get away from it for a while, or change my attitude. I just worked and worked and worked. And I probably did a lot of damage to myself and my game in the process.

"I'm sure I'm going to want to try the Tour again somewhere down the road. But right now, I can't even imagine it."

With the grand perspective of four months, Billy's fate on that Saturday morning in Endicott, when we needed to make a birdie on the last hole to make the cut, seems less important. But it then seemed about the most important thing in my life.

VII

Billy and I met at the En-Joie Golf Club at 6:30 A.M., an hour and a half before our Saturday tee time, so that he could putt, chip, and hit balls. Billy would, of course, take all the preparation for playing one hole that he would for playing eighteen. That was inherent in his nature. At ten minutes to eight we made the walk out to the eighteenth tee. So did Tom Lehman, who needed to make an eagle two on the hole to make the cut. Stan Lisk, the club pro who earned a spot in the tournament through local qualifying, shot an 87 in the first round, and was fifteen over par through seventeen holes in the second round. He didn't bother to show up.

The eighteenth of the En-Joie Golf Club is 400 yards long, with light rough and a few trees down the right side and a pond within driving range down the left. The hole is played from an elevated tee, and a good drive might leave a player as little as a pitching wedge shot or less into the hole. But playing a driver off the tee brings the pond into play. The prudent shot is to hit a three wood, and that's what we did. Billy hit a good one, albeit short, finishing in the middle of the fairway, 170 yards from the pin.

"Just a six iron, huh, Mike?" Billy said, as we stood over the ball, and that was the right club. He pulled the shot, slightly, and the ball finished hole-high but twenty-five feet to the left. I took out the pin and walked to the high back of the green, from where I could watch our fate. Billy was faced with a difficult putt, a double breaker that went up one hill and down another. The ball came off the putter face well, and as it coasted up to the hole it looked as if it might go in. But it didn't. It slid a foot past the hole on the high side and a foot beyond. Billy tapped in; we missed the cut by a stroke.

VIII

If you ever caddie on the pro golf Tour, you might think, at first, that life ends with a missed cut. It does not. On the Saturday afternoon after missing the B.C. Open cut, Billy was at the driving range of the En-Joie Golf Club getting ready for the Bank of Boston Classic. I was out there, too, in hasty preparation for the Labor Day Caddie Classic. In the previous six months I had learned a fair amount about the game—about professional golfers, about the structure of tournament golf, about caddies and caddying, about the mechanics of the swing. But I had little chance to apply these lessons to my own game, and I was not sure if they were applicable at all. Billy gave me a lesson that day on the practice tee, a technical one, and I finally understood it on the back nine of the Caddie Classic, in which I shot a 41. Unfortunately, I went out with a fat 54. My playing partner, "Mr." Bill Tripp, who caddies for Ron Streck, fared no better, and we did not even win back our twenty dollar entrance fee from the $3,500 purse. Regardless, it felt wonderfully liberating to actually swing and play again, and I was looking forward to going home and playing more.

Brad Faxon asked me if I wanted to work for him the following week at the Bank of Boston Classic (where Billy has a regular caddie), and I was tempted to say yes: Financially, I probably could have squeaked by for one more week; there was no rule that said I could stay on the Tour for only six months. I had no pressing commitments elsewhere. I had no pressing commitments at all, which, for a spell (six months, perhaps), is liberating. After that it's not.

But I made the drive east, from Endicott to Sutton, Massachusetts, anyway. More out of habit, I suppose, than necessity. I wanted to make the drive. During my time on the Tour I was never so happy, never felt so free, as when I was driving fast on open roads in a rented car with the windows down and the radio volume up, and I wanted that feeling one last time. I got to Sutton and looked about. Brad was there, and Al Geiberger, and Steve Elkington, and Billy Britton. I stayed for a while, but without a bag I felt more like a member of the gallery. Later in the afternoon I made the drive south, to Woods Hole, and took the ferry to Martha's Vineyard. It was less than a year earlier that I had lived on the Vineyard. I still had my stereo there, and some friends to stay with, and some friends to play golf with.

September is a beautiful month on the island, one of orange sunsets and soft grass, warm water and good waves, and I could happily have taken a job and stayed through the fall. Whatever once felt restricting about the island I could no longer remember. But it was time to go home. I took one ferry from the Vineyard to Woods Hole and another from New London, Connecticut, to Orient Point, New York, on the eastern end of Long Island. My journey, it occurred to me on that last leg, had been a green road home. Green for the fairways and the roughs and the putting greens and the money and the borders of the highways, but also for me—I began green, a beginner, in my salad days. Now, six months later, I was still essentially a beginner, but perhaps less of one.

For six months my home was the road. I thought it would be a lonely place, but it wasn't. I made friends, some only for a week at a time; others, I hope, that will endure.

On my way home I stopped off at the Bellport Golf Club. I ran into an old member I knew from years back.

"I heard you were caddying on the Pro Tour," the member said.

"Yes, I was," I said.

"Geez, that must have been great. That's what I'd like to do for a spell—caddie on the Tour. You know, travel about, see some different places, see how these guys hit the ball. Is it a hard thing to do?"

I struggled for a moment to come up with an answer as succinct as his question.

"If you want to do it, you can," I said.

"Oh, geez, yeah. I wanna do it," the member said.

And then I made the final, familiar drive from the golf course home, past Patchogue Floral, past Dr. Libin's office, and, finally, to the driveway of the house where I had grown up.

AUTHOR'S NOTE

As a caddie I was able to learn about tournament golf; as a reporter I was able to write about it.

Along the way, a great many people allowed me to become a participant in their lives. I hope this book makes plain my respect for them. For all shortcomings I am solely responsible.

My deepest gratitude goes to the golfers who took me on as a caddie: Brad Faxon, George Archer, Steve Elkington, Jamie Howell, Kevin Morris, Larry Rentz, Al Geiberger, and especially Billy Britton.

Lee Roy Pearson III, of Ranger, Texas; Chuck Will, of CBS Sports; and Jeff Parsons, of the Muirfield Village Golf Club, all of whom gave me work along the way, contributed greatly to my caddie education, and have my sincere thanks.

The leading players in the Tour's cast of characters—the golfers, caddies, and officials—are nearly all male. This unfortunate fact is reflected in the book. The book itself, however, would have been impossible without the help of three women: Denise Schwarz, expeditious typist; Sandra Choron, steadfast agent; and Nancy Crossman, enthusiastic editor.

I am also thankful to Nancy's colleagues, particularly Ted Macri, Georgene Sainati, and Kathy Willhoite.

For their photographic contributions I am grateful to Peter Simon, Stephen Szurlej, Amy Mauro, and Nina Bramhall.

For advice and encouragement I am grateful to Elizabeth Marchant Sanchez, Jerry Tarde, William Shawn, and Andrew Shanley.

For hospitality and friendship on the road thanks to Wally Brewer and John Rowland; Andrew Clurman; Stanley and Jean Shepard; Bill and Cathryn Gruttemeyer; Scott and Pam Uffelman; and Kelly Walker. For hospitality and friendship off the road thanks to Paul Underwood, Bruce Menken, Barry Klayman, Mel Damski, and Joyce Zaorski.

My high school golf coach, John W. Sifaneck, died at age forty-four while I was at work on this book. He loved the game, and his enthusiasm was contagious.

Michael Bamberger
Patchogue, L.I.
January 1986